PUBLIC SCHOOLS,
PRIVATE GOVERNANCE

J. Celeste Lay

PUBLIC SCHOOLS, PRIVATE GOVERNANCE

_____

Education Reform and Democracy
in New Orleans

_____

TEMPLE UNIVERSITY PRESS
Philadelphia • Rome • Tokyo

TEMPLE UNIVERSITY PRESS
Philadelphia, Pennsylvania 19122
tupress.temple.edu

Library of Congress Cataloging-in-Publication Data

Names: Lay, J. Celeste, author.
Title: Public schools, private governance : education reform and democracy
in New Orleans / J. Celeste Lay.
Description: Philadelphia, Pennsylvania : Temple University Press, 2022. |
Includes bibliographical references and index. | Summary: "Examines the
post-Hurricane Katrina transformation of New Orleans public schools to
an all-charter system and the consequences of this change for local
democracy"—Provided by publisher.
Identifiers: LCCN 2021040401 (print) | LCCN 2021040402 (ebook) | ISBN
9781439922637 (Cloth : acid-free paper) | ISBN 9781439922644 (Paperback
: acid-free paper) | ISBN 9781439922651 (PDF)
Subjects: LCSH: Educational change—Louisiana—New Orleans. | Public
schools—Louisiana—New Orleans. | Charter schools—Louisiana—New
Orleans. | Privatization in education—Louisiana—New Orleans. |
Education—Parent participation—Louisiana—New Orleans. | Public
schools—State supervision—Louisiana—New Orleans. | Race relations in
school management—Louisiana—New Orleans. | School management and
organization—Louisiana—New Orleans. | Hurricane Katrina,
2005—Political aspects.
Classification: LCC LB2802.N48 L39 2022 (print) | LCC LB2802.N48 (ebook)
| DDC 370.9763/35—dc23/eng/20220215
LC record available at https://lccn.loc.gov/2021040401
LC ebook record available at https://lccn.loc.gov/2021040402

To my girls, Lucy and Kimberly

Contents

Preface and Acknowledgments

I am the product almost entirely of public schools, including college and graduate school and had always assumed my children would go to public schools. In 2012, I embarked on a journey to enroll my child in kindergarten in New Orleans. Things did not go as planned, and my rage led me to this project.

In the wake of Hurricane Katrina in 2005, New Orleans sought to transform its schools from a "broken system" into an innovative, unique, and highly effective system of schools. The city now has the only all-charter school system in the United States. There are ostensibly no neighborhood schools. Further, every parent or child must participate in a process of actively choosing a school. I purposely do not write that parents "choose" their school because many children are not able to enroll in the school of their choice, but rather they are placed in a school according to a computer algorithm that considers parents' preferences, residence, siblings, and a lottery number.

As a political scientist, I became interested in the governance changes and the effects of the dramatic policy change on public opinion. How did such sweeping reforms come to be? Were they merely the result of a destructive "natural" disaster? What happens when you remove electoral accountability from those making critical decisions about schools? Do people think the system is working, especially those who have the most contact with the system? Theories of policy feedback suggest that the changes in governance and the processes that put the new system in place will have predictable effects on individuals' attitudes about the how the system operates. School choice and charter proponents contend that when parents have a stronger voice in this arena, their levels of efficacy and trust will spill over into other areas of government and society. Is this the case here? Have the policies led to a positive feedback?

In seeking answers to these questions, this book combines my scholarly interests with my role as a parent who sat through open houses, filled out applications, and had my four-year-old tested by strangers in a failed effort to enroll in *public schools*. As a highly educated person with a private vehicle and a fairly flexible schedule, I found the search and application process exhausting and confusing. This process made me doubt myself and lose faith not only in public schools, but in the entire city that would allow such a system to be created. I could only imagine how someone with many fewer privileges would maneuver this system, and what its effects on their efficacy and trust would be.

What I found was in some ways even more depressing than I imagined. The people of New Orleans—particularly the parents of K–12-age children—did not lose faith in the system. The dramatic policy transformation did not lead to a negative feedback loop as it had for me personally. Rather, for most parents, political trust and efficacy were already so low, the people so disappointed and discouraged, that they had come to expect this "new and improved" system would work no better for them than the old one had. To be sure, New Orleanians remain optimistic. They desperately want these reforms to work. They look for any positive indicator that things are better, that they've made the right decision to educate their children here. However, they expect that officials will be corrupt, that their voices will be ignored, and that they will have to fight for their children in a system that is built to their disadvantage. Some ask why it has to be this way, but most others have stopped wondering and accept that educating their children is going to be a struggle just like finding affordable housing, using public transportation, and keeping a well-paying job. A growing number are actively pushing back against the system, but that is not the modal response.

I have been humbled to find that my loss of faith was not universal. I had the privilege to have had faith in my government, to believe that I could make things work for my children through information advantages and sheer tenacity. I discovered that the main advantage I have in this system is the privilege to opt out. That privilege, I believe, comes with a responsibility to take a serious look at how this system works and more importantly, to give voice to some of those who have been excluded: the parents who are unable to opt out, who are forced to work within the system, and who want the exact same things for their children that I want for mine.

In writing the book, I am indebted to many people. I am most grateful to those who believed their voices were being excluded and yet trusted me enough to talk to me. I had excellent research assistants. Anna Bauman, Ruoxi Li, Dorothy Slater, and Matthew Wu were some of Tulane's brightest and most intellectually curious undergraduate students, and their help in collecting data and thinking through these issues was invaluable. Two graduate students in the Tulane political science program, Lucia Kovacikova and Bethany Carter, also built databases from which I could analyze local media coverage and legal evolution in Louisiana. I also built on the work of undergrads in my Politics of Education Policy course, especially Lily Milwit, Alyssa Schnoor, Matthew Weber, and Juharah Worku. The librarians at Tulane were incredibly helpful, especially Eric Wedig, and I appreciate conversations with Marta Jewson, an education reporter at *The Lens*. I am also grateful to the Kaiser Family Foundation for sharing its survey data with me and to Debra Vaughn for sharing data from the Cowen Institute. Finally, I could not have done this work without the financial support of Tulane University's Committee on Summer Research, the New Orleans Center for the Gulf South, and a grant from the Lavin-Bernick funds for faculty research. Tulane gets a lot of grief from those opposed to the reforms, for understandable reasons that I discuss in the text, but for each of these grants, I outlined the basic premises of the project and these Tulane-affiliated entities were willing to financially support me.

I am grateful to my colleagues for reading drafts and talking with me about these ideas: Peter Burns, Geoff Dancy, Michael Hankinson, Mirya Holman, Mary Kroeger, Estilla Lightfoot, Casey Love, Anna Mahoney, Domingo Morel, Menaka Philips, Matthew Thomas, and Clarence N. Stone. My colleague Mirya Holman not only read portions of this manuscript but helped me collect data that has been instrumental in my understanding of the dynamics of the effects of reforms. I also appreciate senior colleagues at and beyond Tulane who encouraged me, including Michael Cunningham, Kathy Dolan, Kelly Grant, Sally Kenney, Lee Skinner, and many others. I also appreciate the patience and kindness from Aaron Javsicas, Temple University Press's editor.

My husband and colleague, Chris Fettweis, has listened mostly patiently to my rants about the schools for many years. I also appreciate my children's patience as I worked on weekends, holidays, school breaks, and in the midst of pandemic virtual learning. I hope to help them understand just how privileged they are to be able to take their educational opportunities for granted. The book is dedicated to them and to all the parents in New Orleans who want nothing more and nothing less than a good education for their children.

PUBLIC SCHOOLS,
PRIVATE GOVERNANCE

Introduction

A Total Flim-flam

With the democratic process, you can see what's really
going on. We are losing voice. We are losing control over
what we say we want to happen. As for electing people to
represent us, they no longer have the authority to do so
by law.
—Reverend Willie Calhoun Jr.,
   community organizer, New Orleans

John McDonogh High School, known as "John Mac" to locals, opened as
Esplanade High School in 1912 on the outskirts of the French Quarter
in New Orleans. It was an all-girls school until 1952, when it began to
enroll white boys. It was considered one of the best high schools in the city
until the courts finally required public schools to integrate in the late 1960s
and the city largely abandoned its public schools. By 1975, white enrollment
in New Orleans public schools was half what it had been in 1961, when white
families began to move to the suburbs or enroll in private schools. The next
thirty years was a story of public corruption, disinvestment, and declining
quality in New Orleans public schools, including John Mac.

A former teacher recounted his first year at John Mac in 2002, with its
broken lab benches, cracked linoleum tiles, holes in the floor, jerry-rigged
fixes of major maintenance issues, and mice dropping from the ceiling during class. He also noted the "increasing regularity of daily announcements
that noted the passing of a former John Mac student whose life had met a
violent end."[1] In 2003, in what was described as a gang killing, four young
people entered John Mac's packed school gymnasium with a semiautomatic
assault rifle and opened fire, killing one fifteen-year-old and wounding three
others. The shooting made national news and became infamous in New
Orleans. For white residents, the story of John Mac High School was a quint-
essential example of what was wrong with New Orleans schools: run-down
facilities populated by poor, Black children who were prone to violence and
Black teachers and administrators who cared more about their benefits and

unions than the children they were charged with serving. For the community of alumni, neighbors, students, and parents, John Mac was a victim of the city's neglect, the criminalization of the Black community, and the lack of economic opportunity for Black people that drove violence and "poor performance." The battle over John Mac in the wake of Hurricane Katrina would place these opposing perspectives at center stage.

When Katrina caused the floodwalls around Lake Pontchartrain to fail in 2005, many people believed it was an opportunity to "fix," once and for all, public schools such as John Mac. Eighty percent of the city flooded, and nearly all residents were forced to evacuate, some for a few days, but most for weeks or months; far too many took years to make their way home, and many have never returned. To get the city back on its feet, officials knew they needed schools. Two months after the storm, the Louisiana State Legislature paved the way for the state body authorized to take over failing schools, the Recovery School District (RSD), to take control of nearly all the public schools in New Orleans. A year after Katrina, thirty-five of fifty-six public schools had transformed into charter schools.[2] In 2020, all the public schools were charters.

The most common narratives about how this transformation happened begin with the storm. Several prominent scholars propose that in its devastation, Katrina was a catalyst for change in a city where reforms had been blocked by an intransigent local board and a citizenry that revered its schools so much that it was the "last place on earth one would have expected innovation in the schools."[3] The new system's architects and advocates contend that the reforms were born of necessity to get schools back online quickly in the wake of the hurricane. Moreover, they argue that the proof of its success is in the pudding. Test scores and graduation rates are up, and polls show that parents want school choice and are satisfied with the system. Other narratives focus on the idea of "disaster capitalism": that reformers used Katrina's destruction as an opportunity to take advantage of the Black community's displacement and loss for their own profit and political advancement.[4]

This book tells a different story of how this transformation happened. It is based in theories of political behavior and policy change, focusing on how political minorities disrupt systems to create change and keep reforms in place, and the predictable political effects—exclusion, frustration, and resignation on the part of those most directly affected. I argue that the intentional gradual change in the decade preceding Katrina made it possible for the state to take control of New Orleans schools quickly and easily. The reforms had inched along incrementally at the state level for years, creating an apparatus—the RSD—and a system of measuring performance and an accountability regime that made the takeover logistically possible. Moreover, the rhetoric that accompanied these changes slowly and methodically led elected officials and regular citizens alike to believe that school choice and charter schools were the only way forward and that these neoliberal reforms would rapidly trans-form the city's schools. The reformers believed that the ends would justify the means. If certain groups had to be excluded, silenced, or demeaned to make the system better for young people, then they would be vindicated in the end, and opponents would come around.

These reforms were not unique to Louisiana, of course, but have not re-sulted in the wholesale shift to private governance and management in other cities that we see in New Orleans. It is undeniable that Katrina provided the opportunity for reformers to put their ideas on steroids. I do not entirely dis-pute the existing narratives that begin with the storm. Rather, I argue that they do not tell the whole story. The stage was set and the actors were ready long before the storm. It is important to understand these pre-Katrina moves for many reasons. In addition to the policies themselves are the networks and relationships that were built during that time that were central to the mainte-nance of the reforms after Hurricane Katrina. The patterns of exclusion and the framing of their stories in the media developed during this period provid-ed a roadmap for the immediate and long-term aftermath of the hurricane. Further, the pre-Katrina reforms are a harbinger to other cities undergoing substantial reform—they are one "opportunity" away from a similar whole-sale transformation. Indeed, the architects of this system and its financial backers have been busy selling and financing this model around the United States, using the so-called success in New Orleans as their evidence of what is possible elsewhere.

Contemporary education reform in New Orleans, as in most urban cen-ters, cannot be divorced from its history of racial oppression. The irony of the reform movement is that its architects framed it as a movement on behalf of marginalized, oft forgotten, and overlooked Black children while simul-taneously excluding their parents' voices and ignoring the effects of these policies on the members of this community. Both before and after Katrina, white reformers purposely excluded Black educators, community members, and parents. This was part of a "longer historical narrative in which White institutions generate exclusionary social networks, then disrupt and devalue Black social capital while bemoaning the failure of the Black community to participate in the system."[5] Parents clearly understand that they were and continue to be shut out of policy-making discussions and yet blamed for the new system's deficiencies.

This racial division underscores the notion that functioning democracies require "something like a common identity." If certain members of a democratic polity are deemed less valuable than others, there can be no democratic deliberation or decision making, and thus no legitimacy. The wholesale takeover of the schools in the wake of Katrina was anything but a consensus-building operation. It would have been impossible without marginalizing important stakeholders. Reformers put in place a system that could be maintained only by continuing to place barriers on participation. A system built on such exclusion cannot be described as a functional, legitimate democracy.

This book moves beyond an examination of the political moves in the immediate aftermath of the storm to also focus on how such dramatic changes were maintained. The political system is set up to push back against and prevent major policy change. In the unlikely event that major policy reform occurs, it is easy for actors to revert to old ways of doing things. The interest groups that had held the old status quo in place usually do not simply disappear. I show that reformers managed to maintain the new system through a combination of structural and political maneuvers that continued to sideline the very people about whom reformers claimed they were most concerned.

Finally, the second half of the book focuses on the predictable political effects. Where most analyses of the reforms' effects focus on educational outcomes, I zero in on how the major shifts in governance have influenced the newly empowered, privately selected charter board members and the disempowered parents of public school students. Much of the public opinion research that has been touted as evidence of widespread buy-in captures the attitudes primarily of those who do not have direct experience with public schools. The data I draw on, however, demonstrate that parents are frustrated, confused, and angry about their interactions with this new system. Even so, they are resigned, and most are not marching in the streets or withdrawing their children from schools. They have been here before and, indeed, have come to expect that public services will simply not work for people like them. They do not expect their frustration to be heard or for anyone to care. These policies did not cause this reaction, but they exacerbate the feelings of powerlessness and resignation.

When You Want to Kill a Community, You Strip Away Its Schools

In many ways, the story of John Mac High School exemplifies what has happened in New Orleans. In September 2006 it reopened as a non-charter direct-run school operated by the RSD. According to a teacher who worked there at the time, some classes were as large as one hundred students; there were no computers, textbooks, or water fountains and no school phone. There were more security guards than teachers.[6] Students were subject to searches and were escorted to the bathroom. For nearly six years, neighborhood residents, students, parents, alumni, and community activists worked with the RSD to have the building renovated and prevent John Mac from being "chartered."[7]

The African American communities fighting to maintain local control of schools such as John Mac, which had been nearly all Black for decades, did not trust the people they viewed as outsiders who came into town without any knowledge of the history, culture, or sense of community that these schools helped to maintain. Their opposition to charter schools was not simply a knee-jerk reaction against change. Rather, their reluctance to buy in to the reforms was built on the skepticism that came with decades, if not centuries, of benign neglect and overt racism. Whites had abandoned the public schools years earlier, and now, in the wake of a devastating disaster, it seemed that they wanted to turn these predominantly Black public schools over to outside agencies who were going to replace the Black teachers, administrators, and elected officials who governed and worked in the schools with non-native white folks who had no real knowledge of or concern for the communities they were supposed to serve.[8]

On the other side were the reformers, a group led by, though not exclusively composed of, affluent whites. Some had been elected recently to the local school board. Others had served in appointed positions in K–12 education at the state level. Still others were entrepreneurs with limited experience in education, some of whom were native New Orleanians, but many moved to the city specifically to get involved in the reform movement. The reformers wholeheartedly believed in the power of school choice to improve school quality and wanted to experiment with innovative models of organizing and delivering education, especially charter schools. Many were open about their opinions that corrupt school employees and unqualified or unmotivated teachers were to blame for the poor performance in the schools. That so many of these teachers and administrators were Black and so many of the reformers were white underlies a central feature of the reform logic.

Again, the story of John Mac High School is illustrative. In 2011, John White, superintendent of the RSD, selected a national charter operator to begin running the school even as the principal was following White's directions to propose a plan for teachers, administrators, and alumni to operate the school. The new governance plan was backed by the New Orleans Business Council and the Citizens for One Greater New Orleans, groups composed primarily of white residents of the most affluent neighborhoods in the city. The Future Is Now (FIN) charter operator was founded by Steve Barr, a brash, camera-hungry, "no-nonsense reformer."[9] The RSD and New Schools for New Orleans (NSNO), a charter "incubator," allocated nearly $1 million to FIN to get John Mac off the ground. Barr described what he found at John Mac this way: "This is what seven generations of crap looks like."[10] He announced that all the faculty members would be fired, and he traveled to Washington, DC, and New York to meet with prospective teachers, decisions that led the students to walk out in protest. Barr also contracted with the Oprah Winfrey Network to shoot a documentary about his attempt to turn performance around in its first academic year. The show, *Blackboard Wars*, referred to John Mac as "the most dangerous school in America."

The turnaround story that the show had undoubtedly hoped to chronicle did not materialize. The school's performance score in 2012–2013 was 9.3 out of 150; it improved only to 16.5 the following year. Enrollment dropped substantially after the documentary aired, leading to cuts in staff and salaries. In the middle of FIN's second year as John Mac's operator, in January 2014, the RSD announced that the school would close at the end of that year to undergo extensive renovations and reopen two years later with a new charter operator. Barr left town.

Parents, teachers, students, and concerned citizens rallied and organized to be part of deciding the future of the school.[11] In August 2014, the state Board of Elementary and Secondary Education (BESE) directed the Orleans Parish School Board to convene a work group and bring back recommendations for the future of John Mac. Three months later, however, the BESE abruptly changed course and decided to give the RSD the authority to decide the next school operator. In a scene out of *Game of Thrones*, several community members walked in front of board members repeating "shame" as the board voted to undo the work of the community group. Brenda Square, spokeswoman for the Steering Committee, said that working with the RSD was a "total flim-flam" and "a betrayal of every commitment they shared with the John Mac community." One BESE member who voted against the move stated, "As a black, African American female who sits on this board, I am angry. What you are doing to children that look like me is a disgrace. When you want to kill a community, you strip away its schools."[12]

Later that year, the RSD announced that the newly renovated building would go to Bricolage Academy, a new charter elementary school with a focus on "diversity by design." It would be a different school in every way. Bricolage attracts many middle- and upper-class white families and has been touted for its curriculum focused on hands-on science and arts projects. In January 2017, the gym where the infamous 2003 shooting took place was razed. The newly renovated space opened with great fanfare in 2018.

Some see these events as growing pains in a long-term effort that ultimately has been better for the children in the city. An underperforming, dilapidated school with a history of violence was closed, and, in theory, its students (and those who would have attended) had opportunities to attend better schools elsewhere. The building was restored and reopened as a charter school that had proven its success even without a permanent facility. The important questions, they believe, are whether test scores have improved and whether a greater proportion of students are reading at grade level, graduating from high school, and going on to college. If this is the case, then this painful period of school closures will have been worth it.

To others, the John Mac story (and that of several other schools like it) is a familiar tale of dispossession of Black spaces and exclusion of Black voices. Public schools have long been a focal point for social, economic, and racial crises. In New Orleans, schools "offered residents the means to envision competing futures and the state the mechanism to grant certain futures while denying others."[13] Given the city's history with segregation and the long fight for integration, the public disinvestment from schools, and the deep disparities in educational opportunities between Black and white children, the reform movement that began in the 1990s and continues to the present is deeply racialized. White reformers refused to accommodate alternative perspectives and failed to see that this refusal would, in turn, affect the educational outcomes they say motivate the reforms.

For the John Mac families, their school was not improved. It was eliminated. Their efforts to organize and play by the rules of the new authorities were pushed aside. There are significant costs to their faith and trust in the schools and in city leadership. Many schools, which act as neighborhood anchors, are gone. Both physical and psychological links to the past have been removed. The students who would have attended John Mac have little chance of getting into a school like Bricolage and, for the most part, are still enrolled in schools with below-average performance scores. Even if some educational outcomes are improved, the price paid in the diminution of the experiences of the least advantaged in school governance and civic participation is real, and it is at least worth admitting and deliberating on this trade-off.

The Main Argument

The main argument of this book is that in the years leading up to Hurricane Katrina, there was a slow, deliberate dismantling of the public schools in New Orleans, and the post-Katrina reform processes have predictably left Black parents and residents without a voice and the officials charged with school governance, most of whom are white, with little accountability. In short, the reforms were made possible only by excluding and sidelining the experiences and preferences of the residents who interact most directly and frequently with school authorities, and they have had expected effects on the character of local democracy in the city.

Reformers did not claim that democracy was a worthwhile sacrifice for the possibility of better schools. Although some have argued that reformers were motivated by a desire to profit from a privatized school system or that they were driven by naked political ambition, most conceived of democracy along classically liberal lines, disregarding racial dynamics, inclusion, or democratic deliberation. They often claimed they were helping to expand opportunities, especially for Black parents, and that their policies enhanced individual liberty. Under their system, parents can apply to any school and are "free" from the constraints of a local school district. They have the "right to choose" their schools. In the name of autonomy, charter schools are free to engage in almost any practice they want, creating a quasi-market with innovative variations of schools that should allow parents to find the best fit for their child. If parents are not satisfied with their school, they can "simply" choose another that suits their values.

These liberal values represent an approach to education that is distinct from the perspectives of many within the Black community. In New Orleans, as in other U.S. cities, Black neighborhood associations, church groups, civil rights organizations, and benevolent aid societies have fought for more than a century for resources for public schools serving African American children. These networks serve as a significant form of Black social capital, which was developed in response to the marginalization of the Black community and to "a political culture of white supremacy."[14] The white reform movement does not value these institutions and has continued to marginalize Black parents and educators in the years before and since Katrina. They have put in place a system in which "the entire power structure of public education in New Orleans has been recast to represent the views, beliefs, and desires of a White minority."[15]

This individual-centered, liberal approach to democracy sees government as the primary constraint on liberty. Freedom, however, is often constrained by "the aggregate effects of private decisions on the distribution of opportunity in society and the range of options facing particular individuals."[16] White Americans who hold fast to concerns about government intrusion tend to see the invisible hand of a market as racially and economically neutral. Democracy and equality of opportunity are limited to freedom of choice, with no regard for the varying constraints on the options for different families. Other models of democracy prioritize inclusive participation and shared self-government. These models are messier and more contentious. Deliberation and disagreement are messy and time-consuming and require that those with the most advantage must be willing to share power with those who have the least.

Beyond the fact that the liberal approach is deeply racialized, there is also a substantial difference between theory and practice. Applying to any school one wants is cold comfort if the options are limited or the chance of actually enrolling one's child in these schools is nil. Families that require public transportation, before- or after-school care, and provisions for children with special needs do not have the same options as their counterparts for whom these may be unnecessary or privately contracted. Charter schools may be "free" to decide their own policies, but if these practices routinely discriminate against students with special needs or those whose parents do not understand how the system works, then the disparities from the old system are merely reproduced in the new one, only with less oversight and accountability. The invisible hand has nearly always operated in the United States in ways that leave Black citizens at a disadvantage, and in New Orleans these liberal reforms allow white leaders to "blame Black families for the failure of their model."[17]

I show not only that those who govern the schools are unrepresentative of the public they serve, but also that these folks, despite controlling millions in taxpayer dollars and the most important public service in a city, do not view their roles as public servants at all. Echoing Reverend Willie Calhoun, elected officials have little authority, and Black parents have little voice. Many parents believe they are stuck and are resentful about the consistent claims by reformers that children in New Orleans have flexibility and choices about their schooling. This is not to say that they were happy with the system before Katrina, and they certainly do not want to go back. If policy makers listened to these voices, they would hear an urgent desire for children to go to school closer to home; to spend less time on buses traversing the perimeter of the city; to focus less on assessment and more on recess and the arts and in learning the history of the place where they are being raised. Parents want a human connection rather than an online system with an algorithm that places their children in schools without regard to their families' needs, even as white children continue magically to end up only in the highest-performing schools, just as they did prior to Katrina.

This book relies on the theories of policy feedback to examine the emergence, maintenance, and effects of the first all-charter district. I review that literature in each chapter as it relates to each aspect of the reform process. Policies are not only the product of political struggles; they affect politics in ways that influence future public-policy making.[18] Recognizing that policies themselves "restructure subsequent political processes" highlights that reforms affect political life beyond the intended effects on the problems they aim to solve.[19] These reforms were intended to improve the quality of education and the performance of students in New Orleans schools, but the racial and class disparities in the construction of the reforms are reflected in the disproportionalities in how poor, Black parents and community members experience the policies. Reformers established a new coalition that works to maintain the new status quo and advocate against rollbacks. These processes and outcomes send important messages about deservingness and belonging, especially with regard to race, that, in turn, influence the behavior of beneficiaries and the general public, with important implications for democracy.

An Outline of the Book

Chapter 1 explains the events in the immediate aftermath of Hurricane Katrina. I focus primarily on the activities of a small group of elite, mostly white and affluent New Orleanians in the weeks that followed this devastating tragedy. Within three months, the state had passed a law that redefined failing schools in New Orleans (not the entire state) and authorized the state's RSD to take control of all but about a dozen public schools in the city. The local board also fired nearly all school employees, effectively shutting down the most significant opposition to the forces of privatization and devastating the Black middle class.

Chapter 2 goes back in time to before the storm. Looking at the state laws passed between 1997 and 2005, I demonstrate that the path toward reform began well before Katrina. By 2005, Louisiana had long mandated annual standardized testing and had implemented a grading system for all public schools in the state. The state had paved the way for alternative teacher certification programs to replace traditionally certified instructors and had watered down tenure protections. Most important, Louisiana had developed a mechanism to take control of failing schools and already singled out New Orleans as its target. These moves, approved and implemented long before Katrina was even listed among the named storms for 2005, made it possible for the State Legislature to vote just two months after the storm to change the definition of failing schools and take control of nearly all of New Orleans' public schools.

Considering the pre-Katrina period in this context complicates the story of responsibility and accountability for the reforms. My analysis shows that New Orleans officials in the State Legislature, including Democrats and Republicans and Black as well as white legislators, voted in favor of these proposals. A majority of New Orleans voters also supported the creation of the RSD, giving the state the authority to take control of poor-performing schools. A year before Katrina, New Orleans voters elected a reform-minded school board. Opponents of the post-Katrina reforms often claim that these policies were hammered out in secret and were rammed down the throats of the local community. Though there is some truth to this narrative, it neglects to recognize that many residents, including many in the African American community, supported and helped to put the system into place.[20]

Chapter 3 picks up in 2006 and 2007 and explains how reformers maintained the reforms, often in the face of tremendous pressure to roll back and recentralize some aspects of the system. They ensured state control for a long period when they wrote the law that took the schools, made changes to the system only when forced to do so, kept items off the agenda to engineer acceptable outcomes outside the public eye, and framed their opponents as selfish "defenders of the status quo." These tactics prevented critics from making any headway as they pushed back against charters and private governance. Together, Chapters 2 and 3 cast doubt on the argument that the reforms were merely a practical necessity and there was no intention to exclude certain perspectives from decision making. Although some individuals may not have intended to end up with the system as it looks today, there is a lot of evidence that these policies were planned from tip to tail.

The second half of the book turns to the effects of the reforms not on students' education outcomes but, rather, on governance. Private, hand-selected boards now govern nearly every aspect of K–12 education in New Orleans. Chapter 4 examines these governing boards that handle millions in taxpayer dollars, select school leaders, and are responsible for compliance with federal and state laws. Drawing on my own survey of charter board members, an analysis of meeting minutes, and a look at the compliance of these boards with state meetings laws, I demonstrate that these boards are unrepresentative, lack transparency, and fail to engage the public, and its members are skeptical about their roles as public servants. Even with the serious problems with the elected school board prior to Katrina, these handpicked boards are far from a replacement of the elected board with regard to representation, accountability, and responsiveness. Charter boards provide reformers with a powerful mechanism to maintain the new status quo. The continued marginalization of Black voices, both in terms of those who serve on the boards and in the incorporation of public inquiry and dissent, makes it next to impossible to make meaningful changes to the system.

Chapters 5 and 6 focus on the feedback of these policies on public opinion, especially that of public school parents. I use evidence from publicly available surveys and my own studies, including surveys and focus groups. In general, New Orleanians tend to believe the school system has improved. A closer look at these data indicates serious divisions between Black and white residents and between those with kids in public schools and everyone else, suggesting that direct experience with the system is associated with distinctly different beliefs about its fairness. Chapter 5 focuses primarily on these parents' attitudes and experiences with school enrollment and with school authorities. It shows that parents are frustrated and tired. They believe the system is rigged against them and that the same people who had advantages before the storm have them now. Many parents do not appreciate the (mostly white) folks who have come to the city to "save" them and their children, and they long for high-quality schools in their neighborhoods.

Chapter 6 focuses on how these attitudes about and experiences with schools affect political efficacy and trust. In general, political efficacy and participation in local elections have decreased slightly since Katrina. Trust remains low. The feedback effects are minimal, I conclude, because Black residents had very little trust or faith in city officials to start. The parents with whom I met in focus groups are not surprised that they were excluded from the school decisions and that they continue to be at a disadvantage in this new system. Many are angry, but most are simply resigned. They do not believe things are going to get much better, but they remain hopeful, largely because they feel like they have no other options.

The Conclusion analyzes what this all means for schools and for democracy. One might ask why the attitudes and experiences of parents ought to matter *if the reforms are improving educational outcomes.* If kids in New Orleans' public schools are learning more and achieving at higher levels, why should we care about the civic effects of the reforms? The chapter weighs the evidence about improvement in educational outcomes against the findings in this book. The evidence about growth in test scores and other educational outcomes is mixed, at best, and cannot be separated from political attitudes and behavior. The system requires a high degree of buy-in from parents to work as designed, but their lack of faith and continued belief in its inherent inequality influence the choices they make about where their kids go to school and how they engage with these authorities. The support for the system seems to come primarily from those whose children are not in public schools. Further, given the stratification of public and private schools by race, white residents are unlikely to have any real sense of responsibility for public schools. Michael Engel reminds us: "Democratic values are a necessary, even if not sufficient, condition for defending the existence of public education."[21] As the school system in New Orleans has become less and less democratic, it becomes increasingly difficult for the collective citizenry to be concerned about them and easier to privatize them and, ultimately, to give up on the enterprise of public education altogether.

The Conclusion also provides a few modest policy prescriptions designed to increase participation among parents of public school children; improve trust and strengthen their faith that the system is fair; and make the system more representative, responsive, and easier to navigate. Contrary to reformers' rhetoric, there are a multitude of policy options; it is not a choice between what we have now and what we had before. Reformers have made it next to impossible to unravel the system and return to a traditional neighborhood-based school district. Even so, there are options that would include more voices in the process and provide greater legitimacy of the system. I encourage policy makers to consider our democracy as seriously as they say they consider school performance.

The inequality and racial disparities that continue to characterize public education in New Orleans are a function of the inequalities in the local democracy. Systems that exclude the perspectives and realities of those who are most directly affected by a policy will only exacerbate inequality. To improve support for and the functioning of the system, those who have had a tight grip on power will have to loosen their control. If they refuse, then eventually parents and other community members will find ways outside the traditional political process to influence these outcomes.

The Reforms

What Happened in 2005?

[The exclusion of the public from discussions of opening West Bank schools in the weeks following Hurricane Katrina] is a disguised back-door attempt to push through a prehurricane agenda while the citizens of this city are displaced throughout the country. . . . It is in this time of crisis . . . that the role of public input is crucial. The people of New Orleans are entitled to participate in the process that will ultimately change the landscape of their public educational system.

—**Civil District Court Judge Nadine Ramsey**

On August 29, 2005, Hurricane Katrina laid waste to the Gulf Coast. Initially, after the storm came ashore, a collective sigh of relief could be heard from wherever New Orleans residents had evacuated. The storm had veered just east of the city, and it seemed as if residents would be heading home within a couple of days. Then, in a moment, that sigh turned into collective anguish. In shelters and strange and unfamiliar living rooms, we watched the water pouring over and through the levees surrounding Lake Pontchartrain.[1] We watched as our fellow New Orleanians who had been unable to evacuate waved sheets from their rooftops and boiled in the summer heat at the Superdome and the Convention Center. All these years later, many of us can still be taken back to those traumatizing days in a single second with a picture, a smell, or a sound.[2]

For months—years for many—residents worked to pick up the pieces of their lives. Beyond material possessions, thousands lost their jobs and communities. Only eight of 126 public schools escaped with minor damage.[3] Thousands enrolled their children in schools where they had evacuated: Houston, Baton Rouge, Memphis, Atlanta, and even more far-flung places. If the city were to ever rebuild, it would need schools. Within days of the storm, many advocates and education reformers began to discuss the "opportunity" that Katrina had provided New Orleans to build something new, something better than what had been destroyed.[4] In an infamous piece in a national newspaper that captured both the racism and classism of the moment, "old-line families" insisted that "the remade city [would not] simply restore the old order . . . burdened by a teeming underclass, substandard schools and a high crime rate."[5]

On November 28, 2005, the first public school reopened. The Associated Press noted the event, stating, "Some private schools in New Orleans began reopening in October, but no public school had opened, *with the exception of a few charters that were outside the local board's control.*"[6] This statement should have served as a warning. In 2019, the elected Orleans Parish School Board (OPSB) closed the last two remaining non-charter schools in the city. Every public school student in New Orleans is in a charter school.[7]

How did this happen? How can a major U.S. city eliminate its neighborhood public schools? Scholarship in political science and public policy explains that major, systemic policy reform is rare. There are too many "special" interests. Too many elected officials who fear a major change could disrupt their own electoral chances. Too many veto points where reform can stall indefinitely. The people who are most often directly affected by policies are disorganized and lack access to those in power. Conventional wisdom holds that the reforms in New Orleans start with Katrina, a storm that turned the city upside down. This event is responsible, some scholars and activists contend, for setting in motion the forces that led to these major policy changes.

I contend that the sweeping changes were not the result of a single, life-altering event but, rather, were a function of dozens of incremental shifts made over the decade that led up to Katrina. The hurricane emboldened people who had been about the business of dismantling the public schools in New Orleans, but it was not, by itself, responsible for the seismic shift in governance.[8] By excluding all dissenting voices, the reformers, to be introduced in the coming pages, strategically put in place a system that would be difficult for critics to change in the years after reform. Though there have been some modifications since 2005, the system today has most of the same features as the one designed in those early days after the storm. It has staying power not because everyone in New Orleans supports the new system, but because it was set up to shut out opponents and quiet critics.

This strategy has predictable effects. Other scholars have focused on the educational impacts, which are, of course, essential to any thorough accounting of benefits and harms.[9] This book focuses instead on the feedbacks of the reforms on the elite who now govern public education in New Orleans, the parents whose children make up the school population, and the system of governance itself. Members of charter school boards are disproportionately white and do not see themselves as public servants. They do not envision an important role for the public in public education. Parents, most of whom are Black, have internalized the idea that school choice is essential, but many are not satisfied with their experiences within the system or the schools. They are frustrated and largely resigned to a system that was not built for them. The reforms have eroded key features of a democracy—accountability, representation, responsiveness, and efficacy. But first, this chapter explains what happened in the fall of 2005 and then reviews how these events can be explained with current theories of policy change.

Capitalizing on the Disaster—The Early Moves to the All-Charter System

In the 2004–2005 school year, New Orleans public schools had a graduation rate of only 56 percent, 10 points below the state and 18 points below the national average.[10] The state deemed 63 percent of public schools "academically unacceptable" and ranked the district as the second-lowest performing in the state. Only about 20 percent of Orleans Parish graduates enrolled in college. Schools in New Orleans were also segregated, as white parents had begun to leave the public schools decades earlier. Middle- and upper-class Blacks began to join them in the 1980s. Between 1995 and 2005, public school enrollment in Orleans Parish decreased 25 percent while private school enrollment increased 5 percent; the others left New Orleans for better schools in neighboring parishes.[11] By 2004, one-third of all students in New Orleans attended a private or parochial school.[12] The school district was composed primarily of the poorest and most disadvantaged children in the city: African American children made up 94 percent of the students in the district, although Black people were only 66 percent of the city's population; 73 percent of students qualified for free or reduced-price lunch, while the childhood poverty rate in the city was 41 percent.[13] These disparities make it likely that any reform of public schools would be racialized. Jamila Michener argues that one of the key features of a racialized polity is disproportionality "in the ways policies allocate benefits and burdens to particular racial groups."[14] Any system with such enormous racial disparities in education outcomes will affect policy feedback in terms of how resources are allocated, which interests are better served, and how various groups within society interpret the policies.

In addition to low performance and declining enrollment, the central office had enormous problems: eight school superintendents cycled through between 1998 and 2005. The district was rife with corruption. A 2003 report estimated that the central office had misspent $11 million by inappropriately providing checks to nearly four thousand people and health insurance to two thousand people who were retired, had been fired, or were dead.[15] A 2005 audit by the U.S. Department of Education reported that the district had failed to appropriately document $71 million of Title I federal grant dollars. Also in 2005, the Federal Bureau of Investigation indicted eleven central office employees, including a former school board president accused of accepting bribes, and the district faced the threat of bankruptcy. Business leaders wanted something "draconian" to happen to break the cycle of incompetence and corruption.[16]

Thus, many residents, across racial and economic divides, believed that Hurricane Katrina presented an opportunity to remake the school system. The waters had not receded from most of New Orleans when advocates across the United States began to discuss a "clean slate" for the city's schools. Paul Hill, director of the pro-reform Center for Reinventing Public Education, argued that the situation in New Orleans presented a "green field" opportunity to create a "new collection of public schools that families could choose for their children." Chester Finn Jr., a longtime advocate of school choice, stated, "It's one thing to re-create Galatoire's [a famous New Orleans restaurant]. But to re-create a failed school system would be really stupid." Finn, former assistant secretary of education under President Ronald Reagan, recommended a "system of schools" that would have "multiple operators of diverse schools all subscribing to the same basic standards."[17] Most of the "clean slate" folks recommended the city rely on the goodwill from philanthropists and the private sector to fund new school designs. A few, mostly members of the "old" coalition, expressed reservations about those with little knowledge of New Orleans history or culture having such authority.

Two main options emerged from the early, private discussions among reformers: mayoral control and a state takeover of the Orleans Parish district. Mayor Ray Nagin of New Orleans put a committee together, chaired by Tulane University's President Scott Cowen, that recommended more school autonomy but would have kept a mayor-appointed governing board. This majority-white committee was composed of business and philanthropic leaders; only one member worked in New Orleans public schools.[18] Nagin, however, had lost tremendous capital due to his response to Katrina. Further, a powerful policy entrepreneur, Leslie Jacobs, favored a state takeover. As I cover in the next chapter, Jacobs had spent the previous decade setting the stage for such a takeover, ensuring there was both political will and a legal apparatus for this option. Though the mayor's committee consulted with parents, teachers, and principals nationwide and sought advice from national experts, notably absent from the discussions about the future governance of the district were scholars of education and teachers, parents, and students in the Orleans Parish school system.[19] Those with power and authority seemed to believe there were no local successes on which to build, arguing that a complete break from the past was necessary.

As is common, policies also followed funding. The U.S. Department of Education announced it was awarding $20.9 million to Louisiana through the Charter School Program to "help reopen charter schools damaged by hurricanes, help create 10 new charter schools, and expand existing charter schools to accommodate students displaced by hurricane damage."[20] Private foundations and nonprofits also sought to capitalize on the opportunity to remake New Orleans schools, offering funds only if the city agreed to abandon its "adult-centered" agenda toward a (presumably child-centered) agenda focused on charter schools and public-private partnerships.[21] The Eli and Edythe Broad Foundation, a staunch proponent of neoliberal education reforms, asked that New Orleans consider whether an elected board is "really the most effective structure for the system in times of crisis."[22]

A new reform-minded OPSB had been elected less than a year earlier, and along with the state Board of Elementary and Secondary Education (BESE), it signaled early on that it was open to change. When the first post-Katrina OPSB meeting was held in Baton Rouge on September 15, 2005, one new board member, Phyllis Landrieu, attempted to replace the district's officers. Her motion was voted down along racial lines, with the three African American board members accusing the three white members and one Latina of attempting to disenfranchise Black residents who had been the hardest hit in Katrina.[23] As a result, members of the BESE asked whether the state should be more involved, given the "extraordinary times."

In the meantime, a few schools announced their plans to reopen as charters. Benjamin Franklin High School, a nationally ranked, selective-admission magnet school announced it would reopen as a charter. Two of the nine pre-Katrina charter schools sustained minimal damage and announced plans to reopen.[24] Robert Mills Lusher Elementary School had voted just before Katrina to convert to a charter and expand to a selective-admission middle and high school. In those early months, the OPSB voted to allow Lusher to move its middle and high school into Alcée Fortier High School, displacing a predominantly Black school near Tulane University's main campus.[25] In fact, Tulane provided Lusher with $1.6 million to help it reopen and expand. In exchange, the school agreed that university faculty and staff would have priority for enrollment. The African American community saw the decision to supplant a predominantly Black, open-enrollment school with a selective-admission institution that would give priority to Tulane's mostly white staff as a land grab by whites to occupy culturally and historically significant Black spaces. Lusher Charter High School today serves a substantially whiter and less poor population than other high schools.

In early October, Governor Kathleen Blanco suspended several restrictions on charter schools.[26] That same day, the OPSB voted to reopen thirteen public schools in Algiers, a community on the West Bank of the Mississippi River that was not flooded in Katrina, as charter schools.[27] Two African American OPSB members voted against the move, along with the new interim superintendent, arguing they had been ambushed. Lourdes Moran, vice president of the OPSB, admitted that she had kept her colleagues in the dark about the vote but had floated the idea with a "core group of community leaders in Algiers at an invitation-only meeting" a day earlier, where several people said that "anything that stripped power away from [OPSB] is a positive." Even so, Moran denied that she was "trying to wrest the schools away from district control." Some attendees did not buy it. One person screamed that the move was "a public lynching," and another stated, "While we're still counting bodies in New Orleans, you're giving away the schools."[28]

These early moves made it clear that many officials saw charter schools not as temporary necessities, but as models of the future. City Councilwoman Jackie Clarkson said that a charter school system on the West Bank "could literally set the standard for the way the rest of the system goes."[29] State Superintendent of Education Cecil Picard, who had written the original law authorizing charter schools in Louisiana as a mechanism to thwart privatization, argued that all public schools opening in New Orleans in that first year should only be opened as charter schools, citing the district's financial problems, the federal money available for charters, and the private education associations and philanthropic groups willing to donate money to charter schools.[30]

Fast and Furious

In late October 2005, the OPSB moved forward with plans to charter not only the original thirteen schools on the West Bank but also twenty district schools on both sides of the river. The first public schools in Orleans Parish opened in November and December, only one of which was not a charter school. Then, just after Thanksgiving, Governor Blanco signed into law Act 35, which forever changed the education landscape in New Orleans. In a special legislative session, the governor had pushed a plan that shifted control of any failing public school in a district that is "academically in crisis" from the locally elected board to the state Recovery School District (RSD), a state takeover district that had been created two years earlier. Act 35 changed the standard for failing schools in districts that were in academic crisis to include any school with a performance score below the state average. This new metric included many schools with C and D grades that were not considered failing under the old measure. New Orleans was the only district to which these new rules applied, and the new standard meant that nearly all schools in the city were considered failing. This law allowed the RSD to organize its schools in "whatever manner to be most likely to improve the academic performance of each student in the school" and without regard to attendance zones.[31] The New Orleans delegation was split along racial lines: of the fifteen state House representatives, ten Black representatives were opposed and five white officials supported the bill; three of seven senators opposed the bill, all of whom were Black. Only one Black New Orleans state senator, Ann Duplessis, supported Act 35.[32] These votes reflect the belief that the move to take over New Orleans schools was a racialized assault on local autonomy.[33] Act 35 led the state Department of Education to seize control of 102 public schools in New Orleans, leaving only thirteen public schools under the governance of the OPSB.

One additional event reformed New Orleans schools in a dramatic fashion. Two days after the governor signed Act 35, the OPSB announced that all public school employees who had not returned to work would have their contracts terminated as of January 31, 2006.[34] The board argued that, because the state had taken control of 84 percent of the schools, the district could not afford to pay teachers and administrators it would not have the authority to rehire. This decision led to years of court battles that the teachers ultimately lost.[35] In the short term, however, it meant that thousands of middle-class African American women, who made up the majority of the teacher force in New Orleans, would lose their jobs, making them less likely to return to the city. Those who returned would have to reapply to work as teachers in the new charter school sector. The dominant African American newspaper in New Orleans, the *Louisiana Weekly*, described the effect of this decision: "It was a huge blow to the Black middle class. Replacing the teachers with inexperienced, uncertified, white teachers from out-of-state sent a powerful message about who was valued in the new system."[36]

How Does Systemic Change Happen?

Systemic policy change like this is, if not rare, certainly not the norm. Early political science theories discussed the bias toward the status quo. Charles Lindblom noted, for example, that comprehensive change is impractical and risky for elected officials because of its unpredictability.[37] Similarly, E. E. Schattschneider argued that once in place, policies "stimulate the growth of industries dependent on this legislation for their existence, and these industries form the fighting legions behind the policy."[38] Mancur Olson's work on collective action indicates that the opponents of these industries have to overcome substantial barriers to organization and mobilization.[39] In short, the status quo often serves powerful interests and protects incumbents, making comprehensive policy change an enormous challenge.

In education specifically, the school choice proponents Paul Hill, Christina Campbell, and James Harvey contend, "The normal politics of school systems cannot support fundamental reform" because those who run or benefit from the system are unlikely to work to change it.[40] To reformers, the "fighting legions" against contemporary education reform consisted of what Wilbur Rich refers to as the "education cartel," those who are supposedly most concerned about the protection of jobs and career ladders.[41] Teachers, principals, and central office staff have resisted high-stakes testing, new systems of evaluation and compensation, and the stripping of power from elected boards, especially regarding personnel decision making. Contemporary reformers deride teachers and other school officials as self-serving. But they are far from the only groups to push back against standards-based reform and school choice. In some communities, parents pressure elected officials for their particularistic interests, such as fighting for children with special needs or for special treatment for their neighborhood schools.[42] In New Orleans, most white parents abandoned public schools in the 1970s and 1980s, instead directing their political efforts toward economic development.[43] Their lack of financial, political, and psychological investment shaped the system during this period as much as teachers unions and school boards.

In any subsystem, the dominant coalition, or "cartel," is very stable. It exercises power not only through the formal policy process but also by determining "broad acceptance of certain ways of understanding what items are legitimate issues for the exercise of political power."[44] By defining the problem, the reigning groups in the subsystem shape policy. In education, for most of the second half of the twentieth century, the dominant coalition defined the main problems around racial segregation and unequal funding, and as the national conversation about schools shifted the problem identification toward outcomes and performance, this dominant coalition began to lose power.[45]

The new coalition in education politics did not come to power overnight. The national conversation on public education began to shift away from its focus on equality and integration after the release of *A Nation at Risk* in

1983. This report, produced by President Reagan's National Commission on Excellence in Education, lamented the fall of American public schools, especially as compared with other nations, and spawned decades of criticism of teachers, public schools, principals, and school boards. The report helped to galvanize a movement. A new coalition would eventually form the new education policy subsystem at the national level and within many states, including Louisiana. The players included conservative foundations, right-wing and libertarian think tanks, a growing cohort of young Republican and Democratic lawmakers, the rising Religious Right movement, business entrepreneurs, and education conservatives. Over time, civil rights groups joined the coalition due to their continued frustration with the unequal outcomes from and inputs into the schools that primarily served students of color.[46] Although substantive policy victories at the federal level were slow to come, in the late 1980s and 1990s, state governors and legislators began to gain power and change public policy in ways that would enable major reforms such as those in New Orleans.

During the 1990s, several cities attempted systemic reform, most without lasting success. Urban education reform has been largely characterized by trying to apply best practices without disrupting the underlying system, "movement without progress."[47] It was focused on programmatic reforms, such as new curricula or pedagogy, and personnel changes. With each new idea, new superintendent, or new slate on the school board, cities had high hopes that were usually dashed when test scores failed to skyrocket or when the complete financial picture was discovered. New coalitions came together for a brief period, but systemic reform was generally elusive. Within this framework it is easy to see why most education "reform" occurred at the margins and was neither transformative nor durable.

Overcoming Structural Obstacles to Reform

Given the challenges to systemic or comprehensive policy change, what explains the dramatic changes in the organization of New Orleans schools after 2005? Many scholars and activists point to a single event—Hurricane Katrina—as responsible for education reform in New Orleans. The political scientist Terry Moe, for example, writes, "[Katrina's] physical destruction set in motion a series of events that [destroyed the power of the local vested interests]."[48] Similarly, the economist Douglas Harris claims that Katrina swept "out the political opposition and [swept] in some desperate circumstances."[49] David Osborne sums up this sentiment, claiming that the city got "a chance to start over" and "Louisiana's leaders wiped the slate clean in New

Orleans."[50] Though they acknowledge there were "enacted policies" before the storm, Andre Perry and Michael Schwam-Baird claim, "The absence of evacuated stakeholders changed the political dynamics that held the previous system together," as if the architects of the reforms would have included other people, but they just were not available. They go on to state that the rapid changes "were arguably convenient solutions to the acute needs that arose after the storm. In this regard, New Orleans education recovery can be interpreted as a series of reactions to unfolding events that built on preexisting policies rather than as a process based on pre-established goals."[51]

In this conception, the elimination of neighborhood schools and privatization of educational governance were merely convenient solutions to immediate problems, not the product of decades of stated goals and concerted activity along these lines. The exclusion of important stakeholders was due to the need for expediency and was not an intentional tactic to push through reforms while Black parents, teachers, and school employees were distracted and displaced. In the language of classic policy-making scholarship, Katrina was a "policy window" or a punctuation of the policy equilibrium. In these conceptions of agenda setting and policy formulation, the policy system is generally static, but if policy entrepreneurs can take advantage of a window of opportunity, they can produce large-scale change.[52] Katrina made it politically possible for the long-simmering problems of urban education to converge with solutions (standards-based reform, school choice, and portfolio management) that had been swirling in what John Kingdon calls the "policy primeval soup" to result in major change. It is an example of how an issue can "hit suddenly" and be followed by a "tremendous flurry of activity."[53]

Katrina obviously provided an opportunity for change. However, while the storm spurred rapid and dramatic reform in New Orleans, the years leading up to the hurricane were not characterized by stasis. The equilibrium had already begun to shift dramatically in the decade preceding the storm, when numerous policy changes were pushed through, primarily at the state level, but with at least some support from local leaders. Katrina sped the reform process along and widened its scope, but it was not responsible for setting the changes in motion; nor were the policies passed merely out of necessity or convenience. Louisiana's moves on education in the late 1990s and early 2000s were part of the national reform movement resulting from changing issue definitions and heightened attention on public schooling.[54] During this period, new actors began to "insist on rewriting the rules and changing the balance of power" that would ultimately establish a new equilibrium that would last well into the future.[55] They accomplished their agenda in large part by excluding and ridiculing critics and framing market-based reforms as the only workable solutions to improve the city's schools.

Focusing only on the immediate post-Katrina period the picture shows sweeping change directly tied to the man-made disaster's effects. However, the pre-Katrina period illustrates the power of incremental change that made these dramatic shifts possible. This gradual policy change happens as "the losers [in a policy system] adapt themselves to the new conditions imposed upon them."[56] As they adapt, they look for ways to disrupt the existing system.

An important element is relational. Clarence Stone argues, "Education, like other areas of policy action, is mediated through local politics. . . . Real policy innovation comes about less by simple enactment than by changing relationships."[57] New groups seeking power must work simultaneously to break up stable and powerful coalitions and build new arrangements. Harris calls the reformers in New Orleans a "family" whose private battles about political strategy and control were set aside as they "closed ranks" and moved with "common purpose."[58] In addition to establishing new relationships, policy innovation must upset the existing coalitions.[59] To be successful, there must be sufficient formal authority from elected leaders. The new coalition set about shifting how the problem was framed and, most important, moved the venue for the fight to the State Legislature from the local school board.[60] I show how the new education reform coalition used these tactics to disrupt the traditional power brokers, then capitalized on Katrina to expand the scope of the reforms they had already set in motion prior to the storm.

To the extent that Katrina provided a window of opportunity to solve the problems with New Orleans schools, the convergence was on particular problems as defined by this new coalition. The conflicts about the root problems in New Orleans public schools did not melt away in the immediate post-Katrina period. Rather, the groups of elites who were responsible for the reforms defined these problems differently from groups who had been active in education policy for generations. Because of the reforms these elites had put in place in the decade before the storm, and because they successfully excluded nearly all opposing voices, they gained power to act on their version of reform in the months after Katrina. The entrepreneurs were able "to hook their solutions to problems that seem[ed] pressing or to take advantage of propitious political happenings."[61]

The racial dynamics of the reform movement should not be overlooked. In New Orleans in the 2004–2005 school year, 89 percent of administrators and 73 percent of teachers were Black. Policies that targeted New Orleans educators did not have to explicitly mention race to have a disparate impact on Black people, mostly Black women. Breaking up the "cartel," then, meant destroying the power of middle-class African Americans. That a reform coalition dominated by whites would so disenfranchise Black women in a heavily Democratic and politically liberal city, all while espousing an equity framework, illustrates bell hooks's argument that white liberals can simultaneously disavow prejudice and "support and affirm the very structure of racist domination and oppression that they profess to wish to see eradicated."[62] Rather than embrace their experience and join with Black women in demanding more resources and better facilities, the reformers, most of whom were white, affluent, and well connected, believed they knew better how to fix an education system that primarily served Black children.

The next two chapters explain how the 2005 reforms were made possible by gradual changes over many years, then show how the reformers established a sustainable system that would be resistant to retrenchment. I first go back in time to trace the policy change at the state and local levels. Then, in Chapter 3, I pick up in 2006 to show how the reforms have remained in place despite lawsuits, reports of mismanagement and corruption, and cries of inequity from those who are directly affected by the reforms.

Incremental Change before the Storm

I think the best thing that happened to the education system
in New Orleans was Hurricane Katrina. That education
system was a disaster and it took Hurricane Katrina to wake
up the community to say "we have to do better." . . . That city
was not serious about its education, those children were being
desperately underserved.

—U.S. Secretary of Education Arne Duncan

Several significant, highly controversial, and politically
difficult pieces of legislation, that were attempts to get at the
problem, were passed prior to Katrina. . . . As a result, when
Katrina washed away many of the facilities and the bulk of the
students were forced to relocate . . . the largest portion of the
responsibility for rebuilding the schools fell to the state-run
Recovery School District.

—Louisiana State Senator J. Chris Ullo

Secretary Arne Duncan illustrates the conventional wisdom that Hurricane Katrina marked a beginning for education reform in New Orleans.
I argue, rather, that the city was not sleeping through the many problems
that plagued its education system. New Orleans and the State of Louisiana
had been in the throes of a reform movement for many years when the hurricane came through in 2005. The activities of the state and federal governments in the weeks and months following Katrina, described in the previous
chapter, would not have been possible without the incremental moves over the
decade prior to the storm. This chapter traces the evolution of policy reform
in Louisiana during this period and shows that, while Katrina accelerated and
expanded reforms, it did not mark the beginning of reform.

Dispelling the notion of Katrina as the starting point is important for several reasons. First, it is insulting to the people who worked tirelessly to remedy problems for years, especially throughout the long period of disinvestment
in the 1970s and 1980s. The African American community in New Orleans
continually fought for resources and reforms for years, but these efforts have

largely been ignored in this narrative about Katrina, which frames white re-formers as saviors.

This story also suggests that it takes a major event such as a natural disaster to make significant changes to a policy system. In fact, without the gradual changes that took place before 2005, it would have been more difficult and time-consuming for the state to define schools as "in crisis" and seize control. As other states and cities look to the New Orleans model, it is important that they understand that the 2005 reforms were the result of the efforts of activists and elected officials over a long period. They pushed policy forward in small increments. Katrina gave the movement an opportunity to make a giant step forward.

Finally, this narrative incorrectly assigns responsibility and lets some folks off the hook for their roles in laying the groundwork. With a few exceptions, New Orleans officials and voters supported the reforms put in place in the decade before Katrina. Although the immediate post-Katrina period certainly excluded certain groups, the period before the storm included more voices. I begin the chapter with a look at the work of Black activists and community members in the twentieth century, then take a close look at the activities within the Louisiana State Legislature in the decade preceding Katrina.

The Struggle for Education Equity

African American community activists have been active in the struggle for better public schools for decades.[1] Networks of neighbors, kin, fellow congregants, teachers, school administrators, and parents fought for better schools long before Katrina. Educational inequalities were not accidental and were not a byproduct of housing and land use decisions but were, rather, a means for whites to set up and maintain a system of white supremacy and segregation. According to a recent analysis, from the city's founding, "schools became forts on the frontier, opening new spaces and directing the people and markets that could go there."[2] The era of reform before Katrina and the transformation of schools in the years after the storm are a continuation of how race and education together shape the physical, economic, and social life of the city. Daniella Cook and Adrienne Dixson argue that "reform" is not a neutral, positive term signifying progress; rather, reforms historically are usually "grounded in negative assumptions and stereotypes about people of color" and "render invisible the complexities and richness of the experiences of people of color."[3]

In the early post–Civil War days, African Americans used their votes to push New Orleans to adopt integrated public facilities and schools.[4] Louisiana's majority-Black delegates pushed through a state constitution that encouraged

integrated schools (the only state in the South to do so).[5] Though integration
was short-lived, during the Jim Crow era that followed, the "quest for improvements in education became the only sustained form of protest that the black
community directed against the citadel of white political power and supremacy."[6] In 1900, when the school board voted to deny education to Black people
past the fifth grade, members of the Phyllis Wheatley Club continued to urge
Black parents to send their children to school for sixth grade and beyond. In
the 1930s and 1940s, legal fights led to policies requiring equal pay for white
and Black teachers, until the state restricted public-sector unions in the 1950s.[7]

After the Supreme Court's decision in *Brown v. Board of Education* in
1954, local and state governments stalled integration for years. The African
American community responded to these moves by submitting petitions, fil-
ing applications for admission to white schools, raising money to pay for litigation, and trying to win support from moderate whites. Civic groups such
as the Colored Educational Alliance, the New Orleans Federation of Civic Leagues, and the New Orleans branch of the National Association for
the Advancement of Colored People (NAACP) fought for better educational
opportunities in legal fights over teacher pay and segregation, protests about
the denial of higher education and decent school facilities, and civil disobedience of institutional segregation. In September 1963, the Citizens Committee, led by Oretha Castle, led the largest protest march in the history of New
Orleans.

Their efforts continued well past the 1960s, when schools were finally
integrated. During the 1970s, the federal government helped to build infrastructure and provide necessary services in some predominantly Black neighborhoods.[8] The 1980s, however, saw disinvestment in urban poverty programs, including desegregation efforts. Public services, especially schools,
had deteriorated significantly during the twenty-five years prior to Katrina.
The city's lack of investment was blamed on a recession in the 1980s and the
rollback of the Great Society. In reality, the state's focus was elsewhere, con-
centrating almost exclusively on economic development, including directing
resources toward a casino, an NBA franchise, and expansions of the convention center and the NFL team. In exchange for these projects, New Orleans
lost special project funds for improvements to the schools.[9] As a result, schools
became even more segregated by race: the percentage of Black children in
predominantly Black schools rose during the 1990s and early 2000s.[10]

As schools continued to suffer, Black education activists pressed the city
for improvements to facilities and increased funding.[11] Most elected officials
ignored their efforts. As in other cities, Black activists "have looked at the
local schools as the platform from which to launch their battle against sys-

temic discrimination and subordination," and they continued to fight any-way.[12] In 1988, voters approved a property tax increase but defeated new funds for school facilities. In 1989, the Lower Ninth Ward Neighborhood Council won a major victory when the Orleans Parish School Board (OPSB) allocated $6 million for a new school to be named Dr. Martin Luther King Jr. Elementary School.[13] The school eventually opened in 1995, largely thanks to continuous community activism.[14]

In 1993, activists were successful in pushing the OPSB to approve allow-ing a school's parents, staff, and students to change the names of several schools from those of slave owners and Confederate leaders to those of Afri-can American civil rights activists. Among others, Jefferson Davis Elementa-ry became Ernest Morial Elementary and Robert E. Lee Elementary became Ronald McNair Elementary. By 2005, there was even some uplifting news on achievement: test scores indicated that 79 percent of New Orleans schools had improved their School Performance Scores from the previous year. In 2004, fourth-graders in fifty-five of eighty schools showed improvement in English and math.[15]

The continuous activism belies the notion that Katrina marked the begin-ning of an education reform movement in New Orleans. While Black com-munity members fought continuously, the white elites ignored their efforts. Thus, when white state officials began to actively pursue education reform in the 1990s, they did not see themselves as building on the work of these activ-ists. Further, the victories around renaming schools cost the white business elite very little. Instead, they concentrated on the new fight that was begin-ning to take shape at the state level as part of a national movement for educa-tion reform, focused largely on accountability and privatization.

Placing Reform in Context

The new reform coalition of liberal and conservative politicians, think tanks, and organizations described in Chapter 2 began to see successes at the state level in the 1990s. At the national level, President Bill Clinton's Goals 2000: Educate America Act and the 1994 Improving America's Schools Act recom-mended the use of assessments to hold schools accountable, the creation of uniform standards, and new aspects of school privatization. Federal legisla-tion did not advance much beyond encouraging states to boost standards and accountability, but that changed in 2002 with the passage of No Child Left Behind. This law mandated that schools test all students in grades 3–8 and once in high school. They were to report scores publicly and by several subgroups. Schools that failed to meet state standards would receive increasingly harsh penalties each year and could be closed or required to turn over the staff. The logic behind these policies was that the federal government and states would "hold schools accountable," which, in turn, would motivate teachers and students to "do better." The federal law stopped short of allowing parents to choose private schools, but it did give parents the option to select a different public school if their children were in a failing school.[16]

Many of these provisions had come out of states that had been experimenting with accountability and choice throughout the 1990s. This type of "bottom-up" federalism can result in policy diffusion at the federal level.[17] By 2000, forty-nine states had developed English/language arts standards (up from twenty in 1995) and mathematics standards (up from twenty-five), and forty-six states had created standards in science (up from twenty-three) and social studies (up from twenty). These content standards were usually accompanied by performance standards—the scores to be considered "proficient" or "basic" in a given area. Similarly, by 2000, nearly all states administered tests at least once in elementary and once in middle school. All states had annual "report cards," and forty states reported these results at the school level. Although states had administered standardized tests for generations, until the 1990s few tied test scores to specific consequences. By 2000, seven states were rewarding districts and twenty were rewarding schools for performance; twenty-nine states were sanctioning districts and thirty-two were sanctioning schools for poor performance. It was not only more common to punish than to reward, but individual schools, rather than entire districts, were targets.

In addition to standards and reporting, states adopted several forms of school choice. Where school choice proponents had long championed voucher programs that would allow public money to go to private schools, in the 1990s charter schools quickly gained popularity as an alternative mechanism for school choice. Charter schools are publicly funded but privately managed or operated. They are free to set their own schedules, establish their own curricula, and hire their own personnel. In exchange for this liberation, charter schools are authorized for only a certain period, and their authorizers are supposed to hold them accountable for academic performance and quality management. Between 1991 and 1999, the number of states that allowed charter schools jumped from one (Minnesota) to thirty-seven (the number includes Washington, DC), and the number of charter schools doubled between 1997 and 1999. Three states also passed legislation enabling voucher programs.[18]

Reformers also had their eyes on governance. Locally elected school boards were problems, they believed, because they were beholden to the teachers' unions, which were the most powerful groups to oppose reformers' plans.[19] Between 1989 and 2005, state governments assumed control of more than forty-five school districts in nineteen states.[20] For most reformers, the real problems were in cities, where test scores were chronically low, unions were powerful, and racial minorities looked to the school system for middle-class jobs and political power. The movement on school choice, first with voucher programs and later with charter schools, was concentrated in urban centers.[21] State takeovers took place in large and medium-size city districts such as Boston and Newark. These takeovers were more common in cities in which the Black community had risen in power during the previous two decades.[22] White flight and the loss of low-skill manufacturing jobs placed heavy burdens on cities.[23] Test scores and graduation rates were consistently lower in cities than in the suburbs.[24] To educators, the culprit was obvious: impoverished students and resource-poor districts.[25] Reformers, however, used these disparities to push their ideas about incompetent teachers and corrupt and inefficient central bureaucracies.[26]

Policy Reform Becomes Possible

As reviewed in Chapter 1, the deck is generally stacked against comprehensive policy reform. Eric Patashnik highlights the importance of policy entrepreneurs "manipulating the procedural context of decisions" to push through the status quo.[27] In other words, to deal with the challenges of powerful interest groups, risk-averse politicians, and apathetic publics that work in tandem to prevent serious reform, reformers should focus on changing the rules by which policies are made. This might include formal rules about whether amendments can be offered to bills or strategic decisions about which committee should take up a piece of legislation. Another common tactic is to move the policy venue, where the policy equilibrium is different, thereby giving some actors advantages they could not find in another venue.[28] There are numerous examples of failed federal reforms finding success at the state level. In the case of education, reformers moved their fight from the local level to the state.

As education entrepreneurs focused on state legislatures and appointed boards, there was a possibility that state legislatures could vote for policies directed at cities by overriding the urban delegation. Big-city representatives often claim to be mistreated by their states, as when George Washington Plunkitt complained about "hayseed legislators" in Albany.[29] In Louisiana, there are significant cultural, political, and economic differences between the major urban area—New Orleans—and the rest of the state. New Orleans is home to a predominantly Catholic, African American population compared with the more rural areas that are whiter and more Protestant.

Demographic and political shifts are also changing the relationship between states and cities. As the partisan divide has grown between urban and rural America, with cities becoming increasingly Democratic, the potential for conflict increases.[30] In recent years, there have been several examples of cities' moves toward more progressive policies conflicting with state policies.[31] Georgia Governor Brian Kemp's order preventing municipalities from passing mandates for face coverings during the COVID-19 pandemic is just one recent example. Further, as cities lost population in the late twentieth century, they also lost strength in state legislatures at the same time that direct funding from the federal government was cut dramatically. Although urban-suburban coalitions could offset some of this imbalance, they require strong leadership and innovative strategies that make them difficult to maintain.[32]

Recent scholarship finds that, despite conventional wisdom about conflict between cities and their home states, when urban delegations are unified, they can "manage the state's involvement in city affairs."[33] Gerald Gamm and Thad Kousser show that the reason big-city bills fail at higher rates than those affecting smaller municipalities is that the delegations are larger and more internally divided.[34] Domingo Morel's analysis of state takeovers similarly demonstrates that local leaders are able to represent their constituents better in cohesive state-local regimes than in disjointed regimes.[35] This literature suggests that if New Orleans delegates could unify on education reform, it would be harder for the more rural parts of the state to push their agenda.

In the 1990s and early 2000s, Louisiana followed national trends in adopting education policies focused on accountability, standards, and choice. Though the bills were passed at the state level, they were targeted at New Orleans and, in most cases, passed with the support of at least some of the city's delegation. In no case was the New Orleans delegation united against an education reform that ultimately passed. This chapter traces the advocacy and policy changes in the state and city in the years leading up to Katrina, demonstrating that the hurricane merely sped along and widened the scope of changes that were already underway.[36] The ground undergirding the politics of public education in New Orleans did not shift due to Katrina as dramatically as some have contended.

New Governor, New Ideas

Louisiana got on board the charter school and accountability movement early on. In 1995, the state passed a modest charter school law, a pilot program that its author, State Senator Cecil Picard (who would shortly be named Louisiana's superintendent of education), called "the last line against vouchers and privatization," a clear indication that he believed dramatic change was on the horizon.[37] This law allowed no more than eight districts to apply for charters and required that any group establishing a charter school include certified teachers and at least ten citizens; it also mandated that charter schools enroll low-income students in at least the same percentage as the school system as a whole. Even with a large federal grant for charter schools awarded that same year, the idea did not catch fire immediately: over the next three years, only three charter schools were established in Louisiana.[38]

In 1996, Mike Foster was elected governor after the retirement of the colorful and controversial Edwin Edwards, who had served four nonconsecutive terms as governor over more than twenty years. Like many other longtime Democrats of that era, Foster switched parties when he decided to run for governor in 1995. On education, Foster vowed to replace the elected representatives to the state Board of Elementary and Secondary Education (BESE) with an entirely appointed board. Though this proposal did not succeed, his two terms were marked by major milestones in K–12 education, even though both the Senate and the House were controlled by the Democratic Party.[39]

When Foster took office in 1996, Leslie Jacobs, then vice president of the OPSB and chair of the governor's K–12 education transition team, indicated that the administration had "potentially explosive ideas that could rock the education establishment."[40] Jacobs was a native New Orleanian who had helped build her family's insurance brokerage firm before she was elected to the OPSB in 1992. Foster appointed her to the state BESE, where she served until 2008. A profile published that year claims that Jacobs "spearheaded or influenced every educational reform to flow from Baton Rouge in a dozen years."[41] Foreshadowing the future of power in the state, Foster's team excluded representatives from two of the most powerful groups in education politics: teachers' unions and school boards.[42] Along with Jacobs, Foster appointed the New Orleans native Paul Pastorek to the BESE and named Cecil Picard the superintendent of education. This team would be integral not only to the post-Katrina reforms but also to putting in place the key pieces of legislation in the years before the storm that made those changes possible.

Foster attempted to immediately expand charter schools by giving the BESE the authority to override local district decisions about authorizing these schools; this attempt failed in 1996 but succeeded in 1997.[43] That year, Governor Foster made K–12 education a centerpiece of his agenda. At the end of the session, one legislator called it "the most productive session [he had] ever served in."[44] The governor's "expansive, far-reaching plan" included pay raises for teachers, new spending on classroom technology, more in-service days for teachers' professional development, and, most important from a reform standpoint, a school-based accountability system that included high-stakes testing in the fourth and eighth grades.[45] Foster's school accountability plan included sanctions on low-performing schools, such as removal of principals and faculty. It would set performance standards for each school, with rewards and "corrective actions" beginning in 2000.[46]

Foster also called for loosening the rules put in place in 1995 on charter schools and $5 million for interest-free charter school loans. The governor, not known for his skill in oration, said: "We want things that haven't been done before, but things that have been talked about."[47] House Bill 2065, introduced by a Democrat, raised the cap on the number of charters and allowed those that had been rejected by their local school board to appeal to the state BESE. Other Democrats opposed the move to expand charters. John Travis from Jackson, Louisiana, warned it could "destroy the whole public school system in our state," and Lelon Kenney of Columbia, Louisiana, asked, "Isn't this going to devastate our local school system?"[48] That year, the legislature also passed revisions to the Louisiana Education Assessment Program (LEAP) to make the tests more difficult and to add a provision requiring the BESE to identify and publicly report on schools' performance.[49]

I examined all the K–12 education bills and resolutions introduced in either house of the Louisiana State Legislature from 1997 to 2005.[50] During this period, more than nine hundred bills and resolutions related to K–12 education were introduced. The issues ranged from the usual—curriculum, textbooks, teacher salaries—to newer arenas of education policy, such as accountability, standards, and school choice (see Table 2.1). Seventeen percent of the bills that passed during this period were related to school choice, standards, or assessment. On school choice, Republicans introduced seventeen bills related to vouchers, all of which failed. Given that Democrats controlled the legislature during this entire period, it is not surprising that more Democratic legislation was introduced and passed than that of Republicans. Nonetheless, GOP bills were as likely to pass: 31.5 percent of Republican bills passed compared with 30 percent of Democratic bills. With the exception of voucher programs, Democrats were nearly as likely as Republicans to introduce legislation related to standards, assessment, and school choice. Sixty-five percent of the charter school bills were introduced by Democrats. Just as they had at the national level, the education interests of the two parties began to converge around performance and "success."[51] Further, since this was a period of divided government, Democrats in the legislature pursued objectives the governor supported—again, with the exception of vouchers.

Table 2.2 shows the legislation that was passed by topic across each year in the study period. Although most topics were perennial issues, there were some trends. The bills related to the Recovery School District (RSD) did not

TABLE 2.1. TOPICS OF K–12 EDUCATION LEGISLATION INTRODUCED AND PASSED IN LOUISIANA, 1997–2005

Topic	Introduced by Democrat (Passed)	Introduced by Republican (Passed)	Total Introduced (%)	Total Passed (%)
Charters	24 (12)	13 (4)	37 (4.1)	16 (5.7)
Voucher program	0 (0)	17 (0)	17 (1.9)	0 (0.0)
RSD (state takeover district)	8 (1)	3 (2)	11 (1.2)	3 (1.1)
Standards	50 (7)	39 (14)	89 (9.9)	21 (7.6)
Curriculum	44 (15)	10 (5)	54 (6.0)	20 (7.2)
LEAP/student assessment	42 (3)	15 (4)	57 (6.3)	7 (2.5)
Special education	10 (5)	11 (6)	21 (2.3)	11 (4.0)
Textbooks/supplies	8 (5)	8 (3)	16 (1.8)	8 (2.9)
Student behavior/ discipline	42 (16)	13 (3)	55 (6.1)	19 (6.9)
Student health	14 (1)	8 (3)	22 (2.4)	4 (1.4)
Extracurricular activities	23 (4)	3 (0)	26 (2.9)	4 (1.4)
Transportation	21 (3)	2 (0)	23 (2.5)	3 (1.1)
Teachers (tenure, certification, training, evaluation, salary)	45 (15)	47 (15)	92 (10.1)	30 (10.9)
Local superintendent	7 (3)	7 (1)	16 (1.8)	4 (1.4)
School employees (general)	48 (15)	18 (11)	66 (7.3)	26 (9.4)
School boards	39 (15)	35 (13)	74 (8.2)	28 (10.1)
Taxes	9 (3)	3 (2)	12 (1.3)	5 (1.8)
School property	21 (17)	7 (6)	28 (3.1)	23 (8.3)
State DOE/BESE/ state superintendent	47 (5)	52 (9)	99 (10.9)	14 (5.1)
School attendance	16 (5)	15 (1)	31 (3.4)	6 (2.2)
Other	31 (15)	26 (9)	57 (6.3)	24 (8.7)
Total	549 (165)	352 (111)	903	276

Source: Data from Louisiana State Legislature, compiled by the author.

TABLE 2.2. TOPICS OF K–12 EDUCATION LAWS PASSED
IN LOUISIANA BY YEAR, 1997–2005

Topic	1997	1998	1999	2000	2001	2002	2003	2004	2005
Charter	1	0	5	0	6	0	2	1	1
RSD	0	0	0	0	0	0	1	1	1
Standards	5	1	4	2	3	1	2	1	2
Curriculum	3	1	4	0	5	0	2	3	2
Assessment	1	2	2	0	1	0	0	0	1
Special education	1	1	2	1	2	2	0	2	0
Supplies	4	1	2	1	0	0	0	0	0
Discipline	5	1	5	0	2	0	3	2	1
Student health	0	0	0	0	0	0	2	0	2
Extracurricular activities	2	0	0	0	0	0	1	1	0
Transportation	1	0	0	0	2	0	0	0	0
Teachers	5	0	2	1	5	0	12	3	2
Local superintendent	0	2	2	0	0	0	0	0	1
School employees	1	0	4	0	4	1	9	5	2
School boards	2	2	4	2	7	1	5	4	1
Taxes	0	0	1	0	3	0	0	0	1
School property	2	1	2	1	3	3	2	5	4
State DOE/BESE	4	0	3	1	1	0	3	0	2
School attendance	1	0	1	2	0	1	0	0	1
Other	5	1	6	1	4	2	2	2	1
Total	43	13	49	12	48	11	46	30	25

Source: Data from Louisiana State Legislature, compiled by the author.

appear until 2003 with the passage of Act 9. The creation of a state takeover district was successful the first time it came before the legislature. The focus on standards and assessment tapered off over this period: fifteen bills related to standards and six bills related to assessment became laws between 1997 and 2001, but only six and one, respectively, passed between 2002 and 2005. Bills related to school employees were on the agenda in the later period: nine were passed into law in 1997–2001, compared with seventeen in 2002–2005. Reformers moved from focusing on standards and assessment to governance and personnel.

A New Millennium, More Reform

After the busy 1997 session, Governor Foster and the State Legislature continued to push for education reform for the remainder of his two terms. In 1999, the legislature approved several expansions of charter schools. Act 1339, passed unanimously in both houses, allowed the BESE to authorize the conversion of preexisting public schools to charters; allowed parents and faculty to circumvent the locally elected school board and petition to the state BESE to convert an existing public school into a charter school; lowered the potential for charters to serve at-risk students; and allowed charters to establish admissions standards "related to a school's mission," including academic achievement.[52] Again, it is important to emphasize that these laws were passed unanimously, and certainly not over the objections of New Orleans delegates. In most cases, Black and white New Orleans legislators were on the same page. Another law, Act 757, made dozens of changes to the original charter program, most of which expanded their authority or eased the process of applying, including allowing groups to apply to the state BESE for a charter if their applications are rejected or not acted on by the local district within thirty days. Two House members from New Orleans voted against this act, though all other New Orleans legislators supported it.[53] The result of these laws was to enhance the power of the state and the individual charter schools at the expense of the local school board.

In 1999, the accountability program began to release School Performance Scores (SPS) based on student achievement data.[54] Also in that year, requirements went into effect for students in the fourth and eighth grades to pass state tests to advance to the next grade.[55] In 2001, the state passed laws that would make it easier for out-of-state teachers to be certified and created the Critical Teacher Shortage Incentive Program to encourage more people to enter the profession in math, science, and special education.[56] The legislature also amended the law with Act 20 to allow charters to contract with for-profit organizations to manage schools, including authority over employment decisions. The New Orleans delegation was divided on this bill: one senator (of five) and nine of fifteen representatives voted against it. Diana Bajoie was the only senator to vote against the bill; Bajoie was the first Black woman elected to the Louisiana State Senate. In the House, three white members and six Black members of New Orleans's delegation voted against Act 20; its supporters were all white, except Karen Carter Peterson.

The 2003 session led to several important changes that would come into play in the aftermath of Katrina. Act 9 created the state takeover district by providing that an elementary or secondary school deemed "academically unacceptable" in any city or parish is a "failed school" and "shall be removed from the jurisdiction of" the local board and "transferred to the jurisdiction of the Recovery School District" under certain conditions.[57] Jacobs helped craft the package, stating, "The primary purpose of the bill is to create leverage."[58] The amendment was endorsed by the Louisiana Association of Educators but opposed by the state's other teachers union, as well as by the new superintendent of Orleans Parish Schools, Anthony Amato, and the Louisiana School Boards Association. Although a majority of the New Orleans delegation supported the law, they were split: two senators and six representatives opposed it. Though all but one of those who opposed the creation of the RSD was Black, many other Black representatives supported it.

Act 9 required a constitutional amendment to be approved by the voters in the state. An editorial in the *Baton Rouge Advocate* urged voters to approve Amendment 4, writing, "If [it] passes, obstinate or pathetically inadequate school systems" would have to make some choices:

> Does it make a real effort to rescue a failing school? Or does it face the consequences of a BESE takeover? We suspect that few boards want the humiliation of a BESE takeover. . . . The famously inadequate Orleans Parish system . . . is a managerial and educational nightmare, and its politics are heavily influenced by issues of patronage . . . and by the political realities of protecting union contracts for teachers and other workers. . . . Amendment 4 is an innovative addition to the state's accountability program.[59]

The bill's supporters were explicit that it was targeted at New Orleans. The editorial singled out this majority-Black district as influenced by "patronage" and "famously inadequate." A substantial majority of voters in the state (60%) and in New Orleans (56%) supported the measure, but in precincts in the city where Black people made up at least 90 percent of the electorate, voters rejected the amendment by 59 percent to 41 percent.[60] The OPSB passed a unanimous resolution against the amendment. The Louisiana Federation of Teachers called the takeover a "scheme" that would allow nonexperts in K–12 education to obtain public funds.

Local Reforms

While all this activity occurred at the state level, there were also efforts to reform the OPSB in the late 1990s and early 2000s. Two months before he was up for reelection, in December 1997, Mayor Marc Morial considered trying to take control of the public schools by public referendum.[61] In spite of his statement that the "school system scare[d] the bejesus" out of him,

Ray Nagin, Morial's successor, also floated the idea of having the city take over operations for the schools, citing chronic problems and "administrative incompetence" around the collection of taxes.[62] Ultimately, neither mayor did anything beyond making statements and "thinking out loud."

According to the journalism professor Andrea Gabor, 2004 marked the end of the OPSB until its revival over ten years later. In April 2004, State Representatives Karen Carter (Democrat) and Steve Scalise (Republican), both from New Orleans and both supporters of nearly all the reforms passed during Foster's terms, took direct aim at the city's elected school board with a new law boosting the powers of school superintendents in districts that were "academically in crisis." Citing mismanagement and low test scores in New Orleans, the governor signaled early support for the bill.

Act 193 provided that the label "academically in crisis" refers to a local system in which more than thirty schools are academically unacceptable or more than 50 percent of its students attend schools that are academically unacceptable. Only one district in the state fit the bill: Orleans Parish. The law gave the superintendent power over personnel and contracting and made it more difficult for a local school board to fire the superintendent. The act confined the powers of the OPSB to rejecting or approving budgets, policies, and contracts negotiated by the superintendent. The Committee for a Better New Orleans/Metropolitan Area Committee, headed by Joe Canizaro, a wealthy real estate developer and financier, led the effort to consolidate power with the superintendent. Five New Orleans representatives opposed the bill, and three others were absent during the vote. The votes on the bill represented strange bedfellows: several Black representatives from New Orleans who had opposed some of the earlier legislation supported stripping power from the locally elected board, while four of the five "nay" votes were white members, including one, James Tucker, who had supported many of the previous reforms. The measure passed unanimously in the State Senate.

As the bill made its way through the legislative process, four members of the OPSB tried, and ultimately failed, to fire the new superintendent, Tony Amato, before the law became effective. They were allegedly upset with the new state law limiting their power, but they were also irritated that Amato had allowed the Federal Bureau of Investigation to investigate the board, probes that led to a top official's guilty plea on federal bribery charges and dozens of other indictments and convictions.[63] When the board tried to oust him, Amato was at the height of his popularity. He was chosen as "New Orleanian of the Year" in 2004 by readers of *New Orleans Magazine*, a publication that serves mostly as advertising for tony boutiques and expensive restaurants.[64] As candidates considered running for the school board in August

2004, a poll showed that 70 percent of residents rated Amato as either "excellent" or "pretty good."[65] He fell out of favor quickly, however, when it came to light that he had used school workers and supplies to board up his house for a hurricane. In April 2005, Amato resigned.[66]

In response to the attempt to oust Amato, school board elections in 2004 were competitive. Voters in Orleans Parish "made it abundantly clear that they want[ed] sweeping change in leadership of their public schools."[67] Pre-election polls indicated that fewer than 10 percent of voters had a favorable view of the school board.[68] Three OPSB incumbents were defeated, and two others chose not to run.[69] The board's new members promised to be more committed than their predecessors to serious reforms. The new board did not have a Black majority for the first time in decades; it included three African Americans, three whites, and one Latina.[70] In a contentious runoff election, at least one Black candidate, Torin Sanders, out-raised the incumbent he defeated with the help of the white business community.[71]

In May 2005—three months before Katrina—the state superintendent of education selected a private firm, Alvarez and Marsal, to manage the district's finances.[72] Alvarez and Marsal had operated St. Louis schools, where it closed schools, cut the budget substantially, and privatized certain services. It began a comprehensive audit of the OPSB that summer and found the finances to be "a mess," saying that the district was a "candy jar" for various groups to enrich themselves.[73]

Incremental Change Paved the Way

In the years leading up to Katrina, a new coalition of reform-minded board members, appointed education officials, state legislators from within and outside New Orleans, and the business community gained power in public education politics in the city and the state. The coalition strongly believed that the central office staff was corrupt, inefficient, and incompetent; it also held a lot of contempt for the teachers, whom many believed were largely responsible for the abysmal scores on state tests and graduating students who did not have the skills to be successful. For years, members of this group had largely been shut out of local politics, so they opted to change the venue to the state level, where they made significant but gradual changes to education policy and waited for an opportunity to make dramatic change in New Orleans. This opportunity came on August 29, 2005.

This new set of powerful actors spent the decade before Katrina laying the groundwork for dramatic policy change. Table 2.3 summarizes the major, state-level education policy reforms targeted at New Orleans schools in the decade

TABLE 2.3. EVOLUTION OF EDUCATION POLICY IN LOUISIANA, 1995–2005	
1995	Passage of pilot charter school law
1996	Election of Governor Mike Foster Appointment of Leslie Jacobs and Paul Pastorek to BESE and Cecil Picard as state superintendent
1997	Passage of law to allow BESE to override local districts to authorize charter schools Passage of school-based accountability system Passage of law to raise cap on number of charter schools Passage of requirement that BESE will publicly report on school performance
1999	Passage of law allowing BESE to convert traditional schools into charter schools Passage of law allowing parents to petition for conversion of traditional school into charter school Passage of law allowing a reduction in the requirement that charters serve "at-risk" students Passage of law allowing charters to establish admission standards
2001	Passage of law easing the path to certification for nontraditional teachers Passage of law allowing charter schools to contract with for-profit management companies
2003	Creation of the RSD to take over "academically unacceptable schools"
2004	Passage of law stripping power from locally elected school boards and giving power over most decision making to local superintendents in districts that are "academically in crisis" (only New Orleans fit the definition) Election of reform-friendly majority on the local school board in New Orleans
2005	Katrina lands on August 29 Passage of law that redefines failing schools as those at or below the state average, only in districts that are "academically in crisis" (only New Orleans), and allows RSD to take control of nearly all New Orleans schools

prior to Katrina. By the time the storm's surge weakened the levees that held back Lake Pontchartrain, the state had already set up the potential for it to take control of schools it deemed academically unacceptable. Louisiana had already given charter schools significant advantages in resources and authority to take over traditional schools and establish their own enrollment policies. Standardized tests were being used to grade school performance, and nontraditional teachers had a path to employment. These policy reforms were required for the state to take over nearly all the schools after Katrina. They were also put in place with the support of many New Orleans representatives and voters.

Recognizing the long-term, gradual change contradicts several narratives that have emerged. First, Hurricane Katrina was not the starting point for reform. Though education reformers could not have predicted a disaster of Katrina's size and scope, they were intentional about reforms for many years. The policy entrepreneurs had successfully changed the rules by fighting at the state level, where local interests would have less power, and by reframing the problem with schools around a simple theme: performance. Who could be against high performance for all students? This decade-long initiative succeeded in persuading many in New Orleans that increasing school choice and privatizing school governance would lead to better outcomes and more opportunity for young people.

Another common story about the reforms is that they were simply a necessary response to the devastation wrought by the storm. Katrina Bulkley writes, for example, "New Orleans public schools were transformed in response to the loss of school facilities from the destruction of Hurricane Katrina and the exodus of people fleeing the flooding and chaos, rather than a planned strategy for school change."[74] The pre-Katrina reforms alongside the immediate post-Katrina legislative activity, however, complicate this narrative of passivity. Although reformers may not have mapped out every step as part of an overarching strategy, neither were these policies simply reactive and haphazard. It was possible, of course, for philanthropists and the federal government to get behind a fully funded traditional school district. Charter schools were not the only answer to bringing schools back.

Finally, the story laid out in this chapter shows how a wide coalition that included New Orleans legislators and local board members was responsible for the policy innovations that made the post-Katrina changes possible. Many critics of the reforms point to the exclusion of educators and African American communities in the planning after the storm. While true, many locally elected officials, including Black officials, were supportive of the pre-Katrina reforms. Further, the OPSB elections of 2004 put in place a local board that supported the sweeping changes.

Adoption is, however, only one phase in reform. As difficult as it is to facilitate major policy change, it is equally challenging to maintain the policies in the face of the many forces that would prefer a return to the status quo. The next chapter shows the many tactics reformers used to prevent retrenchment in the years after they successfully pushed through these changes. If critics could water down the reforms or put in place policies that would more closely resemble a traditional school district, whether through small changes or another dramatic shift, all the pre-Katrina work would have been for naught. This did not happen, however. In fact, the system today is more privatized and the public is even less involved than in the early post-hurricane period.

An All-Charter System
Takes Shape

One thing we won't accept is defenders of the status quo
who simply want more time or money. . . . We will do better
because our kids only grow up once, and they deserve better.
—**Louisiana Governor Bobby Jindal**

This will be the greatest experiment in choice, charters and in
creating not a single school system, but a system of schools.
—**Paul Vallas, superintendent,**
  Recovery School District, New Orleans

In 2006, a system of schools was born, but as occurs with any major change, there were significant challenges and no guarantee the reforms would last. Major reforms are often threatened with "the slow death of a thousand nicks" such that retrenchment should have been possible.[1] For one, it is nearly impossible to maintain heightened public interest and media attention. The media also rarely maintain the favorable issue frame that helped push policy adoption. Also, the entrepreneurs who are responsible for touting reform and twisting arms may leave office or move on to other issues. In addition, the forces of opposition do not simply disappear but, instead, often rally and launch a counterattack.

Those who had to interact closely within the system helped to reveal its problems early on. The "portfolio management" system was so different from the old system that the confusion on the part of parents and schools should have enabled opponents of the reforms to capitalize on it and push the system back to the traditional system with which everyone was familiar. From the start, dramatic inequality between the two school districts emerged. Parents sued on behalf of their children with special needs and because of the harsh discipline being meted out in many charter schools. To enroll, parents had to apply at each school, resulting in a confusing and opaque process that frustrated them. Scandals related to mismanagement and noncompliance with state and federal laws belied the rhetoric about how the new system was a departure from the "bad old days."

Even so, the system did not return to normal. This chapter shows that its architects refused to allow opponents any room to pull back on the reforms. Specifically, four tactics prevented policy retrenchment. One tactic was structural—the architects wrote into the law that a school could return to the local school district only after five years, and even then, the state, via the Recovery School District (RSD), would decide whether it would return schools to local jurisdiction. Second, reformers made changes only when they were forced to because of a judicial decree or threats of an impending suit. Third, leaders in the reform movement kept items off the agenda so there would be no public debate and they could engineer acceptable outcomes. Finally, with the assistance of the local media, these folks framed their opponents negatively, as selfish "defenders of the status quo." To be opposed to any aspect of the reform movement meant one would be painted as not caring about the education of New Orleans children.

Race undergirded aspects of each of these tactics. As discussed in the previous chapter, the vote among New Orleans state representatives on the 2005 act that authorized the state to take control of New Orleans schools was divided along racial lines. Thus, Black elected officials from New Orleans opposed the state's takeover and the decision to prevent change for at least five years, while white legislators supported it. Black families of children with special needs brought litigation that led to minimal reforms and consent decrees and fought for reforming the enrollment system. By contrast, white reformers engineered outcomes behind the scenes that would primarily benefit white, relatively affluent families. Finally, media framing is often racialized, and the framing of the reform opponents was no different.

I begin with a review of the events in the early years after the 2005 reforms, as charter schools and networks were established and the two districts (the RSD and the Orleans Parish School Board [OPSB]) developed policies and practices that would establish the new system of schools. Reformers were wildly optimistic because they believed that market-based reforms would rapidly transform the school experience and educational outcomes. It was not that the architects of the system overlooked the need for central oversight and management. Rather, the near-complete decentralization was a key feature of the new system. Over time, reformers made slight modifications, such as a centralized enrollment system and minor changes in disciplinary and special-needs oversight, but largely only in response to lawsuits. The basic structure of the system has not changed since it was put in place following Katrina. In fact, in terms of the number and proportion of children attending charter schools, the system has moved toward greater privatization.

"I Don't Know the First Thing about Running a School"

The authors of the post-Katrina education reforms in New Orleans were confident and clear about their expectations. An illustrative example was James Huger, the chief executive of Premium Parking and a real estate developer who led a private group that founded the charter network Choice Foundation.[2] *The Atlantic* referred to him as a white "scion of Uptown New Orleans gentry," and he admitted, "I don't know the first thing about running a school."[3] His lack of knowledge did not hold him back in 2006 from marketing Lafayette Academy and holding open houses for potential parents at his alma mater, Isadore Newman, a tony private school that claims Peyton and Eli Manning as alumni. He promised parents a private school-quality education for free. Like other reformers, Huger wholeheartedly believed in the power of school choice, claiming that it would "empower" school officials "with consequences."[4] Other local elites, such as Arthur Hardy, a local (white) celebrity best known for his annual *Mardi Gras Guide*, joined the boards of charter schools and touted all the choices for parents.

These folks assumed that without neighborhood schools controlled by what they believed to be a corrupt elected board, parents would select schools based largely on academic achievement. Teachers and principals would step up as they had not in the past, because in a charter system, they would be held accountable. Schools in which students had perennially low test scores would demonstrate they could meet standards to "stay in business."[5] "Bad" schools would either close or model the "good" schools. These policies would ultimately improve the entire system, all while removing inefficient government bureaucracy and harnessing the power of the market for innovative solutions to entrenched problems. Reformers expected a radical and relatively rapid transformation in academic performance. Their confidence also made them unsympathetic to criticism about the process and the content of the reforms.

The enthusiasm belied some serious problems. One week before the RSD schools were set to open in 2006, about 30 percent of the teaching positions were unfilled.[6] Most buildings were still in various states of disrepair. In the waning days before school started, four schools that had enrolled students decided they could not open as planned due to the state of their facilities.[7] Parents often discovered that their pre-Katrina school was closed or that it was no longer accepting applicants only when they attempted to enroll their children. Frustrated parents and grandparents complained when charter schools in their neighborhoods refused to enroll their children.[8]

Parents could preregister their children for school via the phone or the Internet but had to appear in person to complete the process and needed to show their child's Social Security card, birth certificate, immunization records, and any Individualized Education Programs (IEPs)—documents that had been damaged or lost in the flooding for thousands of parents across the city.[9] About one thousand children who had preregistered were eventually dropped from the rolls because parents did not show up in person. During the registration process, parents were asked to select their top three school choices, though children were assigned on a first-come, first-served basis, so the most popular schools filled quickly.[10]

The very real obstacles that parents encountered were discounted by those who saw the new system primarily as an opportunity. Stephen Hales, a respected local pediatrician who would come to sit on multiple charter school boards (and serve in Mardi Gras's most prestigious position—the King of Carnival), wrote a letter to the editor chastising the *Times-Picayune* for its coverage of the challenges schools faced in hiring staff, fixing damaged buildings, and the so-called dizzying new school options. "New beginnings are sometimes messy," he wrote, "but they not only bring with them 'dizzying options,' but also dizzying possibilities. Who could have imagined such a fresh start, and the real possibility that a transformed system of public schools could be part of the recovery of our city?"[11]

A New System Takes Shape

In 2006 and 2007, dozens of schools opened. In those years, there were five different types of schools. In June 2007, the RSD ran or authorized most schools (thirty-nine); of them, twenty-two were directly run, and seventeen were charter schools. The RSD had not originally intended to directly operate schools but ended up doing so as a result of the dearth of "high-quality" charter school operators. This required the RSD to "quickly reorient its structure to become a district able to open and operate schools."[12] The OPSB operated five schools and authorized twelve charters. And the Board of Elementary and Secondary Education (BESE) authorized two charter schools. In total, 57 percent of public school students were in charter schools.

Inequities emerged immediately between the different types of schools. The Cowen Institute for Public Education Initiatives, launched in 2007 to

TABLE 3.1. DIFFERENT POPULATIONS SERVED BY
PUBLIC SCHOOL OPERATORS, 2007

	% Identified as Special Education	% Identified as Gifted	% Qualified for Free or Reduced Price Lunch	% Black
RSD direct-run	7.3	0.0	68.7	97.5
RSD charter	6.6	2.0	90.6	96.6
OPSB direct-run	7.6	11.0	75.8	93.8
OPSB charter	4.0	24.0	69.8	67.3

Source: Cowen Institute for Public Education Initiatives 2007.

provide research on the school system, published its first *State of Public Education in New Orleans* report in June of that year, writing, "The RSD and the schools it operates have been hampered by operational disadvantages, inexperienced leadership, and insufficient district staff. . . . The emergence of public school choice is a promising element of the new system, although it is currently constrained by a lack of schools, inequitable access for students, and limited information."[13] There were disparities both between the RSD and the OPSB and between charters and non-charters within these districts. As shown in Table 3.1, in 2007 only 4 percent of students in OPSB charters had special needs, compared with much higher proportions in the other schools. In contrast, 24 percent of students in OPSB charters identified as gifted, compared with *zero* in the RSD direct-run schools. The OPSB charters were also less poor and more white than the others. In fact, there were almost no white children in any other type of public school. These figures underscore the importance of selective admissions in the OPSB charter schools. All the OPSB charter schools had some elements of selectivity, such as applications, writing samples, volunteer requirements for parents, interviews, and behavioral contracts, and half had admissions tests and early deadlines.[14] These disparities are good indicators that the reforms were deeply racialized, if not in intention, then certainly in effect. It can be no accident when a system is created in which nearly all the white students are located within the one type of school that also has so few students with special needs and so many gifted students and is generally less poor than the other types of schools.

The RSD struggled throughout 2006–2007 to fill important staff positions, and its direct-run schools were relegated to some of the worst facilities in town. As of May 2007, nearly two years after Katrina, only two schools operated by the RSD had the facilities to prepare hot meals, even though about 75 percent of its students were eligible for free or reduced-price lunch.

The RSD estimated it had a staffing gap of about one hundred teachers and eighty-eight support staff in February 2007. As a result, students were not receiving the support services they needed, especially psychological counseling and special needs services.[15] A 2008 legislative audit showed that the RSD had overpaid some former employees; it did not control movable property, resulting in theft of more than $55,000 in supplies; and nearly half the time, vendors were not paid within ninety days (as required by Louisiana law) due to cash flow problems.[16] It is important to recall that the RSD was the state's solution to corruption and mismanagement in the OPSB.

In the decentralized system where schools could decide which students to accept, the RSD direct-run schools quickly became the schools of last resort for students the other schools did not want. These students were nearly all Black; they also were more likely to have special needs, require transportation, and have other difficulties that made them undesirable to charter schools. By law, the RSD could not have selective admissions and had to accept any student living in Orleans Parish. Over the early years, families returned to the city whenever they could secure housing and employment, often without regard to the academic calendar. In the 2007 spring semester, the Cowen Institute reported, one hundred new students enrolled in the RSD schools *each week*. Charter schools, especially those authorized by the OPSB, had enrollment caps and did not generally accept new students after a certain point in the school year. However, those schools could also ask students to leave midyear for failure to meet behavioral or academic standards; when children left, they nearly always went to RSD direct-run schools. These forces made it difficult for teachers at RSD schools to meet academic standards or get to know their students and their situations.

As the RSD direct-run schools struggled, the OPSB and RSD charters did much better. RSD charter schools differed from OPSB charters in some important ways. The state prevented charters authorized by the RSD to give priority to children living in a geographic attendance zone, but OPSB charters could have these priorities. Because OPSB schools were located in more affluent, white neighborhoods and were higher performing to start, this policy fueled and perpetuated racial and economic disparities. The RSD charters and direct-run schools were also required to provide public transportation, generally in the form of yellow school buses. Several OPSB charters, however, opted not to provide public transportation for students, saving money that could be allocated to teachers, school materials, or facilities.

The 2007 Cowen Institute report found that the "current system does not provide all students with access to high-quality public schools."[17] Ten

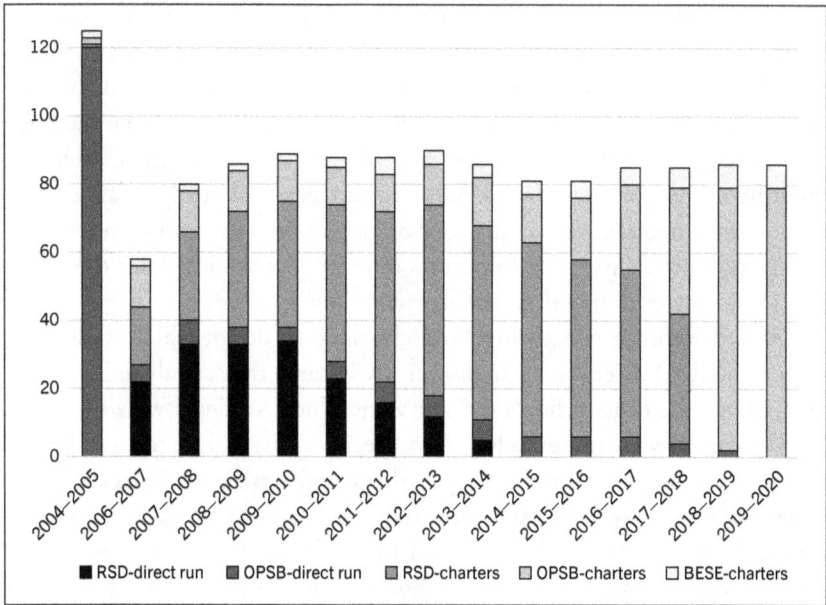

Figure 3.1. Number of direct-run and charter schools by operator in New Orleans, 2004–2020 (*Source:* Data compiled by the author from the Cowen Institute for Public Education Initiatives' *State of Public Education in New Orleans* reports for each year. The 2004–2005 data are from the Louisiana Department of Education; the 2015–2016 data are from National Alliance for Public Charter Schools 2016.)

schools (17%) had selective enrollment policies; thirty-two (62%) had enrollment caps; and nine (16%) had no traditional bus transportation. By April 2007, the enrollment deadline had already passed for the next school year in 36 percent of schools, meaning that students who returned after May would be ineligible to enroll in these (predominantly higher-performing) schools. In a period of recovery and economic crisis, families who did not or could not plan six months ahead to get over these hurdles were shut out of the best schools in the city.

In 2009, Paul Vallas, superintendent of the RSD, announced that over the next few years he wanted to transform all the direct-run RSD schools into charters.[18] As Figure 3.1 shows, the number of direct-run RSD schools fell every year after 2009; by 2014, Vallas's plan had been fulfilled. In 2018–2019, the RSD returned its schools to the OPSB, leaving only the OPSB and the BESE as charter authorizers. Since that year, more than 90 percent of public school students in New Orleans were enrolled in charters (see Figure 3.2). By 2019–2020, 100 percent of the city's public school students were in charter schools.[19]

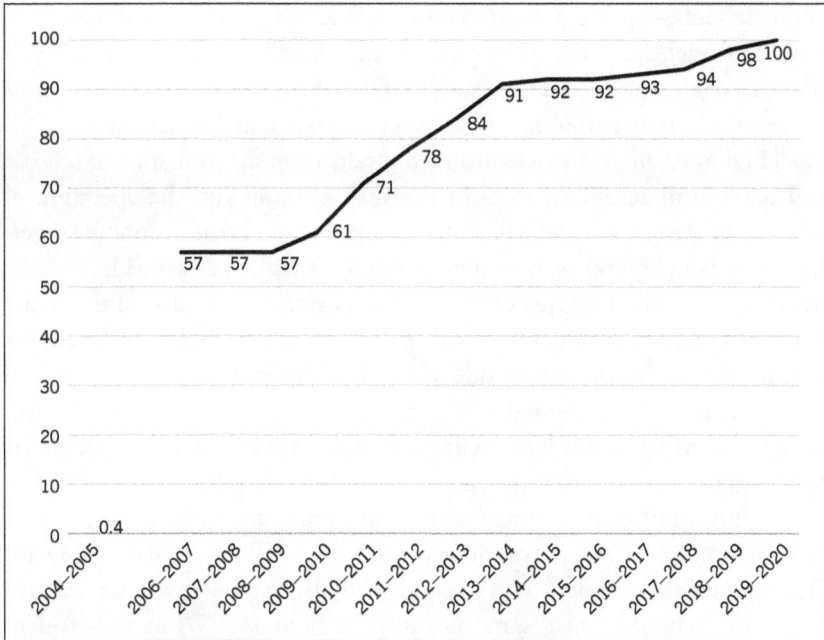

Figure 3.2. Percentage of public school students in charter schools in New Orleans, 2004–2020 (*Source:* Data are compiled from the Cowen Institute for Public Education Initiatives' *State of Public Education in New Orleans* reports for each year. The 2004–2005 data are from the Louisiana Department of Education; the 2015–2016 data are from National Alliance for Public Charter Schools 2016.)

Ensuring Sustainable Reforms

The new system was intentionally decentralized. Some scholars argue that decentralized governance tends to enhance some forms of democratic participation, but this narrative tends to overlook the ways in which decentralized systems have been harmful for racial minorities.[20] It was local school boards and states, not the federal government, that fought racial integration. Decentralized systems that govern health-care access, voting rights, unemployment insurance, abortion access, and minimum wages also disproportionately work to the disadvantage of the poor and communities of color.

This new style of education governance is called the portfolio management model (PMM), defined as "a district that provides schools in many ways—including traditional direct operation, semi-autonomous schools created by the district, and chartering or contracting to independent parties—but holds all schools, no matter how they are run, accountable for performance."[21] This governance model is a major departure from Progressive-era public schools, which emphasized bureaucratic control and the professionalization of teachers, as well as its predecessor, which focused on close connections between schools and their communities.[22] In PMM, the central office becomes mostly an authorizer—the entity that opens and closes schools. This model relies on market mechanisms to produce competition among schools and maximum autonomy in both parents' selection and the operation of schools. By design, schools will come and go: the ones that cannot meet performance benchmarks or have low enrollments will be closed.[23] In PMMs, school quality will improve not only (or even primarily) because of the choices parents make about where to send their kids to school, but because the district intervenes "in the supply side of the market equation."[24] "Bad schools" will ultimately come to model the practices of "good schools" to survive, which, according to this logic, will improve the system. This style of governance ignores the fact that the "good" schools are largely, if not exclusively, those with significant advantages at the start and are much more likely to be composed of greater proportions of white and affluent students. Edward Goetz writes about "opportunity neighborhoods," but one could replace this term with "schools" for the same meaning: "It is not that White and affluent people have come to occupy favored [schools but, rather, that] those [schools] are favored because the inhabitants are White and affluent."[25]

The early years after Katrina have been referred to as a "Wild West" where there was almost no oversight and schools could do whatever they wanted. In 2007, there was no system-wide tracking of students' behavioral issues or academic history. Parents had to maintain their children's academic records to demonstrate the grade they should be in and where they should be placed. Each charter school contracted on its own for food service, transportation, and myriad other services, creating enormous inefficiencies and wasteful spending without economies of scale. The disparities presented in Figure 3.1 were not the result of parental choices alone. Black parents did not eschew OPSB charters; rather, parents claimed that OPSB direct-run and charter schools turned away students with special needs, lower academic performance, and problematic disciplinary histories. Because of the laser focus on test scores, schools had incentives to select only "good" students who would perform well on state tests.[26] Indeed, many of these issues became the basis for lawsuits that ultimately forced reformers to concede to certain changes. A variety of groups tried to pressure policy makers to recentralize, to exercise some oversight of charter schools' practices. It was a critical test of the sustainability of the post-Katrina policies. The remainder of this chapter examines how reformers were able to maintain the new status quo in the face of inequality, scandal, and growing opposition.

Policy Design to Prevent Reversion

One of the main methods by which reformers prevented retrenchment was in the policy design itself. The idea behind the Recovery School District was that it would take over failing schools, transform them, and then return them to local authorities. The 2003 law that put the RSD in place, however, left control over the return up to the state Board of Elementary and Secondary Education.[27] Similarly Act 35, the 2005 law that redefined failing schools in New Orleans and transferred their authority to the RSD, specified that schools transferred to the RSD would remain in its jurisdiction for not less than five years. During the fifth year, the RSD would recommend to the BESE whether the school should continue in the RSD, be closed, or be returned to the local school district from which it was transferred. This provision staved off debate about jurisdiction for five years. In 2010, the question of jurisdiction emerged, and many critics of the new system argued it was time to return to local control. In an op-ed in the *Times-Picayune*, the architect of the reforms, Leslie Jacobs, implored State Superintendent Paul Pastorek—her former colleague—and the Louisiana BESE, on which she used to sit, to "continue the current arrangement" rather than return all the public schools to the OPSB.[28]

A few months after this opinion piece was published, Superintendent Pastorek devised an ingenious plan. Schools that met academic thresholds would be able to choose whether to opt for local control. The RSD schools that were still failing after five years would also be able to petition to the BESE that they be taken (or retaken) over by the OPSB.[29] In both cases, the school's governing board would vote on whether to return to the OPSB or petition to return.[30] Pastorek and the BESE could rest easy that the charter boards, whose members were hand-selected, would not elect to return to OPSB oversight. Charter leaders were averse to OPSB oversight due to their perception of its corruption and ineptitude and their concern that they would lose autonomy. Most would never elect to return. To the public, however, Pastorek's plan resembled a compromise. Although several schools were eligible to return to the OPSB because of their academic performance, none elected to do so until 2014, when the Friends of King Schools, a local charter network, elected to return Dr. King Charter School to the OPSB, largely in response to the network's dissatisfaction with the charter renewal process in the RSD.[31]

Pastorek's plan only put off questions about the continued presence of the state takeover district. In 2011, Jacobs released a plan from an ad hoc task force she had put together—again, not elected and not inclusive of all views—that would have created two appointed boards to sit alongside the OPSB. The three boards would have distinct authority and share power over the system of schools.[32] While the BESE did not adopt this plan, it demonstrates the continued role that Jacobs and other reformers played behind the scenes and their continued reliance on the same tactics of exclusion they had used in the pre- and immediate post-Katrina periods.

The debate took on a new dimension when the RSD finally got out of the business of operating schools in 2014. The Louisiana State Legislature first debated a measure to unify the RSD and OPSB in the 2015 legislative session, but the bill failed in the House (31–61) after passing in the House Education Committee by only one vote. It was introduced by a New Orleans House member (Joe Bouie Jr.), but only three of ten Orleans Parish representatives supported what had become known as "unification." All three supporters were Black, and the other seven were either absent or opposed returning the schools to the OPSB.

Then, in a stunner, the state elected a Democratic governor in November 2015. John Bel Edwards was a moderate Democrat who had served in the Louisiana House for only seven years but had risen quickly to serve as the House minority leader. As a legislator and gubernatorial candidate he had expressed skepticism about charter schools, the rating systems for schools and teachers, the mechanisms that allowed the state to overrule local decisions or take over local schools, and the statewide voucher program that his predecessor, Governor Bobby Jindal, had put in place.[33] He voted in favor of unification of the RSD and the OPSB in 2015. Teachers and school boards supported his candidacy. Reformers were, for the first time in nearly two decades, uneasy about their power. Writing in *U.S. News and World Report*, Gerard Robinson, a fellow at the American Enterprise Institute, tried to quell this anxiety by noting how hard it can be to roll back the policies that were put in place by Edwards's predecessors: "School choice advocates are rightfully concerned about the future of choice in the Pelican State. Regardless of the election's results, Jindal's tenure created some lasting policies that will make completely thwarting parental choice efforts in Louisiana a herculean feat."[34]

These concerns spurred reformers to action as they tried to push through acceptable reforms before their opponents could get organized. According to the pro-reform education news website The74Million.org, "There was concern that if the political sands shifted and . . . the new, charter-hostile governor, John Bel Edwards, gained enough allies, reform proponents could lose the ability to help shape reunification."[35] During the 2016 legislative session, New Orleans Senator Karen Carter Peterson, who had cosponsored legislation in 2004 that paved the way for the post-Katrina state takeover, introduced a bill to immediately transfer authority from the RSD to the OPSB. Peterson told the newspaper *The Advocate* that the legislation was the result of "weeks of negotiations" and that the local New Orleans delegation "agreed with charter school operators to make modest changes in the bill" to transfer authority.[36] Again, these negotiations were largely out of the public eye, and charter school leaders had a privileged position. Black parents and educators continued to be shut out of the conversations.

The law required the OPSB to develop a plan for unifying its twenty-four direct-run and charter schools and fifty-two RSD-authorized charter schools over a two-year period. The superintendent was authorized to recommend and implement charter authorization actions, which the OPSB would have the authority to review and could overturn only with a supermajority. The law requires all schools to participate in common enrollment and common expulsion systems and provides for limited geographic preference but otherwise preserves charter schools' autonomy over budgeting, curriculum, personnel, and other aspects of schooling. A Unification Advisory Committee composed of the OPSB and RSD superintendents and several charter operators developed the transition plan in consultation with a much larger Unification Task Force. The task force consisted of four committees: System-wide Services and Resources; Facilities; Authorization, Accountability, and Planning; and Transparency and Community Responsiveness. Like other aspects of education reform, the task force's work was racialized: the committee charged with "community responsiveness" was composed primarily of African American residents (twenty-three), while the "authorization" committee included eleven Black residents, compared with twenty white men and women. In other words, white folks dominated the group that made the most important decisions about authorization and accountability, while Black folks were brought in to discuss how to frame the ideas within the Black community. A few community meetings in which residents could give opinions and ask questions were well attended, but beyond hearing these comments, this group developed the details of the unification process on its own. No locally elected body had any real power in the process, and unlike in the creation of the RSD, the plan did not require a public referendum.

The new OPSB would set and measure accountability, monitor school performance (including sanctioning and closing schools), "manage school choice and equity," and manage site location of facilities. It would not manage individual schools or networks, hire school leaders or other personnel, make decisions about curriculum, manage school operations, or set school budgets. These activities would be done by the schools or networks themselves. Thus, the unified school district would be mostly a charter authorizer, and even though its members were elected, the public would continue to have little ability to influence school policies, personnel, or other important decisions. In essence, reformers got nearly everything they could have wanted, and for most schools nothing changed after transferring from RSD to OPSB "control." The policy was designed so that critics would have almost no ability to change the underlying logic of the system.

Squashing the Power of Teachers

Another example of how reformers used political structures to prevent any reversion to the traditional system is in the laws directed at teachers. Lasting reform is a function of diminishing opponents' political cohesion. Alexander Hertel-Fernandez refers to policy feedback as a "political weapon" that "emphasizes how organized interest groups or politicians can deliberately press for changes in policy that eventually diminish the political resources available to their opponents."[37] They do this by passing legislation to make it more difficult for opposing interest groups to attract and maintain members, by creating barriers for their opponents to engage in politics through voting or contributing to campaigns, and by limiting the government's ability to carry out programs that benefit their political opponents. The state canceled its contract with the United Teachers of New Orleans (UTNO), and in July 2006, the OPSB allowed its thirty-two-year contract with the union to expire without a new agreement. Each charter school or network was "empowered" to hire, promote, and fire teachers at their discretion. Because of the way they are hired and evaluated, teachers in an all-charter system do not have the incentive to organize. Further, in the wake of the mass firing after Katrina, highly experienced (and tenured) teachers were replaced by new white teachers who were often hired through alternative certification programs such as Teach for America.[38] This decentralized system convinces them that their long-term fate "depends upon their own productive efforts, rather than on their success at winning favors and advantages through political lobbying efforts."[39] Teachers can negotiate only as individuals, leaving them vulnerable to charter schools' practices.

This arrangement was not enough for many reformers. In the years after Katrina, the Louisiana State Legislature passed several laws to further diminish the political power of teachers. Act 1 in 2012 changed the law on tenure and evaluations. To earn tenure, teachers would need five years of ratings as "highly effective" rather than merely a three-year probationary period. These ratings became largely based on students' test scores. Tenured teachers would now be able to lose tenure if they were rated "ineffective" for even one year and could lose their jobs for poor performance. To regain tenure after a poor rating, teachers would need five consecutive years of high ratings. Nontenured teachers could be terminated by the superintendent much more easily. This law also repealed teachers' minimum salary schedule; empowered districts to establish salaries; and removed local school boards' authority over personnel decisions in favor of delegating the authority to principals, subject to the approval of the superintendent. Act 1 also removed protections based in seniority and tenure in cases of reduction in the teaching force. This law, and others passed during this period, dramatically reduced the power of teachers as a political force. Further, these policies led many teachers to leave the profession. About 6.8 percent of teachers left each year between 2006 and 2011, but that figure jumped to 8 percent in 2012 and 10.5 percent in 2013.[40]

In multiple ways, reformers used political structures to "buffer the reform from pressures to change course."[41] The law gave the RSD five years to turn schools around, and it afforded that entity the power to recommend whether to transfer authority to the local district. These legal maneuvers belied the rhetoric about the reforms. If reformers had really believed that competition, choice, and accountability would turn around New Orleans schools, then there is little reason to build in so much control or to diminish the power of critics. The law could have required schools to revert automatically to local control after five years, but reformers would have needed more confidence in their turnaround model. When critics complained about the RSD maintaining control well past the five-year mark, the "compromise" was to allow the hand-selected charter boards to decide whether to go back, a move reformers knew would result in few, if any, transfers. The controversy about how and when to unify the two districts also shows how successfully reformers were able to use political structures to restrict the available options to those that were acceptable to those in power. Reformers ensured they were able to avoid local control as long as possible and, when threatened by a new administration with which they might not be as cozy as the last, in a deeply racialized process, reformers quickly passed a law that ensured the new "unified" district would have very little real authority. By putting these political structures in place, reformers knew their system of schools was safe from any policy retrenchment.

From Their Cold, Dead Hands—Forced Change

One challenge to the reforms came in the form of lawsuits on behalf of particular classes of individuals who had been negatively affected by the reforms. Reformers found they had to give in on certain aspects of decentralization, but they did so as slowly as possible. Parents of children with special needs alleged that charter schools in New Orleans failed to serve this population adequately.[42] A 2010 report to the RSD demonstrated significant disparities in the percentages of special needs students at charters and non-charters and between the RSD and the OPSB. In the OPSB, the proportion of special needs students at some charter schools was as low as 1 percent, while the direct-run schools had much higher proportions. Many families claimed they had been actively steered away from certain schools and that those they attended were failing to provide the services their children were entitled to under federal law. Charter schools claimed their behavior was resource-driven; that small schools cannot afford to pay for expensive special services that only one or two students may need.[43]

In 2014, nearly ten years after the hurricane, the Southern Poverty Law Center (SPLC), on behalf of ten families, reached a deal with the OPSB to improve special education services. The consent decree requires the Louisiana Department of Education to keep close track of how charter schools in New Orleans serve and discipline students with special needs.[44] A year later, the oversight report found that the charter group Lagniappe Academies had held back one-third of its students, refused to screen them for special education services, and created a "Do Not Call" list of families whose children the school did not want to return.[45] Outside the normal processes and schedule, and over the objections of many parents, the RSD abruptly chose to close the school, sending families and teachers scrambling for a school for the following year. According to a report from the Center for Popular Democracy and the Coalition for Community Schools New Orleans,

> The situation at Lagniappe shows exactly the problems with the state's oversight structure for charter schools. The state relies on a largely self-reporting oversight structure that is easily manipulated by the schools themselves—sometimes for multiple years, as happened at Lagniappe. Upon discovering that a serious problem exists, rather than developing a solution that gives the school's students and teachers some much-needed stability—such as bringing in a different charter operator, or returning the school to local control—the state's solution for struggling schools is to close them, effectively punishing students and families for problems outside of their control. Lagniappe Academy is a story of how the state is failing Louisiana students, not protecting them.[46]

The RSD claimed this closure as an example of its willingness to hold schools accountable not just for performance but also for compliance with the law. However, the next year's oversight report showed that ten other charter schools had been flagged for failing to provide services to students with disabilities, and none of those schools' charters had been revoked, leading to questions about the fairness of the charter authorization process.[47] Kevin Lawrence Henry Jr. finds, for example, that in 2011 nearly 90 percent of Black applicants for charter schools were denied, while more than 60 percent of white applicants were approved.[48] His research shows that authorizers preferred "no excuse" narratives, which were more often propagated by white applicants, over the more communitarian proposals put forward mainly by Black charter applicants. Matthew Candler, who led the charter recruiting process for the nonprofit New Schools for New Orleans, admitted in an interview with the economist Douglas Harris, "I wasn't very open to community groups as [school] operators. . . . I confess that I did not really think about local [community members as] 'producers' or potential school leaders."[49] These statements, along with the real disparities in the authorization process, indicate that it is not the neutral, benign, color-blind process that advocates of an all-charter model claim. The story of charter authorization, according to Henry, is "a story of racism in education policy."[50]

The lack of oversight on discipline issues also led several social justice-oriented organizations to call for reform. A 2010 report from Families and Friends of Louisiana's Incarcerated Children and the National Economic and Social Rights Initiative found that the RSD issued out-of-school suspensions to 25 percent of its students during the 2007–2008 year, more than twice the statewide rate and more than four times the national average.[51] The expulsion and suspension rates went up by nearly 250 percent, peaking in 2009.[52] Another report indicated that from 2001 to 2014, Black students were twice as likely to be suspended as white students, and Black students received longer suspensions for the same types of infractions.[53] In response to a lawsuit, again filed by the SPLC, the RSD agreed in 2010 to make policy revisions prohibiting the use of fixed restraints and handcuffs after an armed security guard at Sarah T. Reed Elementary School handcuffed and shackled a first-grader to a chair.[54] In 2012, the RSD issued a new policy that would apply to all its direct-run and charter schools that required schools to submit documentation to an expert before expelling a student.[55]

These changes were put in place only after years of complaints and formal lawsuits were filed. Reformers were forced to centralize and exercise oversight to comply with federal antidiscrimination laws. Even so, recent evidence casts doubt on this system's ability to exercise appropriate oversight even when required by law. In 2019, independent monitors discovered the state had been monitoring the wrong New Orleans schools for special education services. Ten schools that should have been monitored based on the court settlement were not being watched, and some schools were being monitored unnecessarily. It is not clear whether the RSD and OPSB were or are understaffed, under-resourced, or simply incompetent. However, that so many in authority are philosophically opposed to centralized bureaucracy likely hampers efforts to hold charters accountable. It should be noted that a cornerstone of the stated philosophy of charter schools is accountability. In practice, few schools likely worry they will be seriously sanctioned because of a failure to comply with the law.

A New Enrollment System

Reform advocates would likely point to one major reform as evidence that they have been open to change. In 2011, the RSD rolled out a unified enrollment system, called OneApp until 2021 when New Orleans Public Schools changed its name to NOLA-PS Common Application. I refer to this system as OneApp throughout the book because that is how it was known during the time of this study. In the early years, parents had to complete an application at every school of interest. As in the college admissions process, students could be accepted into multiple schools—or none. School and system officials claimed that, because parents could apply to any school, the system was fair, and they resisted attempts to centralize enrollment, claiming that any bad behavior would be mitigated by the free market. However, the lawsuits related to students with special needs demonstrated that this was not the case and that, indeed, schools were engaged in discriminatory behavior.

Upon OneApp's rollout, state officials such as Superintendent John White and Caroline Roemer Shirley, executive director of the Louisiana Association of Public Charter Schools, claimed that it was a response to public feedback. When announcing the launch, Superintendent White cited parents' complaints and "serious concerns" about access for students with special needs. Likewise, Andrew Vanacore, writing in the *Times-Picayune*, claimed, "After years of complaints about how headache-inducing it can be to enroll a child in public school in New Orleans, state officials have officially launched a long-promised single application."[56]

Notably, White also admitted, "Critics of the charter school movement across the country have held up the [SPLC lawsuit] as a cautionary tale, accusing charter schools of producing higher test scores by simply dumping the students who are struggling."[57] The process of moving to a centralized enrollment system involved contracting with a private entity to develop the system without hearing from or working with parents who would use it. Yet reformers claimed they were being responsive to the public. It was a bonus that this allowed reformers to eliminate one of their opponents' strongest and most defensible positions.

The evidence is far from clear that OneApp created the equal playing field that was touted. First and foremost, for several years OneApp applied only to schools in the RSD. Parents interested in the higher-performing schools governed by the OPSB or BESE still had to apply separately. The algorithm's priorities for students in particular groups are another unequitable aspect of OneApp. Siblings of current students are given priority, and some schools have preferences for children in the neighborhood, or for those whose parents work for universities, or for other special populations. The system also allows for schools to maintain selective preferences, such as admissions tests and earlier deadlines. Despite the rhetoric about a random lottery, some children have a better chance at some schools than others.[58]

Though an improvement over the Wild West period when schools had free rein to pick their students, OneApp has not worked out exactly as its designers planned. On the demand side, according to a 2014 survey, families who chose their schools after OneApp was introduced reported greater difficulty than those who chose before OneApp.[59] Most families rank far fewer schools than they are allowed (originally eight; now twelve). Further, many families fail to complete OneApp in the main round, which indicates either that they do not know it is the only way to enroll one's children in public schools or they do not believe applying is worthwhile.[60]

On the supply side, reports routinely emerged that schools enroll students outside OneApp. In 2013, two popular high schools "quietly admitted at least 85 more students to their freshmen classes" even after they had told officials they were full.[61] Even after OneApp was in place for a few years, a survey of New Orleans school principals showed that one-third admitted to "cream skimming" behavior, such as failing to advertise open spaces, holding invitation-only open houses, and making exceptions for certain types of students.[62] In 2018, the OPSB issued a warning letter to a charter network, Einstein Charter Schools, about enrolling twenty-six students outside the OneApp system.[63] Everyone seems to know someone whose child got into a coveted school at the last minute, after rejection notices had already gone out, or who was given an opportunity to retake an admission test or send in a late application, even though these are supposedly prohibited.

The RSD reported that most families get into the schools they prefer via OneApp, but a deeper dive into the data reveals this picture as more complex. In 2015, 54 percent of those who applied in the first round received their first-choice school, and 75 percent got one of their top three choices. The RSD's reporting neglected to note that 20 percent of applicants were not matched to any of the schools they ranked. Further, the match rates are much lower for those applying outside kindergarten and ninth grade, the transition years when the largest number of spaces are available. Then, only 42 percent of applicants were matched to their first choice; 64 percent were matched to one of their top three choices; and *one-third were not matched to any of the schools they ranked.*[64] As more of the high-performing OPSB schools have been added to OneApp, the match rates have declined. In 2018, with only a few schools not included in the enrollment system, about one-third of those who applied failed to get into one of their top-three schools.[65] As I show in Chapter 5, parents continue to complain about the enrollment process. OneApp was a concession on the part of reformers, but on their terms. Its mechanics remain a mystery to the public, and most parents lack trust that it is fair.

Keeping Controversy off the Agenda

Another mechanism for establishing sustainable reforms is to manage conflict by keeping items off the agenda. E. E. Schattschneider highlighted the way that powerful political minorities often maintain their advantage by keeping political conflict "so private that it is almost invisible."[66] Peter Bachrach and Morton Baratz referred to this as the "second face of power," noting that one of the major exercises of power is when elites keep their most important issues out of the public eye and away from official policy-making processes.[67] It is usually difficult to find evidence of this technique because it is hard to show that something did not happen. However, in one example, official actors were surprisingly forthcoming with information about their behind-the-scenes activities that would continue to give selective-admission OPSB charters preferential treatment.

Transportation has proved to be a perennial issue highlighting the problems with a decentralized school system. Between 2004 and 2013, the cost of busing students to public schools rose by 67 percent, even though enrollment declined. Costs skyrocketed because more students were attending schools outside their neighborhoods and because each charter school or network contracted on its own with transportation providers.[68] It is worth noting that school choice was commonplace even before Katrina: in 2004, more than half the students in New Orleans public schools did not go to the school in their neighborhood.[69] In practice, children could attend almost any school they wanted. The major difference is that students were guaranteed placement in their neighborhood school, but today students can be placed in a school across town even if parents select a school near their home.[70]

In 2004–2005, students traveled an average of 1.9 miles from their homes to their schools. In 2011–2012, the average was up to 3.4 miles.[71] A 2018 report documents that the average bus trip was thirty-five minutes, but a quarter of bus rides lasted more than fifty minutes, with some as long as ninety minutes.[72] In 2017, *The Lens* reported that students were picked up at 4:52 A.M. in eastern New Orleans to ride over two hours across the river to Eisenhower High School in Algiers.[73] Safety has been an important, though less publicized concern. In 2014, six-year-old Shaud Wilson was killed crossing a busy four-lane road in Gentilly to get on his bus. Several routes make stops on some of the city's busiest roads.[74]

Beyond the rising average cost and long bus rides were the disparities across the districts. To maximize their autonomy, charter schools authorized by the OPSB and BESE were not initially required to provide transportation; they also had many fewer students with special needs who are more expensive to bus because they are required to have an escort and to be transported in smaller groups. These policies exacerbate racial disparities because African American adults are less likely to own cars and more likely to rely entirely on public transportation. In 2007–2008, the BESE charters spent *nothing* on transportation while the OPSB charters spent 2.9 percent of their general fund. The RSD charters spent 5.4 percent, and, reflecting their status as schools of last resort, RSD direct-run schools spent 6.4 percent of their general fund on busing.[75] At OPSB charters, however, parents were often on their own. Some students had two-hour commutes on city buses and streetcars that they paid for privately, and some parents took their children out of well-regarded "A-rated" OPSB charter schools because they did not want them riding public transportation or waiting at public bus stops by themselves at 5:30 A.M.[76] As the media began to report on these disparities, it became increasingly difficult for officials to do nothing. However, recentralizing transportation and forcing all schools to contribute to these expenses and share bus routes would not only infringe on their autonomy; it would also cause schools that had very limited transportation expenses to pay up.

In 2015, the OPSB adopted a new policy it claimed would address the disparities in both OneApp participation and transportation. All *new* charter schools authorized by the OPSB would have to provide transportation and participate in the OneApp enrollment system. New schools could not have neighborhood attendance zones and would have open enrollment, except for nonacademic admission criteria tied to the school's mission (such as foreign language ability for a language-immersion school). Existing selective charter schools, however, got away mostly unscathed. Existing open-enrollment charters would be required to provide transportation for students in grades K–6 and the option of bus tokens for those in grades 7–12, and these schools would have to participate in OneApp and reduce their neighborhood preferences to no more than 67 percent of school enrollment. Selective-admission charters, however, would be required to participate in OneApp *upon their renewals* and provide transportation (or bus tokens) *to parents who requested it*, and they could not have neighborhood preferences. These schools also remained able to maintain their own waiting lists rather than participate in OneApp's "backfilling" process for empty seats.[77]

Henderson Lewis Jr., superintendent of the OPSB, stated that these changes came out of more than two years of work with his office, school leaders, parents, and community stakeholders.[78] If policy makers were primarily concerned about inequity, why would the school board continue to treat selective-admissions charters more favorably than others? Certain school leaders had worked behind the scenes to shape the policy changes and mitigate the negative effects on their schools. A few weeks before the OPSB passed these new rules, Kathy Reidlinger, the chief executive of one of the city's premier selective-admissions charters, Lusher Charter School, announced at a meeting of her board, "We've been continually told by Dr. Lewis is [*sic*] not to cause harm to any school. He made a commitment to us that he will continue to work the policy until it meets the needs of *all the charters*."[79] Notably, according to Reidlinger, the superintendent was intent on meeting the needs of *the schools*, not *the students*—an accusation reformers often levy against teachers' unions. As of 2020, Lusher still maintained its own application and did not provide transportation. Joining OneApp and providing transportation to its students threatened to dramatically reshape the school's enrollment and demographics.

As a charter authorizer, the OPSB could have decided to require *all* schools to provide yellow school bus transportation, immediately join the OneApp, or eliminate neighborhood preferences. It did not, largely because powerful brokers negotiated a settlement behind the scenes. Leaders of the city's selective charter schools agreed to join OneApp at their schools' next charter renewals, years down the road, in exchange for maintaining their selectivity, continuing to avoid providing transportation for students, and controlling their own waiting lists. It was a sweet deal. Open-enrollment schools would not be able to do this. Selective schools "gave up" their neighborhood preferences, but in the case of Lusher, Reidlinger had hinted for years that the school would eliminate these priorities. Because they were automatically enrolled, the neighborhood kids were the population over which the school had the least control. Students who otherwise would not have scored highly enough on the kindergarten admission test to be admitted could enroll if they lived in the neighborhood.[80] By keeping reforms off the agenda and operating in obscurity, leaders of the selective charters that disproportionately serve white children achieved their desired outcomes.

Framing Critics as Problems

Finally, to push reforms and prevent backsliding, advocates must be careful about how they portray their goals and those of their opponents. They must often tarnish the public image of groups formerly held in high regard. Until recently, teachers have been one of the most revered groups in the United States, which, along with the organizational power of their unions, gave them power in education policy.[81] The rhetoric among those in the contemporary reform movement characterizes public school teachers as lazy, self-interested, well-compensated (mostly) women who selfishly stand in the way of good ideas that will benefit children. In New Orleans, there is a racial element, as well, because such a high proportion of pre-Katrina teachers were Black women.

In addition to demonizing teachers, reformers lambasted anyone who criticized the reforms. Governor Jindal and many other reformers seemed to pull from the same talking points, commonly referring to any critics as "defenders of the status quo."[82] The most important actor in helping to frame the narrative around reformers and their critics is the news media. Local media frame stories and events and prime the audience through selecting what, how, and when issues and events are covered.[83] The media's selective inclusions, omissions, emphases, and tone shape public interpretations of events, people, and institutions.

A frame is the "central organizing idea for making sense of relevant events and suggesting what is at issue."[84] Framing helps readers make sense of the story and fit the new information into existing schema.[85] In simplifying complex issues into easy-to-use frames, the media are able to influence public perceptions about and support for policies and officials.[86] Rebecca Goldstein shows that national media frame market-based education reforms "as the only solution to address the failures of public education by attacking teachers' unions" and positively covering market-oriented school reform efforts.[87]

The media influence the audience's support for policies, candidates, and more, especially when the source is perceived as credible, such as in the city's newspaper of record.[88] Media effects are strongest when issues are new and the audience lacks strong preexisting beliefs.[89] According to Dennis Chong and James Druckman, "Strong predispositions reduce framing effects by increasing one's resistance to disconfirming information."[90] Readers who are involved in education or education reform are unlikely to be swayed or influenced by editorials, but for most New Orleanians, the post-Katrina reforms established a new and unfamiliar system of schools. For example, reporters often had to define the term "charter school" in early news articles. Such ignorance gave the media significant power to shape attitudes.

Within frames, media prime readers through the use of language, images, and tone. Primes call "attention to some matters while ignoring others, . . . influenc[ing] the standards by which governments, . . . [and] policies are judged."[91] In recent years, national and local media have routinely written that school choice "empowers parents" and that charter schools and other contemporary reforms "put students first."[92] The positive words and phrases, often accompanied by photos of adorable children in school uniforms reading or raising their hands to answer a question, shape how the audience responds to these issues and policies. Who could be against adorable children?

The media also shape narratives by choosing the sources of their information. Local reporting often focuses on the viewpoints of policy makers and the public's response rather than in-depth analyses of problems.[93] The voices of teachers, school administrators, parents, researchers, and community activists are often stifled, whether intentionally or not, as the media focus on officials' views.[94] When non-official actors are included, they are more likely to be portrayed as self-interested, while elected officials are "fighting for all children."[95] One reason for this is that the local media are critical actors in promoting the city's long-term economic interests.[96] Cynthia Gerstl-Pepin also suggests that members of the media "subscribe to tacit cultural assumptions that may exclude the concerns of the economically disadvantaged, minority groups, or other marginalized groups."[97] There is much evidence of racial and class bias in reporting, with implications for agenda setting (where issues that affect white, middle- and upper-class residents are more likely to be covered) and coverage (with the selection of images, words, and tone) that influence public perceptions.[98] The depiction of welfare beneficiaries and immigrants, for example, tends to focus on negative images of people of color; these images have significant effects on public and elite opinion.[99]

New Orleans's newspaper of record, the *Times-Picayune*, was a long-time critic of the OPSB and supporter of the education reforms that had paved the way for the state takeover of the city's schools. In the first post-Katrina editorial related to schools, published on October 10, 2005, the paper's editorial board criticized two African American members of the OPSB.[100] The editorial team also disparaged the school board as a whole and expressed hope that the hurricane would lead to substantive shifts in governance: "It may be that the hurricane will force the dramatic reinvention of city schools, which seemed unlikely to ever happen under normal circumstances."[101] Six weeks after the storm, the newspaper signaled its support for a major shift in governance.

Over the next three weeks, three *Times-Picayune* columnists wrote pieces supporting charter schools, school choice, and replacing the OPSB with a different governance system.[102] In early November, the newspaper published an op-ed by OPSB President Torin Sanders, whom it had criticized for questioning the rapid movement to privatize public schools. This was the first critical voice to be expressed on the editorial page since the hurricane, and even then Sanders focused on how Katrina had provided the opportunity for the board to reset, to gets its finances in order, and to refurbish dilapidated buildings.[103] That same day, however, the *Times-Picayune* ran an editorial saying the exact opposite: that the OPSB would not be able "lead that renaissance" to "create top-notch schools."[104]

Over a ten-year period (Fall 2005–Fall 2015), there were 153 editorials in the *Times-Picayune* related to the New Orleans K–12 school system or state education policy that would affect New Orleans.[105] Of these, 75 percent were positive in tone toward reforms around expanding charter schools, school choice (including vouchers), raising standards, rising performance scores, or praising specific individuals backing these reforms. There were only twenty editorials in this ten-year period in which the newspaper had a negative tone about the reforms.[106] Nearly half of these—eight editorials—were published in 2006 and 2007 and were critical of the RSD's leadership.[107]

Fifteen commentaries were mixed in tone, meaning that even when the editors reported on something negative, such as declines in performance scores or lack of oversight, the critique was tempered with discussion of how the general trends were positive. One example includes a May 2011 editorial in which the newspaper criticized the RSD and OPSB for failing "to set up an effective central mechanism to help parents navigate" all the new school options, but tempered its criticism with, "Many New Orleans children have benefitted greatly from the variety of choices afforded by the RSD and the charter schools overseen by the RSD and the OPSB."[108] In September 2011, an editorial commented on the legislative auditor's report about the lack of oversight in the RSD, which the newspaper referred to as "shortcomings." Although the report was damning for the RSD, the *Times-Picayune* editors devoted considerable space to "debunk[ing]" arguments of "charter critics."[109] Similarly, when the scores from the National Assessment of Educational Progress came out in 2011, Louisiana was again near the bottom of all U.S. states. Nonetheless, the editors wrote that, under Governor Jindal, "we're moving in the right direction."[110]

The paper painted an overwhelmingly positive picture of the reforms.[111] When absolute test scores continued to be far from laudatory, the newspaper commented on growth. If reports emerged about scandals involving cheating or financial malfeasance, the editors spun the stories as positive examples of oversight. One of the most important components of the positive message was to continually highlight just how bad the system was before Katrina and how everything had gotten better because of the reforms put in place in 2005.[112] Beyond the editorials, the vast majority—fifty-four of sixty-three—of *Times-Picayune* op-eds about the reforms in this ten-year period were also exceedingly positive. There was one critical op-ed each year, except in 2006 and 2008, when there were none critical of the reforms.[113]

Thus, readers of the major mainstream newspaper in New Orleans in the ten years following Hurricane Katrina would have heard nothing but good news about the new school system. Any criticism of the changes was softened with rhetoric about improved performance, and negative news and views were either ignored or downplayed. The positive narrative was likely due to some combination of interests and beliefs. The *Times-Picayune*'s interests were aligned with the reformers, not the critics. The reforms gave the city something positive to tout nationally. They brought in millions of dollars from foundations and federal grants. They made New Orleans a model and made the reformers famous in some policy circles. The *Times-Picayune* was more than happy to contribute to selling the reforms as part of the post-Katrina renaissance. But it is also likely that the editors were guided by their beliefs. The paper had long supported education reform and had been a vocal critic of the OPSB.

Conclusions

This chapter has demonstrated the tactics reformers used to maintain the 2005 reforms in the face of changing leadership, confusing new processes, lawsuits, and criticisms. They ensured charter critics could not pull back the reforms through policy design elements and agreed to give in only when forced. Reformers also worked behind the scenes to ensure that new policies would be beneficial to them, thereby keeping controversial issues off the table. All this was undergirded by an assault on their opponents, who were defined as selfish and stuck in the past.

These tactics show how intentional these actors have been at each step. The plan might not have been laid out completely from the beginning, and it is likely that some early proponents of some of the state-level reforms are surprised at where we are now. Nevertheless, at each stage there was an organized effort to engineer particular outcomes. Throughout, the voices and perspectives of those who had the most interaction with the system were excluded and marginalized. In some cases, champions of reform openly blamed Black parents for what they perceived as poor choices and misguided beliefs. Even if reformers were well-intentioned and truly believed these moves were ultimately in the best interests of the children who made up the New Orleans district, it is notable that folks from this community were never part of any serious planning process.

The next part of this book examines the effects of the policies and the political processes described in these pages. I first consider the responses of the elites who were endowed with the power to govern the new system: the members of charter boards. This examination points to another important tactic reformers used to achieve their goals: putting the right people in place to administer the reforms. The new system would be governed by hand-selected, private boards, not elected officials who might have to answer to wider constituencies. These folks were also true believers in the underlying philosophy of the new system, and those who designed the reforms could rest easy that these board members would do little to upset the apple cart.

Private Governance
of Public Schools

With the lack of one central authority, the obstructionists cannot
gain a foothold. While charter board meetings are subject to the
open meetings law, they are not televised, there are too many
meetings to monitor, and truly interested parties now participate,
preventing the obstructionists from gaining control. This structure
was the only way to terminate the OPSB central office employees,
eliminate the collective bargaining agreement and leverage the
opportunity to start anew.
—Linda Johnson, president, Louisiana BESE

The average citizen is in no position to know what is the best
policy for fine schools. Would a hospital put patients and their
families on their boards to determine operations and who is hired?
—Anonymous charter board member

The testimony of Linda Johnson, president of the Louisiana Board of Elementary and Secondary Education (BESE), before the U.S. Senate in
2006 showed that those who put the reforms in place understood they
needed leaders who were likewise committed to the new way of doing business. If the people on the ground were not similarly committed to decentralization and school autonomy, then all the work in preparing the way and
capitalizing on Katrina's opportunity could have been lost. Charter schools
allowed reformers to ensure the survival of the new system because they are
governed by their own private boards. In place of an elected board, which was
viewed as corrupt and incompetent, hundreds of volunteers serve on more
than forty private charter boards. Charter boards are responsible for hiring
school leaders, managing compliance with state and federal laws, overseeing
the financial management of their schools, and following the authorization
process. Charter founders select an initial board, and new members come
on at the discretion and invitation of current board members. These boards
control millions of taxpayer dollars and one of the most important public services in the city. They also have been one of the major players in maintaining
and expanding the system of schools and resisting policy retrenchment. New

policies lead to new political coalitions, which can also bring in new policy makers "as old groups fade away."[1]

Charter board members are deeply invested in maintaining the reforms, for both ideological and political reasons. These folks tend to believe in the market model and have incentives to ensure that authority remains in their hands and that their schools are perceived as doing well.[2] Further, by virtue of how they are selected, charter board members are shielded from public accountability. These dynamics contribute to their attitudes about their roles and their behavior in these positions. As they serve on the boards, these actors learn lessons about their value in the larger political community, as well as the roles and value of the public they serve. This chapter examines these boards, especially as related to how well they serve the public.

Some advocates have argued that charter boards effectively replace an elected board without sacrificing important elements of democratic decision making. Because of the number of boards, there is an opportunity for hundreds of residents to participate in the direct governance of a school or network of schools. These folks do not have to run for office and thus are theoretically beholden to no one, politically or financially. They may be more committed to the principles of education reform and may be at greater political liberty than elected boards to make tough choices about academic performance and accountability.

Through the use of a survey of charter board members and analysis of data on compliance with transparency laws and meeting minutes, this chapter demonstrates that the boards in New Orleans are unrepresentative and lack transparency. They fail to fully comply with state laws about the disclosure of public information. Boards act mostly on financial issues and matters related to board governance (new members, bylaws); very little of their work is focused on academics or school policy. Finally, board members see their role much like a board of directors of a private corporation, with responsibilities only to those they directly serve. They are not concerned about public accountability, and many view the "public" with suspicion and contempt. This information not only tells us about the operation of charter boards and the maintenance of the new system but suggests how the privatization of a major public good affects important democratic values, such as participation, accountability, and representation.

School Governance and Democracy

The transfer of authority away from an elected school board is not unique to New Orleans. Many cities have seen greater centralization through mayoral control and state takeovers, while others have witnessed more school-based autonomy through charter schools and voucher programs.[3] In either case, the result has been to transfer power away from popularly elected school boards. When power is centralized, it usually shifts to different elected or appointed officials. It is still possible for voters to hold these officials accountable and to have their interests represented.[4] When power is decentralized, however, it moves from public control to private hands, leaving little opportunity for public engagement or accountability.

Elected school boards have been thought to play an essential role in preserving local control of schools and giving citizens an active role in school governance.[5] These elections allow citizens to express support or dissatisfaction with their schools or school leaders, and "being able to voice such concerns provides community members with a sense of connectedness to their schools," even if they do not have children in schools.[6] School board elections are considered by many an important accountability check and a form of social capital. Finally, unlike other local offices, school board members tend to see their work as community service and not as a stepping-stone to higher office.[7]

Further, as a public good, public education may be best distributed through democratic processes. Lorraine McDonnell claims that school governance "determines how students are socialized, for it is in this area that decisions are made about what should be taught and who is entitled to educational benefits."[8] Beyond teachers and parents, citizens have an interest in public education because everyone is taxed directly or indirectly to pay for schools, and for social, economic, or moral reasons we all have an interest in seeing that young people get an adequate education. Kenneth Strike writes, "So long as there are broad public interests in education and so long as education is provided at public expense, there is no real alternative to vesting sovereignty over education in a legislature."[9] Elected boards can maintain a democratic character, argues Strike, while still giving schools significant autonomy by operating as the "voice of the political community."

Finally, when elected boards allow public deliberation and respect the expertise of teachers and administrators, they convey to these groups that their voices are welcome and respected. Citizens are likely to be more efficacious and participatory when they believe their officials are listening. Using an experiment, Jonathan Collins recently showed that when they watch a school board meeting with public participation or public deliberation, trust in local officials and the willingness to attend future school board meetings rise.[10] It is impossible for all parties to support the outcome of every decision, but when they deem the process fair, they view the decision as legitimate.[11]

The method of selecting representatives and the extent to which citizens see "people like them" in positions of authority influence how members of the community interact with their public servants.[12]

Critics of school boards argue that the quality of local democracy via elected school boards is far from ideal. One of the chief concerns is that these boards are beholden to narrow political concerns, especially teachers.[13] Although school board elections were put in place in the nineteenth century to remove politics from schooling decisions, some scholars now argue the separation of school governance from general municipal governance "effectively substituted a politics of the people with a politics of the elite."[14] Local district control, as opposed to a more centralized structure, also "creates a forum for the occasional exercise of bigotry and xenophobia; localism . . . serves as a barrier to changes in the distribution of students and resources."[15]

Beyond the narrow interests of certain groups, the public at large often exhibits little interest in school politics. Turnout for school board elections is typically very low, especially when they are not held at the same time as state or federal races, and school board elections are generally noncompetitive.[16] Except in small communities, citizens do not actively participate in school board meetings.[17] It is important not to overly idealize the elected board as a bastion of democracy and to seriously consider the potential benefits of other types of decision-making bodies.

If the public is not particularly engaged in school politics and the elected board listens primarily to a set of narrow interests, then a different governance structure may be not only more effective, but also more democratic. Stacy Smith contends that elected school boards marginalize minority groups, and charter boards offer "the opportunity of incorporating diverse stakeholders in positions of formal decision-making authority."[18] Unlike on elected boards, charter boards' face-to-face deliberations among a group of citizen-volunteers dedicated to the same cause, Smith writes, put them "in a strong position to successfully replace representative governance with direct democratic decision making."[19]

As privately selected volunteers, charter boards are removed from the narrow political interests that supposedly plague elected boards. Charter school boards are more democratic than elected boards, some argue, because they can be held directly accountable by the parents and students they serve.[20] If unhappy, parents can simply vote with their feet and find another school for their children. Further, there is some evidence that parents in choice schools compared with assigned schools are more likely to participate in the Parent-Teacher Association, volunteer in schools, discuss schools with their neighbors, and trust the teachers.[21] This chapter examines whether these assertions bear out in New Orleans. Are charter boards more democratic? I examine three central elements of democracy: representativeness, accountability, and effectiveness.

Who Serves on Charter Boards? Are They Representative?

A long-standing debate in political science centers on descriptive representation and whether people of color and white women are better represented by officials who share these identities.[22] Although descriptive representation ("standing for") is not perfectly related to substantive representation ("acting for"), they are linked.[23] Representatives of color are more likely than white officials to vote in a way that is consistent with their constituents' interests.[24] Several studies have found strong collective representation for Latinos and African Americans: the greater the proportion of Black or Latino school board members, for example, the more policies favor minority students.[25] Black representation on school boards is also related to greater Black representation in the composition of school administration and teachers.[26] Descriptive representation signals to the public that there is more opportunity for minority groups to be engaged and to be heard, contributing to a sense of empowerment and efficacy.[27] As will be explored more deeply in the next chapter, citizens' direct experiences with government affect their attitudes and behavior.[28] If their experiences are more likely to be positive when they are able to work with people who share important descriptive characteristics, it may have mobilizing effects.

Elected school boards provide some of the best descriptive representation of any government institution in the United States. A 2009 survey showed that 80 percent of elected school board members in the United States were white, 12 percent were African American, and 3 percent were Latino.[29] Minority representation increases according to the size of the minority voting population, the size of the jurisdiction, and in ward-based rather than at-large electoral districts.[30] Nearly 22 percent of board members in the largest districts are African American, and 6 percent are Latino. Nationally, board members are also more likely to be men: 56 percent in 2009, down from 61 percent in 2002. Like other elected officials, U.S. school board members are better educated than the average American, especially in large districts.[31]

It is not clear whether the same types of people would serve on a charter school board as those on an elected board. Because these schools are often created by people in the community and board members do not have to run for office, one might expect that these boards would be more representative of their communities. However, the mode of selection makes board diversity less likely. Charter school founders are generally responsible for putting together an initial board when they apply for authorization.[32] When there is attrition, the original board typically selects replacements, leading to an insular process that serves "to narrow the range of interests represented by charter school boards."[33] Further, finding and maintaining people with relevant expertise, diverse qualifications, and sustained interest in public education can be difficult. In New Orleans, where there are more than forty boards, there must be hundreds of members every year. There is also an issue of the cost and efficiency of this labor. The knowledge and expertise required to govern a charter school is immense, and with hundreds of individuals serving at any time, there is likely to be greater inefficiency and duplication of efforts, not to mention wide variation in quality. If this is offset, however, by better representation or functioning, it may be worth it.

We do not know much about the composition of charter boards. A few studies indicate that charter board members are less racially diverse than those of elected boards.[34] In Washington, DC, charter board members are more likely to be women, but in other places, boards had higher proportions of men. In Washington, DC, charter board members are very well off: 88 percent earn more than $100,000 per year, and 51 percent earn more than $200,000.[35] Outside New Orleans, a significant proportion of charter board members were currently or formerly employed in the education sector.

I collected several forms of data to examine questions about charter boards' representation, priorities, and compliance. There is no central database of charter school board members in New Orleans, but schools and networks are required to list the names of their board members on their websites. I conducted an online survey of charter board members in early 2016. More information about the survey's sample is in the appendix.

As in other cities, whites are overrepresented on charter school boards in New Orleans.[36] As Figure 4.1 shows, charter school boards in New Orleans are not as diverse as the elected school board, the Orleans Parish School Board (OPSB). Nearly 60 percent of charter board members were white. The OPSB is elected through ward-based districts and the board in place when these charter board data were collected in 2016 was composed of four African American and three white members. White citizens were much more overrepresented on private charter boards. Both the elected board and private charter boards were unrepresentative of the public school population, but charter boards were more skewed. Men made up the majority (54%) of both the elected and charter boards.[37] For charters, a plurality were white men:

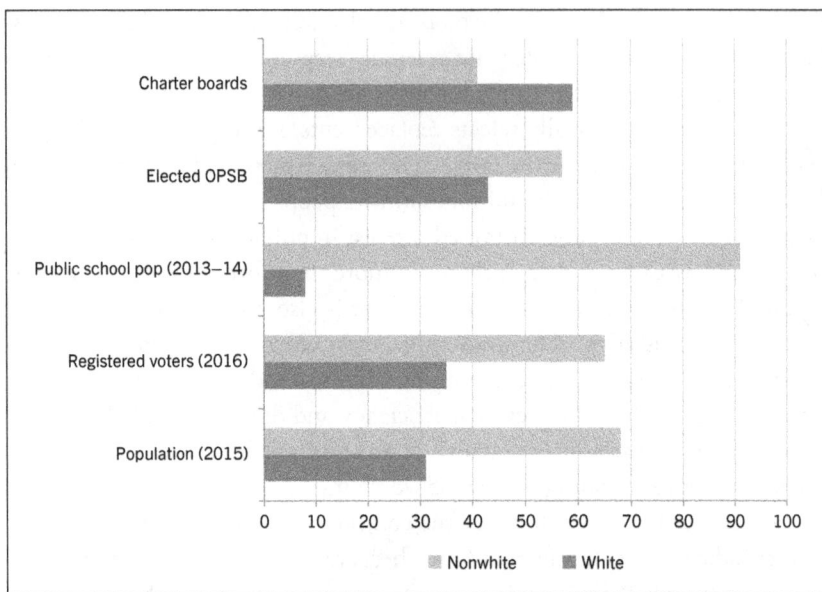

Figure 4.1. Racial composition of charter boards compared with elected board and population, 2016 (*Source:* Data compiled from original survey by the author.)

37 percent were white men, 22 percent were white women, 24 percent were nonwhite women, and 17 percent were nonwhite men. The vast majority of nonwhite members were Black.

Fewer than 10 percent of board members have experience working in the public schools. Women (and in New Orleans, Black or Latina women) are more likely to actually choose schools and to be involved in schools.[38] Only 24 percent of charter board members are women of color, meaning that most of the parents who do the choosing, volunteering, and communicating with teachers and schools may doubt whether their interests are being represented.[39]

Board members are selected because of their expertise in certain areas, such as accountants who can handle budgeting or lawyers who can work on compliance with state or federal laws. The members are not plucked from the community at large. Instead, they represent the elite. One important area of expertise that is largely missing from charter boards is in education. Only 8 percent of charter board members currently worked in or were retired from teaching or school administration.[40]

Charter boards were composed of members of all ages. About one-quarter were in their thirties and another quarter were in their forties, and about one-third were older than sixty. About half were born in New Orleans, and nearly everyone else had lived in the city for more than ten years. Although many newcomers have moved to the city to be a part of education reform, they are not sitting on charter boards. The survey indicates that, like those in Washington, DC, charter board members in New Orleans were affluent. Nearly half of charter board members had household incomes of more than $100,000 per year; 5.5 percent made more than $500,000 per year. This is potentially troubling not only because of the lack of representation, but because of the city's high levels of poverty and inequality combined with the large number of charter board members needed in an all-charter city. There are only so many highly paid, highly educated professionals in the city who are willing to serve in this capacity. This raises serious questions about the sustainability of a model that relies on a continuous supply of these folks.

The vast majority of charter board members were either founding members or were asked to serve by another board member (38.9% and 41.6%, respectively). Only 10 percent of board members who were surveyed applied or volunteered for their position. Given the insularity of social and professional networks, it is unlikely these boards will become more diverse over time on their own. In September 2015, the OPSB passed a requirement that every governing board must include either a parent or legal guardian of a currently enrolled student, and in 2016, the OPSB amended it to allow a parent, a recent graduate, or parent of a recent graduate of the school. Charter leaders were opposed to this decision. Some held that having parents on the board was a conflict of interest, as if the other board members were objective observers; others believed charter schools should have complete autonomy over their membership. In 2018, the investigative online news site *The Lens* noted that boards were adding parents and alumni but did not have figures about the proportion of boards that were complying with the new rule.[41] This rule makes it possible for board members to be forced to look beyond their own networks, but much depends on how boards go about selecting parents.

It is possible that board members would prefer more diversity but have a hard time finding people. To examine this question, I reviewed a sample of charter board meeting minutes from July 2016 to January 2017. There were a total of 249 meeting minutes from thirty-eight boards during this period. Of sixty excerpts pertaining to member recruitment in the meeting minutes, only five comments mention a desire to increase the demographic diversity of the board.[42] Recruitment efforts focused on occupations or a general request for members to "reach out to colleagues" in their own networks. In contrast, the analysis of the public comments made at board meetings shows that 13 percent focused on the lack of representation and 17.4 percent more on the difficulties in accessing the board. Boards do not appear to be particularly concerned about diversity or the extent to which they represent the public. The public that is engaged with charter boards, however, would like for the boards to be more representative and accessible.

It is worth noting that the composition of the OPSB (now called NOLA Public Schools [NOLA-PS]) changed as a result of the 2020 election. There is now only one woman, who is white, and only three (of seven) of its members are Black. Three new members of the board are white and the fourth is Latino. The 2020 elections were the most competitive since Katrina, yet none of those who won campaigned on significant change or increased public involvement. In the most competitive races, pro-reform interests from outside Louisiana contributed substantially to the winners' campaigns.[43]

Effectiveness: What Are Board Priorities?

A 2010 report by the pro-reform Thomas B. Fordham Institute finds that elected school board members tend to place a priority on "intangible" outcomes, such as helping students "fulfill their potential" or "preparing them for a satisfying and productive life," as opposed to "readying them for the workforce or for college."[44] Budgetary concerns are also more important to board members than student achievement or community engagement. To this pro-reform group, these priorities are misplaced. Frederick Hess and Olivia Meeks disparage school boards as operating primarily as "fiduciaries of a public trust rather than change agents on behalf of a compelling societal agenda."[45] Arnold Shober and Michael Hartney's study of elected school boards similarly indicates that board members are divided in their priorities, but districts where members are more focused on academic performance are more likely to have higher levels of student achievement. The direction of the causal arrow is unclear, of course.

Because of the politics of charter schools, charter board members may be more focused on student achievement than on fiduciary responsibilities and are more likely to have an education agenda around school choice and performance.[46] However, charter schools, especially in New Orleans, grew out of not only concern for low student performance, but also frustration with corruption and irresponsible financial management. State takeovers of public schools, premised on low performance, often end up being focused mostly on financial concerns.[47]

In the survey, New Orleans charter board members selected what they believed to be the top three responsibilities that are most important for the board. By far, the most commonly selected item was "budgeting/financial management," chosen by 79.8 percent of respondents. A majority (56.8%) also selected "compliance with state laws" and nearly a majority (47.3%) selected "developing policies that align with the mission." About 20 percent selected "school performance." Charter board members reported that they expected school leaders and staff to handle academic performance and that their job was to ensure the school is legally and financially sound.

These survey responses mirror the analysis from the minutes of the meetings. A third of total votes in charter board meetings (345 votes) between July 2016 and January 2017 dealt with financial matters; 28 percent were related to board policy. Votes on matters of academics or student life made up only 7.5 percent of the total. In sum, whether school boards are publicly elected or privately selected, the chief priority is financial matters and budgeting. If charter board members have an agenda focused on school performance or academics, it is not manifest in how they see their responsibilities or in the actions they take on the boards.

Charters and Financial Malfeasance

One could very easily argue, however, that in a city with a history of corruption and where a board president was charged and convicted of bribery, close attention to the budget is certainly not a bad thing, especially if it corresponds to responsible financial management. However, it is not entirely clear that charter schools do considerably better in this regard than elected boards of the past. In 2015, two top leaders of ReNEW SciTech Academy stepped down amid cheating allegations. It was then revealed that they had inflated the school's special education population to obtain more funds to fill a budgetary hole. They "blew up the education plans of 49 students, adding an average of 1,032 minutes of extra help, which total 2.5 days per week" and brought in $180,000. At the same time, the leaders ignored other special needs students, saying in emails that these kids were a "secondary priority to students who were more likely to pass the state assessments."[48]

The state pension program for teachers has gotten a few charters into trouble. The same network that inflated the special education figures, ReNEW, did not enroll all eligible employees in the pension system, resulting in shorting the state by more than $375,000; it also enrolled ineligible teachers, contributing nearly $350,000 that should not have been taken from teachers' salaries. In 2014, it was discovered that James Singleton Charter School had not enrolled all its teachers and had doctored records to avoid paying $600,000 to the state.

The former elected board chair was not the only person to commit a crime. In 2010, the former financial manager at Langston Hughes Academy was charged with stealing about $660,000 from the school by writing checks to herself and making withdrawals from the school account.[49] She was sentenced to five years in federal prison. A Lusher Charter School employee wrote herself $25,000 in checks from the school; she returned the money, and although her certified public accountant (CPA) license was revoked, she was never charged.[50] Nearly $26,000 went missing from Lake Area New Tech Early College High School in 2014, and that same year, an employee at the Knowledge Is Power Program (KIPP) New Orleans stole nearly $70,000 by taking and forging checks for vendors.[51] In 2020, the business manager of Warren Easton Charter High School absconded with more than $70,000 of student activity funds.[52]

To be clear, these violations are not unique to New Orleans, or to charter schools. However, given the claims about how charter schools remedy the problems of traditional school boards and in the central office structure, I argue we should hold charters to similar, if not higher, standards. If these were traditionally elected boards, their skeptics would almost certainly view these incidents as evidence of their ineptitude. That same standard should hold for charter boards. Charter boards can select financial professionals as members who have fewer schools to oversee and have the expertise to reduce mismanagement.[53] The reasons for upending the New Orleans system included not only the district's low performance, but its culture of corruption. These incidents cast doubt on the notion that charter schools, because they are governed privately, are inherently less corrupt. In fact, the lack of oversight from the authorizers leaves the discovery of this malfeasance largely to the local media, and there are few, if any, consequences. Authorizers have not shut a school down solely or even primarily because of financial mismanagement.

Reliance on Board Members' Donations

The analysis of the meeting minutes also picked up a phenomenon unique to charter boards: donations from board members are a dominant topic of discussion at meetings. During the limited period that was examined, about a third of boards solicited donations or connections from members during board meetings. One school passed a bylaw requiring annual financial donations from board members, and four other boards discussed doing so. These types of requirements are likely to exacerbate the issues around representation, since the average community member or public school parent in a city as poor as New Orleans will be unable to contribute financially to a charter board. School fundraisers tend to be a mechanism by which affluent parents can improve their children's resources, but they exacerbate inequalities.[54] Requiring board members to financially contribute may act as a similar mechanism to keep poor and middle-class board members out.

Compliance with State Laws and Board Structure

Advocates of educational privatization claim that public school systems are mired in bureaucratic red tape, costing valuable resources and stifling innovation. One of the chief advantages of charter schools is that they are free from some of the regulations of traditional public schools. Further, those regulations to which they are subject theoretically should be handled more efficiently and thoroughly in a system with market features. Because charter boards are publicly funded, and due to their roles as a quasi-government that oversees the delivery of this essential public service, they are subject to state laws requiring transparency of public information. However, charter boards often use their public-private status to "maintain proprietary status over information that in traditional schools is considered public."[55] These schools are associated with reduced efforts to inform the public at large.[56]

The Lens has conducted multiple investigations on the compliance of charter boards with open meetings and public information laws. In 2010, its investigative reporters found that a "large number" of these boards failed to comply with their requests for basic information about board members and meetings.[57] Five years after Katrina, many boards were confused about whether they were public bodies at all. In 2011, *The Lens* revisited the issue of compliance, finding that only six of forty-three charter school boards "could show they even come close to complying" with an open budgeting law.[58] Oversight of this compliance falls to the authorizing bodies, which at the time included the RSD and the OPSB. That year, fourteen schools were up for reauthorization, and all but one had failed to comply with the portion of public meetings law requiring them to send public notices to the media. All were renewed without any comment about the open-government law.

In 2016, *The Lens* repeated its investigation into the transparency of meeting information. This was eleven years after the system was set up and more than two years after the state had clarified its law requiring that all public bodies post meeting minutes online. Only seven of forty boards were regularly posting minutes for full board meetings; no board posted committee meeting minutes.[59] After the noncompliant boards were contacted, all but three posted their minutes within two weeks but did not include committee meeting minutes. The minutes that were posted were missing many required elements, such as who was present and how each person voted on each item.

In January 2017, I collected similar data as *The Lens* to examine how charter boards were keeping up with these requirements after having updated their websites just six months earlier. Louisiana law requires that charter boards post information on their websites about board meetings, minutes, and school personnel. Using the websites, I coded whether charter boards provided the dates, times, and places of all meetings, including committee meetings.[60] I also coded whether boards and their committees provided an agenda for the last scheduled meeting and whether the last three months of meeting minutes were posted online. Boards were also required to list the name and contact information of their custodian of public records.

Finally, to determine the level of compliance with state laws about inclusion on these documents, I examined the meeting minutes. The minutes must include the time, date, and location of the meeting; the attendance or absence of each member; and the individual votes for each member on each item on which there is a vote.[61] This analysis also checked whether there was information that is not required by law but is useful for a citizen who wants to know who sits on charter boards and how he or she may contact these individuals. This information includes board members' biographies, photos, and an email address or other contact information.

In January 2017, charter boards had no reason to assume they would continue to be monitored, and, indeed, compliance was highly variable. Nearly all charter boards (93%) provided the one piece of information they are legally required to supply about their board members: their names (Table 4.1). No additional information is required about board members, and most boards provide little else. With only 15 percent of boards providing email addresses for board members, it would be difficult for a parent or concerned citizen to contact the boards. Nationally, Hess and Meeks find, 83.9 percent of elected school boards in the largest districts include an email address for every board member on the district web page. The elected OPSB website includes email addresses for every member.

Most boards comply with the state requirements about posting board meeting information. On average, boards post 2.34 of the three pieces of information needed to attend a meeting (time, date, and place), but nearly a third (31.7%) of board websites are missing at least one required element. Nearly 15 percent of boards supply none of this information on their websites, making it impossible for parents and other members of the public to attend board meetings.

It is more difficult to find the required board documents. On average, boards publish about two-thirds of these three required elements (last meeting agenda, three months of meeting minutes, and the name of the custodian

TABLE 4.1. COMPLIANCE OF CHARTERS WITH
STATE PUBLIC INFORMATION LAWS, 2017

	Number of Boards Providing This Information	Percentage of Boards Providing This Information
Member Information		
Names	38	92.7
Emails (not required)	6	14.6
Photos (not required)	7	17.1
Biographies (not required)	19	46.3
Meeting Information		
Date	35	85.4
Time	31	75.6
Location	30	73.2
Required Board Documents		
Last meeting agenda	31	75.6
Three months of minutes	26	63.4
Custodian of records	29	70.7
Committee Meeting Information		
Schedule	11	26.8
Agenda	13	31.7
Minutes	6	14.6

Source: Charter board survey by the author.

of records). More than half the boards failed to provide at least one of these types of documents.[62] Many of those boards are often praised among charter advocates for their success. Three boards provided none of the required materials. Six months after they were called out in local media for their failure to comply, most boards went immediately back into noncompliance. The rates of compliance are lower than with elected boards in the nation, where 74 percent of the largest districts have board minutes and documents available on the web.[63] Advocates and board members often claim that boards simply "aren't aware" that they have to provide this information, in spite of the many investigations into their behavior.[64]

In looking at the structure of board decision making, the meeting minutes indicate that, as in most legislatures, the important work takes place in committees; the full board often merely accepts the recommendations of its committees.[65] In New Orleans, information about committees is very hard to find. In many cases, the only way to tell whether a board had committees was to read the minutes from the full board meetings, as few websites included lists of committees, their members, and information about these meetings. Based on the minutes, most boards have committees: about 83 percent have a finance committee; 72 percent, a governance committee; nearly half, an academic committee; and 41 percent, a development committee. Smaller percentages have committees on facilities, strategic planning, marketing, outreach, legal, and personnel. On average, boards post fewer than one of the three required elements about committees: information about committee meetings, meeting agendas, or meeting minutes. Given that full boards often adopt committees' recommendations without discussion, the lack of transparency around these committees is troubling.

Aggregate data are helpful in demonstrating the widespread nature of this problem. For individual cases, dozens of stories have been published in local media about charter boards' violations of state transparency laws. In May 2012, the Algiers Charter School Association failed to notify the media of its meeting, then held the meeting in a private office building. Two months later, the group held its meeting publicly but went immediately into executive session without appropriate rationale. Protestors complained, "They're not letting us be heard. . . . We're not being respected."[66] In October 2016, the same board failed to include on the posted agenda a vote on the most controversial decision these boards make: to relinquish a charter for one of its schools.[67] The measure passed with parents and other community members having no ability to influence the process. This also happened at New Beginnings School Foundation in 2016 when it voted to close Gentilly Terrace Charter School without noting anything about a potential closure on its public agenda.[68] It does not appear that any of these issues came up when these schools sought reauthorization.

In 2016, Lusher Charter School was faced with an attempt by its teachers to form a union. Emails received through public records requests later revealed that the president planned to get around public notification requirements by using a "walking quorum," wherein one or two people would step outside if the meeting size approached a quorum.[69] This is a clear violation of state law. The emails also revealed extensive substantive discussions taking place about the measure via email—another violation of law. Meetings of public bodies must be held in a public session. The board secretary made a fairly obvious statement that she was not an "open meeting expert" after she claimed to believe only the vote was required to be held publicly, not the discussion. The OPSB supposedly looked into these potential violations and decided that no further action needed to be taken.[70]

Charter boards can largely flout these state transparency laws and do whatever they want. Charter authorizers do not exercise oversight, and these issues never matter for reauthorization. This behavior demonstrates to citizens that those in positions of authority simply do not care whether the public has access to the boards. If the public cannot find information about meetings or decisions, or if boards routinely discuss important matters in private or in executive session, there is no opportunity for the public to express opinions or ask questions. These public bodies are not only unrepresentative; they often actively attempt to shut the public out of important discussions that directly affect them.

Public Accountability

Accountability is a mantra among charter school supporters, who contend that their schools are better because they are held accountable for meeting performance standards. If their students do not succeed, charter schools are closed. Charter schools hold administrators and teachers accountable, all while unleashing their "entrepreneurial spirit" and "professional creativity."[71] Advocates argue that charters heighten accountability because parents can choose another school if they are not satisfied.

These conceptions of accountability, however, assume that public schools are primarily (if not exclusively) intended to serve only the children who attend them. Traditionally, public schools are thought to be *public* goods that serve the entire community. They not only educate young people but also act as anchors for neighborhoods and communities as both physical places for communities to gather and psychological links to the past and future. They are funded through taxpayers, most of whom do not currently have children attending public schools. Those who work in schools were considered public servants, not only teaching children basic skills, but socializing the next generation as citizens and members of society.

As public institutions, the officials responsible for making decisions about public schools ought to be accountable to the public, not only to those who attend their school. This has traditionally been accomplished through elections of school board members and in open meetings, where community members can ask questions and comment on important issues. Nonelected board members could theoretically still be accountable by welcoming and encouraging public deliberation, taking seriously public opinion, and appreciating their role as public servants. Research on charters in cities other than New Orleans finds that elected school board members have a greater sense of responsibility to the general public than do charter board members.[72] Research by Michael Ford and Douglas Ihrke shows that charter board members are less likely to consider the input of members of the community in their decision making.[73] Melissa Stone and her colleagues find that charter board members in Minnesota feel most accountable to their authorizers: fewer than 20 percent said they felt accountable to the public or taxpayers.[74]

The results are similar in New Orleans. My survey asked respondents an open-ended question about the public's role in their activities: "Given that charter boards are not publicly elected, in what ways can residents of New Orleans hold boards accountable?" A plurality (40.2 percent) said that the primary accountability mechanism is attendance and public comment at meetings—an ironic response, given the difficulties with finding information about board meetings. Board members' second-most-common answer (16.2 percent) involved indirect accountability through the elected boards (OPSB and BESE), even though they have limited power over charter boards. Eight percent of respondents mentioned that the public can view the public documents related to the board meetings and decisions, something boards are even worse at providing than information about meetings. Further, "viewing" documents is far from any reasonable conception of democratic accountability.

Nearly 11 percent of respondents wrote that parents have the right to exit their school. These board members fail to see any role for the public at large, who may not have children at all or whose children are not enrolled in their school. In this conception, schools are much like restaurants or retail clothing stores: if you don't like it, leave. New Orleans has a limited number of A-rated schools, and nearly all use selective enrollment. The "high-performing" charters set their own caps and admission standards, which means that, even when parents are attracted to them, the idea that parents can vote with their feet is much more theory than practice.

Beyond logistics, the idea that people should pick up and leave when they are "dissatisfied" has serious implications for engagement and democratic participation. There is no sense that people should work to make their schools better or that the students and parents form a community to which they should feel some allegiance or sense of responsibility. This conception maintains power and decision making solely in the hands of private entities. The only choice people have is to accept the outcomes or find another option. If all the options are closed off or similar to those parents find unacceptable, then there is nothing left but to acquiesce. This flies in the face of everything we know about what makes schools positive learning environments and welcoming institutions for children and what we believe about governance in a democracy.[75]

Several respondents made their views about the public's (in)ability to hold them accountable very clear. One noted, "Assuming there are avenues under State law to hold charter boards accountable, you can be assured that the general public is not aware of them." Another doubted the public even cares to exercise accountability: "I'm not sure the general community cares enough to pursue any kind of accountability." And one board member quoted at the beginning of the chapter expressed disdain for the public's role, claiming that few citizens know enough about education policy for their views to have value.

These comments, especially in light of my results related to compliance with open meetings laws, suggest that charter school critics are right to be concerned about public accountability of private boards. Board members claim that public meetings and comments allow community members to be involved and exercise accountability, but many boards do not post their meeting information, deliberate in private, and fail to provide information publicly about their decisions. Some board members are openly circumspect about the general public's capacity or even right to be involved in school governance. Without the ability to vote them out, the public is truly unable to hold these private board members accountable.

Governance in a Post-political City

A look at the types of decisions charter schools make without public input also demonstrates how little concern these boards have about an engaged citizenry. The degree of public engagement in the creation and maintenance of charter schools varies considerably.[76] Although the state BESE requires charters to have policies that ensure parental involvement and public comment, there is little oversight of these provisions. In 2013, Barry Landry, spokesman for the Louisiana Department of Education, said that the state does not monitor these policies but will respond to individual situations as they arise.[77]

In New Orleans, charter authorizers have closed or transferred charters without parental input and over the objections of parent groups. In 2013, the RSD and the Algiers Charter School Association decided to merge the L. B. Landry and O. Perry Walker College and Career Preparatory High Schools against parents' and students' wishes. In one public meeting, more than one hundred people showed up to express their opposition to the plan. Landry had been renovated, but Walker had the stronger academic program. Leslie Jacobs, former member of BESE and architect of the New Orleans reforms, stated that the decision to merge the schools was largely about resources: Landry had room for Walker's students, and with a smaller post-Katrina population, it did not make financial sense to run the two schools separately. She chalked the opposition up to the "strong ties" that native New Orleanians have to high school alma maters.[78]

Two years after the Landry-Walker merger, the RSD changed its process of selecting school operators to be inclusive of community voices. When it announced that four schools would be closed in 2015, it allowed any public organization in the city to apply to run them. Although some participants said they had to fight to be heard, in the end, many believed this was a fairer and more transparent process. Even so, the leader of the RSD had final authority and was not in an elected position. Community participation is allowed but may or may not be meaningful.[79] Alice Huff refers to this type of politics as "post-political":

> At the heart of post-political concerns is the argument that politics as it is frequently practiced actually reinforces the ideological and structural workings of the current social order. It does so by retaining formal democratic institutions and procedures while shifting the contexts of power and decision-making into arenas that are 1) easily accessed and dominated by corporate interests, and 2) insulated from the effects of citizen engagement and dissensus. . . . Complex urban dilemmas are framed as issues that can be resolved through increasingly privatized governance and/or through "stakeholder democracy" in which a range of social actors engage in discussion and consensus building.[80]

In other words, "stakeholder democracy" *looks* democratic. The *people* were brought in; their views were *considered*. But in the end, they had no authority, and there was no incentive for those with the power to listen to those whom they believed to be tied to the past because of nostalgia or who did not understand the considerations deemed to be more important.

In a traditional system, these parents might have been similarly out of luck with the elected board, which could have outvoted them. It is certainly not the case that traditional public school systems are perfect models of democracy. Democracies do not have unanimous decisions, meaning that some groups will be dissatisfied with the outcome. The difference is not in the outcome, but in the process. Dissatisfied parents in the charter system have no real recourse. They can "vote with their feet," but again, there are too few high-quality schools, and there are no schools in which their voices would carry much weight. With an elected board, they would still have had the option of voting for other leaders in the next election. That likelihood might have altered some of the decision making of the board that chose to merge these schools. In 2013, when more than one hundred parents and community member petitioned to transfer Sarah T. Reed High School from the RSD to the OPSB instead of closing the school, OPSB President Ira Thomas promised he would stand with them and encouraged them to attend the next meeting to express their opposition to the closure.[81]

Giving people a voice without power is a way to legitimize decisions of the powerful. Those with authority can say it was an open process and then do whatever they were always going to do. The people have no recourse. They cannot vote out the charter board members, and without this accountability, the boards can make any decision they want. The only "option" for parents is to find another school in a system that does not offer many good options.

Conclusions

Private charter boards in New Orleans have replaced the elected board in most of its traditional functions. These boards are, however, less representative of the public than the elected board. Charter board members are more likely to be white, particularly white men. Few work or have worked in education. The priority placed on personal donations to the school or network reinforces a lack of diversity in the boards' composition. The lack of diversity introduces political biases in terms of support for the general reform movement and in favor of the market model. It is unlikely that a charter skeptic will ever be asked, or allowed, to sit on any of these public bodies. This creates problems not only with "group think" potential, but also with representation. Further, with such limited oversight from charter authorizers and a priority on wealthy board members, how can the public be sure that board members' business or financial interests do not conflict with the interests of the schools they are serving?

This chapter also demonstrates that oversight is seriously lacking. In the early years, there was great misunderstanding about the "publicness" of these bodies. Many viewed them as other nonprofit boards. Over the years, state laws clarified these rules, generally requiring charters to provide the level of transparency of other public bodies. Their reluctance to provide this information did not simply stem from ignorance of the rules, however. Board members believe there should be a very limited role for the general public. Many members define the public very narrowly as those parents whose children attend their school. Members of these private boards do not see themselves as needing to be accountable to a larger public. Others view the public skeptically, arguing that the public has no interest or expertise in public education and, essentially, that the public should leave policy up to the experts. Never mind that most charter board members lack any background in education.

There was great irony in the debate around requiring parents on the board. Many charter leaders argued that parents could not be objective and would see school policy strictly through a personal lens. Reformers met the one move to improve the representation and accountability of these private boards with skepticism about a commitment to the common good—*on the part of parents.* The board members, however, did not question their own commitment to the public, despite years of evidence about their lack of transparency and their obvious lack of representation. Finally, the logic of school choice expects parents to be self-interested. This works fine, apparently, on the demand side. But when parents demand to be involved in making policy, their self-interested behavior is a problem.

Reformers could not have a stronger, more supportive group of people governing the system they put in place in 2005. These well-connected folks are the stewards for the post-Katrina system. They have proven they are willing to make unpopular decisions against the will of the parents and children they serve. They admit their disdain for "the public" and see no problem with having a group with limited expertise holding considerable power over this public service. Parents and other members of the community do not have to read between the lines to see that they are unwelcome, and even when they manage to find a way to express their opinions, those with authority do not have to hear it.

The lack of descriptive representation sends a signal to the public about who belongs, whose voices are most valued. Political trust and political efficacy are higher among women and people of color when they see that their representatives share these characteristics.[82] It makes it harder for public school parents—the majority of whom are Black or Latino—not only to feel comfortable expressing their views to the boards, but also to see there is any point in doing so. The lack of diversity on the boards, not just in terms of race but also with regard to income and occupation, also reduces the likelihood that board members will have different experiences and perspectives from one another and from those whose interests they represent. The process for selecting new board members makes this cycle self-reinforcing.[83]

The architects of the reforms and their hand-selected board members had no intention of designing a system in which public deliberation was a central element. In fact, as Linda Johnson, president of the BESE, stated in 2006: "There are too many meetings to monitor, and truly interested parties now participate, preventing the obstructionists from gaining control." One can infer who Johnson had in mind by "obstructionists" based on who is selected to serve on the boards and who is underrepresented, as well as how difficult these officials have made it for the public to even know what the boards are doing. The political scientist Jamila Michener argues that racial disparities in "the ways policies allocate benefits and burdens to particular racial groups" have widespread effects, including "how policy is constructed by political elites, perceived among the public, [and] experienced by beneficiaries."[84] In the policies and practices around charter boards, reformers have exacerbated the racial disproportionalities in New Orleans schools. Most of those with power are white, affluent, and well educated, while most of the students and families are Black, poor, and less educated. Thus, when leaders make contemptuous statements about the people who are excluded from deliberation, it is hard to argue that there is not a racial undertone. These comments also highlight reformers' high degree of racial paternalism. They do not value public input, and they believe they know best what Black, poor children need from schools. They would say that the ends (high-quality schools) justify the means (denying rights and access to those who make up the school system).

If they really wanted public involvement and general support, charter boards and authorizing bodies could open up their meetings, seek community participation, and elect board members from the neighborhoods in which their schools are located. They could assume that community members and parents add value to the work of building and maintaining a high-quality school system rather than seeing the "general public" as an ignorant nuisance. Charter leaders' attitudes, the disproportionate representation of the boards, and the difficulties with finding meeting information feed back in several ways: Black parents and community members see they are not valued and are more likely to disengage; likewise, most white citizens are off the hook with public schools because they can assume that people like them have it covered; the boards have little incentive to comply with meetings law, which keeps the system closed; and the lack of public engagement justifies board members' beliefs about the general public's ignorance and apathy. The next two chapters examine the effects of these policies and practices on Black parents' support for the system and political efficacy and trust.

They Choose, We Lose

I would just sit there and kind of pull my hair out. How can
people try to rebuild their lives and figure this out, and have to
trust this system that has completely failed the citizens of New
Orleans for the last fifty to sixty years?
—New Orleans parent

Parents' comments and other sources belie the common narrative that has emerged of widespread public support for the systemwide change after Katrina. In 2009, the editors of the *Times-Picayune* wrote that "the reinvention of public schools . . . is often touted as a bright spot of recovery" and referenced a recent poll that "[put] numbers to those beliefs."[1] Of another poll that year, Leslie Jacobs said, "It would be hard to get better numbers for apple pie and motherhood."[2] Despite the public relations campaign, a close look at surveys of New Orleans residents shows, while they strongly support school choice, opinion on whether the schools have improved and other elements of the system is much more mixed.

Within these data also lurk some significant differences between parents and nonparents, and between African American residents and others. These gaps are rooted in their distinct experiences in the public schools before and after the storm. Despite all the reformers' language about "green fields" and "starting over," parents did not approach the schools as a blank slate. Their experiences as students and as parents in New Orleans public schools shaped how they interacted with the institutions and their representatives. As a result of the trauma and loss that accompanied Katrina, parents of public school kids were under tremendous stress in getting themselves and their children back on their feet in new neighborhoods and an entirely new system of schools. The result was a mix of tentative hope, fear of the unknown, and a reticence to trust authorities who seemed to be selling something that the reformers themselves were not buying.

This chapter examines the general support for the education reforms, including school choice, charter schools, and perceptions about improvement. Then I focus on two specific types of experiences that shaped parents' reactions to the reforms: enrollment practices and the treatment of children within schools. Nearly all parents supported the idea of school choice. However, in practice, parents often found that enrolling their children in schools was much harder than they believed it should be, that good options were not equally accessible for all families, and that some schools and officials made it clear that their children were not wanted. These opinions did not always come through in public opinion surveys, but in more intimate settings, the frustrations and disappointments of public school parents were obvious.

The next section delves into the political science literature on policy feedback, which points to the role that policies, once enacted, play in the public's attitudes and behavior, especially that of target populations. In both their design and the processes of passage and implementation, policies send important messages about deservingness and belonging that, in turn, influence the behavior of beneficiaries and the general public.[3] This chapter demonstrates that public school parents, especially Black parents, in New Orleans are frustrated that they have limited options for their children and that their voices continue to be excluded.

Policy Feedback and Mass Publics

In political science, theories of individual political behavior largely rely on a social-psychology framework.[4] The process of political socialization whereby children learn about politics from their parents, peers, and community members shapes individual preferences about party identification, ideology, and general political orientations toward participation, efficacy, and trust in government.[5] Partisanship and other social identities form the basis for political attitudes and behavior. Though many studies acknowledge that beliefs and opinion are responsive to government performance, most scholars of political behavior contend that one's preconceptions and identities provide the lens through which one processes information about officials' performance.[6] There is less acknowledgment that experience with the government influences political behavior.

In contrast, policy feedback scholarship contends that preferences are also shaped by experience with government and government programs, and various aspects of policy design affect the messages that individuals receive about their status in society.[7] Specifically, policies both confer resources and have "interpretive effects" on mass publics.[8] In terms of resources, a public policy such as Social Security grants economic security; Medicare provides health-care protections for the elderly; low-interest loans for college offer a means for poor students to obtain a postsecondary education; and public education provides skills that are useful in the economy. Such resources have direct and indirect effects on civic participation.[9]

Interpretive effects are the indirect effects on individuals' political and civic participation through political efficacy and trust.[10] As Anne Schneider and Helen Ingram point out, the treatment of a policy's target groups depends on the relative power of the group and how the group is socially constructed.[11] Public policies that target positively constructed groups with power (such as the elderly) are different in design and effect from those that target negatively constructed groups without power (such as undocumented immigrants or drug offenders). For instance, policy makers and the public see Social Security beneficiaries as powerful and deserving and cater to their interests with benevolent policy tools and designs.[12] The elderly learn that government is responsive to their needs and see value in voting and organizing, activities that reinforce their political power.[13]

In contrast, programs such as Medicaid and Temporary Aid to Needy Families also provide a measure of economic security, but they teach very different lessons to beneficiaries and to the public more broadly. Beneficiaries learn that the public sees them as worthy of government support only under certain conditions and that advocating for themselves is largely ineffective. "Stingy benefits" and "demoralizing messages about dependence and lack of deservingness result in political participation levels among welfare recipients even lower than would be predicted from their already low average education and income levels."[14] These demoralizing messages and the lack of adequate benefits make it less likely that beneficiaries will be active in politics and advocacy.[15] The effects of these messages spill over to close associates of the beneficiaries, serving to further depress engagement among this population.[16] Thus, policy makers continue to ignore their needs and devalue their contributions. The public, likewise, has negative constructions of welfare recipients, which reinforce a sense of both undeservingness and neglect among policy makers. It is no surprise that these policies are deeply racialized, such that white Americans associate welfare, Medicaid, and other means-tested programs with Black and Latino families.[17] Negative attitudes about these groups and these programs are intertwined and reinforce one another to perpetuate disparities and disadvantage.

Effects of Policy Design

Important distinctions in the policy type and design influence interpretive effects. Typically, universal programs such as Social Security and veterans' benefits convey more positive messages about deservingness than means-tested programs such as food stamps or welfare. Targeted public assistance programs also vary in the "ways they structure authority relations."[18] Programs that engage beneficiaries in a participatory process and those with clear rules that protect clients' security and autonomy elicit more positive feedback effects than those in which beneficiaries are subject to supervisory discretion.[19] For example, caseworkers often monitor how beneficiaries of poverty programs use their payments, while there is less oversight of individuals receiving benefits from universal programs.[20] There is a continuum of feedback effects: feedback is most negative when policies are characterized by strict supervision and control and most positive when there is democratic participation. In between are bureaucratic authority systems in which there is a centralized administration that treats individuals equally.

In addition to the social constructions of the target populations, the universality, size, and visibility of the benefits influence whether there are feedback effects and whether they are positive or negative.[21] In theory, public school systems are universal, serving parents and children from across economic and racial groups, and they have multiple positive spillover effects on their communities. Everyone, even those with no children, benefits from high-quality public schools. Public education is enormous in size: in most communities these schools serve the vast majority of children, and education is the single largest government outlay at the state and local level. Further, its locally elected, ward-based governance systems are the most representative institutions in the nation and give citizens ample opportunities to have their voices heard.

Given these features, we should expect to see positive feedback effects from public schools. Eric Patashnik contends, however, that compared with programs such as Social Security and Medicare, which confer targeted resources on distinct groups, "One should not expect [general-interest] reforms to stimulate significant feedback effects *in the mass public*" because the benefits are "too diffuse, invisible, and distant."[22] He contends that general-interest reforms generate feedback primarily on policy elites, especially interest groups. Because the resources conferred by public education are vast and spread out over the population and across space and time, the education system's policy feedback effects are primarily interpretive. As a universal program characterized by democratic participation, these effects ought to be fairly positive as compared with means-tested programs with strict supervision directed primarily at the poor.

I argue, however, that the New Orleans school system is not a universal program. After the 1970s, when courts began to enforce racial integration, the city's white and middle-class Black residents abandoned public schools and failed to support adequate resources for them. Today, a majority of white children in New Orleans attend private schools, and the public system is dramatically poorer and less white than the city as a whole. In terms of policy feedback, public education in New Orleans ought to be considered a targeted program, focused on poor Black and Latino families. No degree of change or reform would directly affect the affluent or white residents of New Orleans. Public school parents, by contrast, experience directly the interpretive effects of these policies. Much like those who interact with the criminal justice or welfare systems, this community's experiences with the school system send a message about their place in the system and influence their support for and trust in schools.

In addition to its targeted nature, the changes in governance chronicled in the previous chapter have decreased the democratic nature of public education in New Orleans. The school enrollment process in the immediate years after reform and prior to OneApp more closely resembled a system of supervisory discretion, in which street-level bureaucrats within each charter school or network controlled admission. There was no transparency, and decisions were unequal and arbitrary. With the introduction of OneApp, enrollment moved closer to a bureaucratic system that supposedly applied equal treatment and even a random lottery number to every applicant. This system ought to have more positive effects than what it replaced, but much depends on the implementation and the information that was communicated to parents.

This chapter first examines evidence about the general support for the system to get an idea of which features of the system are most and least popular among which groups of residents.[23] Then I focus on the enrollment experience and parents' reports of their children's treatment within schools.

Support for Reforms

Before considering support for education reform, it is important to understand residents' attitudes about the public schools before Katrina. The University of New Orleans routinely surveyed the city for its Quality of Life study. Figure 5.1 shows that, in the two decades before Katrina, only 1–2 percent of residents rated New Orleans public schools as "very good." Instead, either a plurality or

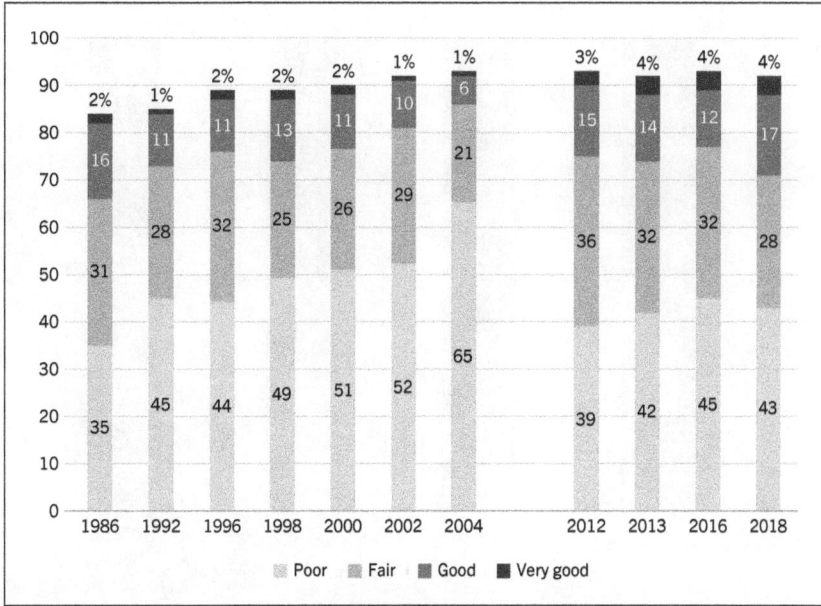

Figure 5.1. Pre- and post-Katrina ratings of public schools by New Orleans residents
(*Source:* University of New Orleans Quality of Life surveys. Reports with top-line data are at https://scholar works.uno.edu/src_pubs/index.html. After Katrina, the options included "very poor," which had not been an option prior to the storm. I combined "very poor" and "poor" so the scales are comparable.)

majority in each year of the study said the schools were "poor," the lowest rating on the scale. Attitudes worsened over this period: in 1986, 35 percent of residents gave the schools a "poor" rating, and in 2004, 65 percent did so, even though there was some indication of improvement in New Orleans's schools immediately before Katrina. The increasing negativity tracks the reform movement at the state, which was accompanied by rhetoric and media stories about the poor-performing schools, especially in New Orleans. In the years after Katrina, there is some evidence that attitudes improved, but only slightly. Well after the reforms were put in place, the plurality still rated schools as "poor."

The Kaiser Family Foundation surveyed residents four times in the first ten years after Katrina.[24] These surveys indicate that although the ratings did not dramatically improve, New Orleanians believed there was progress on schools. In 2006, only 9.7 percent said that "a lot" of progress had been made on strengthening the school system, but this grew to 27.2 percent in 2015 (Figure 5.2). One would not expect much progress in the first year after the storm, but ten years later, a little more than one-quarter of New Orleanians saw improvements. Even so, in each year but 2006, about 20 percent of residents reported there had been no progress at all on strengthening schools.

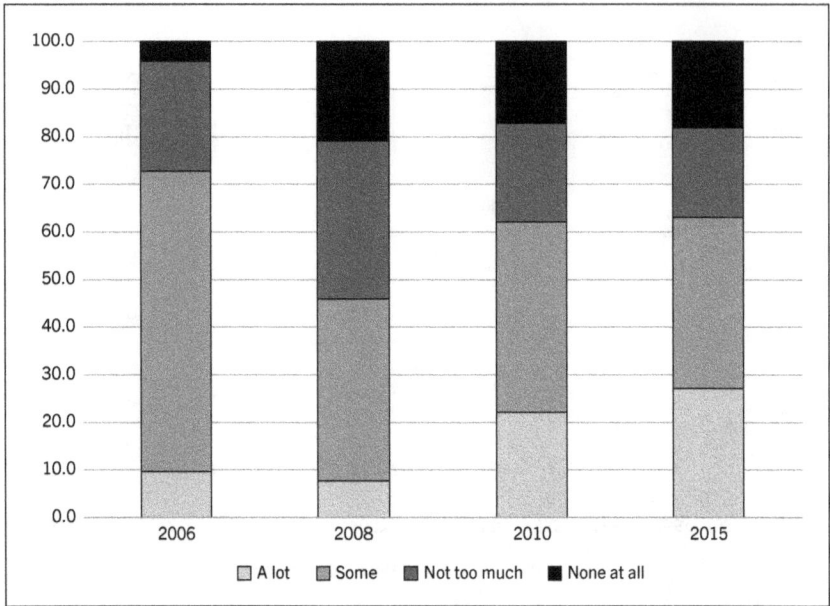

Figure 5.2. New Orleanians' perceptions of progress on strengthening public school system (*Source:* Kaiser Family Foundation polls.)

This also highlights how data can be used for political purposes. Reformers tended to focus exclusively on the growth in positive attitudes, ignoring the fact that 20 percent of residents continued to believe there was no progress.

The Cowen Institute for Public Education Initiatives has contracted public opinion surveys in almost every year since 2007. In general, the trends here also show that people believed the school system was getting better. Figure 5.3 shows that this peaked in 2011, with 66 percent of the sample indicating that the system was improving. Those who believed the system was getting worse constituted the smallest portion in every year (2009–2018); however, the proportion has been stable. Between 15 percent and 20 percent of those polled in each year said the schools are worse. In the early years of this poll, respondents undoubtedly compared the current system with the pre-Katrina system. It is not surprising to see, however, that the portion of those who believe things are staying the same has increased as New Orleans has moved farther from the storm.

The Cowen polls point to other positive perceptions of the reforms. Majorities of residents in all years indicated that charter schools and open enrollment have improved public education in New Orleans. Only about 15 percent of the public argued that open enrollment—the ability to attend a school

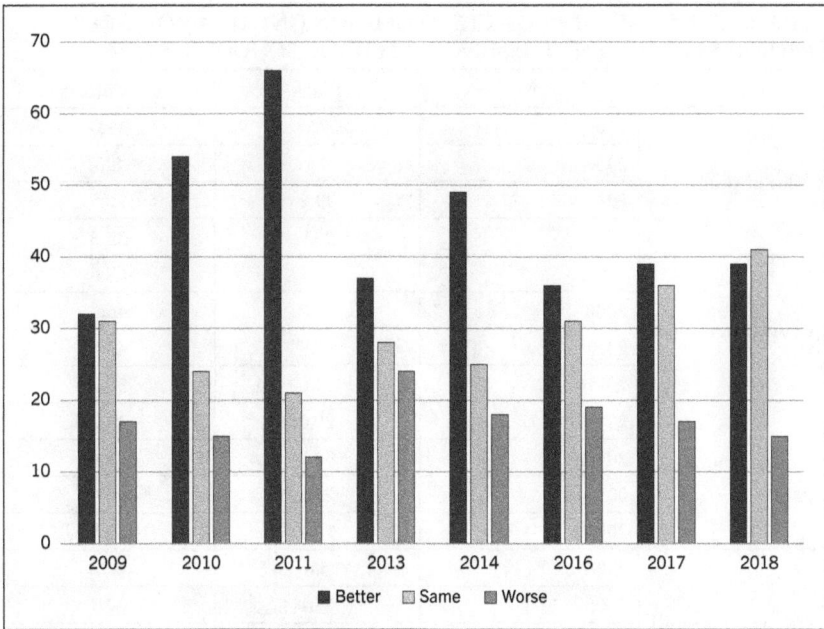

Figure 5.3. New Orleanians' perceptions of whether the school system is improving, 2009–2018 *(Note:* The Cowen Institute survey in 2015 did not ask the question in this way and is therefore not included in this analysis. *Source:* Cowen Institute polls from each year.)

regardless of where you live—has had a negative impact on public education in the city, although it is not clear that the term "open enrollment" is understood in the same way by everyone. In 2011, nearly all respondents (91%) strongly agreed that it was "important" that they "be able to choose what school my child attends." That year, 87 percent of those polled strongly agreed they were satisfied with their decision about where to send their child to school. These findings were touted by local charter leaders and those in the media as evidence not only that the reforms were turning around the performance of the schools, but that they were popularly supported.

It's Complicated: Subgroup Differences

There is also evidence of significant differences in attitudes between various subgroups, such as parents and nonparents and whites and African Americans.[25] Looking at the Kaiser Family Foundation surveys, there were significant racial differences in opinion about progress on strengthening the public schools. Both Black and white residents are more positive over time (see Table 5.1). However, in every year and in every category, Black New Orleanians are

TABLE 5.1. RACIAL DIFFERENCES IN OPINION ON THE AMOUNT OF PROGRESS ON STRENGTHENING THE PUBLIC SCHOOL SYSTEM			
		Black	White
A lot of progress	2006	7.5	11.0
	2008	7.4	8.3
	2010	19.2	26.5
	2015	23.9	33.8
Some progress	2006	57.8	68.0
	2008	30.7	46.2
	2010	37.8	43.8
	2015	33.0	38.2
Not too much progress	2006	29.0	18.2
	2008	36.7	28.4
	2010	22.8	18.4
	2015	23.4	13.5
No progress at all	2006	5.6	2.8
	2008	25.1	17.0
	2010	20.2	11.4
	2015	19.7	14.5

Note: The relationship is statistically significant at $p < .01$ for each year.
Source: Kaiser Family Foundation surveys, 2006–2015.

less positive than are whites.[26] In 2015, nearly one-quarter of Black residents said there had been "a lot of progress" on strengthening the schools, compared with one-third of white respondents who said the same. That same year, about 20 percent of African Americans contended there had been no progress on schools, while only 14.5 percent of whites reported this belief.

The Cowen Institute's polls also show that, from very early on, parents demonstrated less support and more ambivalence than nonparents. In its 2007 *State of Public Education in New Orleans* report, the institute reported that 39 percent of community members believed the public schools were "better now than they were before Hurricane Katrina," but only 27 percent of parents and 17 percent of teachers agreed.[27] Similarly, when a mixed sample of parents and community members were asked each year from 2015 to 2018, about 60 percent reported they agreed that "charter schools ha[d] improved public education" in New Orleans; however, when the Cowen Institute exclusively polled parents in 2019, a much smaller proportion (49%) believed that charters had improved education.[28]

When asked to grade the public schools, residents of New Orleans have

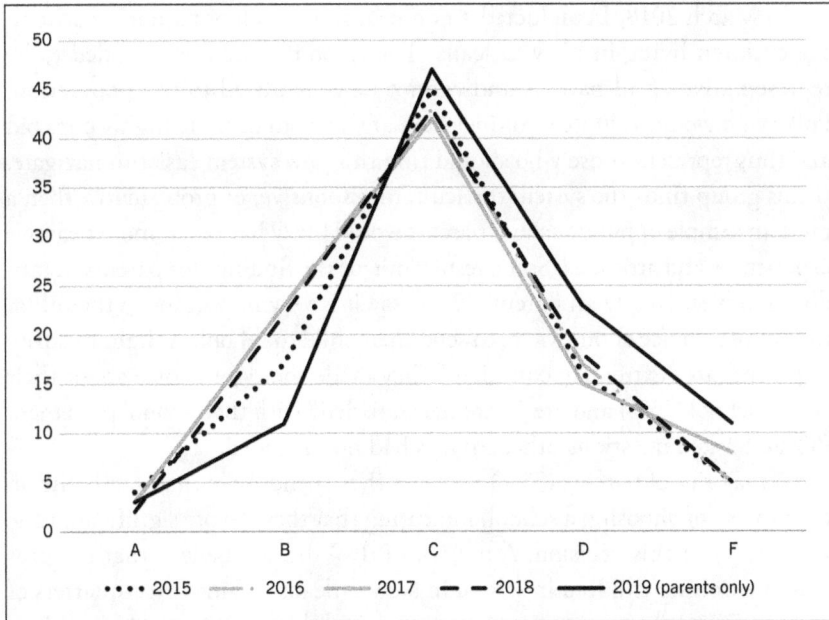

Figure 5.4. Grades residents assign to New Orleans schools, 2015–2019
(*Source:* Cowen Institute polls from each year.)

stable attitudes along a normal curve (see Figure 5.4). The 2019 poll of parents only indicates more negativity: 34 percent of parents graded the schools a D or F, while 14 percent believed the schools had earned an A or B. In contrast to the questions about whether schools are getting better or have improved, there is some indication that parents' low grades are driven by white and private school parents. Black parents were slightly more positive than white parents in both 2017 and 2019.[29] In 2017, the Cowen Institute reported that 41 percent of parents of public school students graded the schools A or B, compared with only 17 percent of private school parents. White parents were significantly more likely to rate private schools as superior (68%), and only 28 percent of private school parents had ever applied to a public school.[30] These results support a recent study showing that Black Chicagoans are much less supportive of school closures than are whites, even as white residents report having very few experiences of their schools being closed.[31] For white parents in some urban centers, the public school system is something they hear about from others or read about in the news—not something with which they have much direct experience. When evaluating these systems, it makes sense to get more information from those with direct experience, who interact regularly with it.

In March 2018, I conducted a non-probability poll of parents of school-age children living in New Orleans. The responses are not intended to be representative of all parents and cannot be generalized to the population. Folks who would volunteer for inclusion are likely to be more highly engaged and thus represent those who should find this new system easier to navigate. If this group finds the system difficult, unresponsive, or problematic, then a random sample of public school parents would likely have even more negative experiences and attitudes. Some results mirror the findings for parents in random samples. Nearly all parents (95%) say it is very important to them that they have a choice about where to send their child to school. A slight majority of parents are "extremely confident" they made the right choice about their child's school (55%) and are "extremely satisfied" with their school placement (52%). I asked questions other surveys had not included.

A majority of parents (55%) reported they spend more than ten hours on the process of choosing a school, indicating that they devote significant time and energy to this decision. A majority (51%) did not believe that the process of enrolling children in school in New Orleans is fair. Three-quarters of parents (77%) disagreed that there are enough high-quality public options in New Orleans. Fifty-seven percent believed "if you know the right person, you can get your child into any school you want." And 60 percent of these parents strongly agreed that they would like their child to attend a high-quality public school in their neighborhood. In sum, these attitudes reflect dissatisfaction with several aspects of the system among a group of parents who regularly interact with the system, but whose participation in a voluntary public opinion database mean they likely have advantages in maneuvering the system.

There are also significant racial differences between Black and white parents on these questions (see Table 5.2). Only 2.4 percent of Black parents were opposed to a high-quality public school in their neighborhood, compared with 14.5 percent of white parents. Although a high proportion of white parents (45%) disagreed that the enrollment process is fair, a substantial majority of Black parents (58%) believed this. The differences were starkest about the question related to whether certain people can get their children into any school they want. Some 68 percent of Black parents agreed, compared with 42 percent of white parents; moreover, only 13 percent of Black parents disagreed, while 38 percent of white parents disagreed with this idea. When one considers the significantly higher levels of dissatisfaction in their school placement and less confidence in their choice among Black parents, the evidence suggests that the experience of school choice and enrollment is very different for parents in different racial groups. There is a 27.6 point gap

TABLE 5.2. RACIAL DIFFERENCES AMONG PARENTS IN ATTITUDES ABOUT SCHOOL ENROLLMENT IN NEW ORLEANS, 2018

	Black Parents	White Parents
I would like my child to attend a high-quality public school in my neighborhood.**		
Agree	80.5	78.2
Neither agree nor disagree	17.1	7.3
Disagree	2.4	14.5
N	82	55
The enrollment process is fair.*		
Agree	19.9	14.5
Neither agree nor disagree	22.2	40.0
Disagree	58.0	45.4
N	81	55
If you know the right person, you can get your child into any school.**		
Agree	68.3	41.8
Neither agree nor disagree	18.3	20.0
Disagree	13.4	38.2
N	82	55
How confident are you that you made the right choice for your child?**		
Not at all confident	8.5	0.0
Moderately confident	46.3	27.3
Extremely confident	45.1	72.7
N	82	55
How satisfied are you with your child's school placement?**		
Extremely satisfied	43.9	67.3
Moderately satisfied	36.6	27.3
Moderately dissatisfied	11.0	3.6
Extremely dissatisfied	8.5	1.8
N	82	55

Notes: Numbers in cell are percentages within each category. Differences measured with Pearson's chi-square.
* $p < .05$
** $p < .01$
Source: Author's School Choice in New Orleans survey.

between white and Black parents in the likelihood of being "extremely confident" in one's choice and a 23.4 point gap in being "extremely satisfied" with the school placement.

Given the racial differences in enrollment in public schools and the disparities in who was involved in planning and implementing the reforms, it is not surprising to see racial differences in attitudes about the system. Despite the rhetoric about education reform as a civil rights issue, the concerns and experiences of Black parents and their children have been sidelined. Those who govern charter schools maintain this exclusion. For most white New Orleanians, public schools are a "potent but distant symbol" rather than a proximate concern.[32] White children are more likely to attend private than public schools, limiting white New Orleanians' experiences with the public schools as students and as parents. Only about a quarter of white parents report they even consider public schools for their children. The feedback effects of the New Orleans school system on white parents are necessarily different from those of the Black families who directly interact with the public system.

In New Orleans, public schools continue to primarily serve poor, African American children. Black parents are conflicted. They want to choose their children's schools, but they also want high-quality neighborhood schools. They are mostly satisfied with their children's school placement, but much less so than white parents. Black parents do not believe the enrollment system is fair. The racial differences also raise questions because of the methodologies used in most surveys. Most of the Cowen Institute's studies do not have enough parents of public school children to be able to make inferences about this important population. Further, these surveys sample on registered voters and use a phone survey.[33] Therefore, even when they oversample parents—or, in the case of 2019, when they survey only parents—the sample continues to overrepresent whites and underrepresent racial minorities, especially Latinos and Asians.

Aesha Rasheed, founder of the New Orleans Parent Organizing Network, advised, "I think we need to listen not just to those who are able, and can navigate the system in a kind of Darwinian way, but those who are struggling. And those kind of people won't be reflected in a poll."[34] For these reasons, I convened several panels of focus groups in 2017 to go into more depth than is possible in phone and internet surveys. Groups were made up of either public or private school parents.[35] When asked about enrolling in schools and about experiences within schools, parents became very animated, and we had robust discussions.[36] I also report on focus group data collected in 2012 by the Cowen Institute. The remainder of this chapter focuses on these conversations.

OneApp and School Enrollment

The common application known in New Orleans as OneApp rolled out in 2011. OneApp was ostensibly designed to solve multiple problems associated with decentralization of the enrollment system. On the supply side, it should prevent schools from gaming the system, from selecting their students and directing the "problem kids" away. Schools would no longer be able to accept applications on their own, and school assignments would be based on parents' preferences, a random lottery number, and schools' published priorities (e.g., for siblings or neighborhood residents). The application, controlled by a central authority (the Recovery School District [RSD] at first, now the Orleans Parish School Board [OPSB]), ought to run bureaucratically, treating clients similarly and without regard to income or race. These types of systems tend to have positive feedback effects on mass attitudes and behavior, compared with those perceived to be arbitrary and unequal.[37] If schools cannot accept or deny students outside OneApp, it should prohibit them from withholding seats from "undesirable" students. A central application should also standardize the necessary documents and application due dates, creating more equality and transparency. These features should increase trust in the system.

On the demand side, OneApp was also intended to make the enrollment process easier for parents. Given how different the new system was from the old one, the information costs were high: parents needed to learn about a variety of schools rather than just the one in their neighborhood. Enrollment in the period between 2006 and 2012 required parents to participate more fully to make sure their children were eligible, including supplying various documents to multiple schools with different due dates and distinct requirements.[38] Parents without access to private vehicles, flexible schedules, or an internet connection were at a distinct disadvantage. OneApp was supposed to make these struggles a thing of the past, as parents would be able to complete a single online application for all schools in the RSD.[39]

To apply, parents give basic information about the child and rank up to twelve schools.[40] Students are assigned on the basis of these rankings, available seats in the chosen schools, any special priorities schools may have, and a random lottery number assigned to each child. Most schools give priority to the siblings of current students; others set aside a portion of seats to children within the neighborhood, to staff members' children, or to special populations. For example, many of the French immersion schools give preferences for the children of French nationals.

A centrally controlled, bureaucratic system that assigns students a random lottery number would seem to send a neutral message about one's place in the community. Although this algorithm does not allow for democratic participation or engagement, enrollment is not left up to the discretion of school officials. In theory, lotteries give each person who "plays" an equal chance at winning. Parents might not like the outcomes, but they should perceive a system like this as fair and unbiased.

However, there were significant inequalities from the initial rollout of OneApp that distorted the elements that were supposed to make the central application fairer than its predecessor. Schools authorized or operated by the OPSB and the Board of Elementary and Secondary Education (BESE) were not initially included in OneApp. They also were, and are, the highest-performing schools in the city. Instead, only the lowest-performing schools—those in the RSD—were initially included. The name of the program and the rhetoric around it suggested OneApp meant there was a single application. But parents who wanted to apply to one of the best schools in the city had to complete OneApp *and* continue to apply individually to these other schools. Further, even schools that participated in OneApp were able to set their own priorities. These features made OneApp far from a truly equal, purely bureaucratic tool in which all children had the same opportunity to enroll in all schools. I expect to find, then, that parents' interactions with this enrollment system led mostly to negative feedback effects: less support in the system; more cynicism; and feelings of inadequacy, frustration, and resignation.

Confusion and Misinformation

Confusion dominated views of the process in both 2012 (when the system was new) and 2017, with high levels of misinformation among parents. For example, parents commonly thought that because they had applied early in the process, they would be given priority. Others were mistaken about some of the requirements for schools. This parent, for instance, chose in 2012 not to apply to her first-choice school because she had heard misinformation:

> Parent: If your child doesn't have a certain grade point average, your child can't get in. . . . The school I really wanted him to get in was KIPP [Knowledge Is Power Program], a charter school, but KIPP did not accept him because he didn't have a certain grade point and I think that's wrong.
> Moderator: They told you that when you went to apply?
> Parent: I heard it from parents.

The OneApp process itself also confused parents, particularly the process of ranking schools. While children are accepted into only one school on One-App, some parents thought that a child could be accepted into many of the schools they ranked on the application, and they would later have the option to select the one they liked best. They seemed to believe OneApp was similar to the Common Application for colleges and universities. A parent in 2012 articulated this belief this way:

The OneApp tells you to name eight schools, but in reality your child is not getting accepted to all these schools. . . . The first choice, if there's an opening, that's the school your child is going to. You don't have the option to choose what school you want to go to. . . . They don't explain that. . . . I thought when they said I could pick eight schools, I thought my student was a high honors so she would get accepted to all eight so I could go from that and pick one.

In both 2012 and 2017, the most common adjectives parents used about the enrollment process were "confusing" and "difficult," and many talked about how angry and frustrated they were with the process. Many parents said things like, "It's enraging to me"; "It makes me so angry"; "I'm just *done!*" Pluralist theory suggests that these dissatisfied parents will band together. They have clearly been victims of a "disturbance," in the language of David Truman, and have significant incentives to improve their situations.[41] Accordingly, they should form interest groups and apply pressure on policy makers. Instead, there were two major reactions to the anger and frustration they felt about school enrollment: resignation and the individualistic pursuit of self-interest. One mother discussed an important observation she made when she applied to the popular, high-performing, selective-admission Lusher Charter School:

I was on top of the early registration. . . . [My son] went to take the test. I made an observation that it was, like, I would say, 90 percent Black boys taking the test that day. . . . A friend from high school . . . was there with her son. . . . We [never got] the test scores. They just said he didn't get in. So I thought maybe he just didn't cut the mustard. . . . I let it go. But the high school friend, she called to ask for her son's test scores, and they couldn't provide them. She wrote a letter, and they said they could retest him, and [then] he got in. . . . I didn't want [my son] to be branded that his mom is a troublemaker. Why would I want him to get in this environment where it seems like it's not an enrollment process; it's an exclusion process? . . . Maybe they by design had all the Black boys take the test on this day so they won't bother to even save these. My other friend had his whole church congregation praying that his son would get into Lusher. That's just too dramatic.

These comments reveal many aspects of what are common beliefs and experiences among the African American women who make up the majority of public school parents. First, New Orleans is not like a big city; everywhere one goes, they know someone. This is an important feature of community life, as well as information sharing. New Orleanians' networks are broad and deep, making word of mouth an important mechanism for information sharing.

Second, as is common with folks who are routinely disadvantaged, this mother did not blame the system at first. Instead, she assumed her child legitimately did not pass the test. Then, when she saw how her friend managed to successfully petition to get her son into the school, she hesitated to do the same thing because she did not want herself or her child "branded" a troublemaker. It is quite common for school officials to view Black parents' involvement at schools as interference, while white parents are often welcomed.[42] Black parents must walk a fine line when they approach schools. As a result, there is often a lack of trust, and there are low levels of involvement.[43] Ultimately, the mother rationalized that she did not want to fight this battle because the school obviously did not want her son or others like him. Her response was to accept the outcome and move on. Fighting had the potential to cause more harm to her child and ultimately would not be worthwhile if the school truly did not want to enroll children like her son. This sentiment was shared by many parents in these focus groups—a belief that if the school did not want their kids, then as parents they did not want the schools, regardless of the schools' performance scores or reputations.

These perceptions have impacts on the system's operation and parents' interaction within it. First, the logic of school choice depends on parents' selecting the "best" schools. If parents avoid choosing high-performing schools because they assume these institutions do not want their children, then school choice cannot operate as intended. Further, the "best" schools are able to continue to under-enroll some kids. Also, the reporting on the proportion of applicants who are placed in their first-choice schools depends on parents' ranking their true preferences. If parents systematically opt not to rank a preferred school because they believe they have no chance, this reporting under-represents true "matches." Second, parents and their kids see where they are welcome, with implications on their engagement and trust in these and other public authorities. Why would people have faith in or place demands on a system that does not value them or their children? Instead of leading to group mobilization, these perceptions are often associated with disengagement and distrust.

Scholars of poverty policy have long found that poor people—who make up the majority of public school parents in New Orleans—"are mainly quiescent and surprisingly accepting" of authority, even though they are greater in number than the affluent.[44] The reluctance to become politically active or push back against power brokers is due both to their greater economic and political vulnerability and to the belief, based on experience, that it is a waste of time because officials do not care about their plight. As John Gaventa noted about coal miners in Appalachia, "Power works to develop and maintain the quiescence of the powerless. . . . Patterns of power and powerlessness can keep issues from arising, grievances from being voiced, and interests from being recognized."[45] The interpretive effects of policy feedback help us understand the reluctance of the poor to join pressure groups or protest movements to advocate strongly for changes that would make policies function better for them.

Although many parents choose to accept outcomes they believed to be unjust, some parents fought the system. They called and complained, went to board meetings, and demanded meetings with school officials. Importantly, when parents engaged in this way, they usually did so on behalf of *their* children. The system is designed to encourage this mind-set, where "education is a private good, an investment one makes in one's child or oneself to 'add value' to better compete in the labor market, not a social good for development of individuals and society as a whole."[46] Although there are parent-focused advocacy groups in New Orleans, the parents in my study, who, while not community leaders, were deeply engaged and had strong opinions, rarely discussed forming or joining collective groups. Even though many mentioned feeling sorry for those who are less advantaged than they, there was a sense of acceptance that this is just the way it is. It is not fair, but for many of these parents, the best one can do is to do right by their children and hope that others are doing the same. One mother in the 2017 focus groups told me:

> A child can get a . . . great education just about anywhere if the parent is doing their job. But the problem here is that . . . the kids who have the least—parents who aren't going to advocate for them—are the children who need the most. You know, they need to be in the best situations. And what we've got is, if a parent is willing to get out there and fight and push and go to fifteen different schools and fill out applications. . . . But it's the rest of the children, the children whose parents are absent or don't, can't help, won't help, or whatever, those kids need the better schools. They need the best support.

Parents recognize the inherent unfairness in a system in which people compete for limited spots in "good" schools, but there was no discussion about collaborating or trying to make things better for *everyone*. The instinct to fight individually instead of collectively is not born of selfishness or laziness. Rather, it has been ingrained in the American ethos and is a feature of these specific reforms.[47] Ingram writes, "Paternalistic eligibility rules now signal that poor people's problems are of their own making. The only way out of poverty is through individual effort."[48] Even when the poor play by the rules, the only options available to them—especially to poor Black families—for housing and public education are substandard. Further, enrollment policy requires parents to educate themselves about how to apply to and get their children into their schools of preference. There is little proactive community outreach, and the system has no default options or opt-out provisions—all of which would make it easier for parents to enroll their children in school.[49] It is, then, no wonder that so many parents feel like they are in a sort of "Hunger Games."

The social stigmas and policy designs alongside the political structure in which there are dozens of privately run charter boards mean that it is only rational for public school parents to see collective action as futile. What are parents supposed to do when the people with authority are not elected officials but, rather, selected volunteers, most of whom are white and rich and have demonstrated little respect for them or their involvement? What is the recourse when enrollment is based on a computer program, and the "good" schools have successfully arranged it so they can continue to select the students they want? Instead, parents expend their efforts individually, trying to improve life for their children. This inevitably exacerbates inequalities.

The focus on improving circumstances at the individual level as opposed to collective advocacy is related to parents' relative comparisons with others in similar situations. They commonly expressed that they were less disadvantaged than others, such as the mother who said, "I know the system pretty well. And it still was really discombobulating and frustrating for me, so I can't imagine it for someone who doesn't know how to read very well or doesn't have internet access." Individual responses and perceptions are less likely to lead to political mobilization than are group-based responses.[50] Even parents who had discussed significant difficulty in enrolling their children in school routinely said or agreed with others who expressed that they were not in as a bad situation as others. It is difficult to motivate someone to organize and fight a system when she believes she is "blessed."

A Rigged System

Parents were not frustrated and angry because they just did not want to go to the trouble of learning about schools and filling out forms. Many repeatedly stated that they wanted to have a choice about where to send their children to school, and these parents spent a lot of time researching schools, saying things like, "It's a full-time job." Instead, the frustration and anger stemmed from a sense of injustice, a belief not only that the process was exhausting, but that it was rigged and that the work put into choosing a school was all for naught:

> Parent: I do my homework and have been very persistent so I feel like I know what I'm trying to do. . . . Researching is fine, making the decision is fine, but the process of enrolling your child for me has been nightmarish. . . . Last year we did all the testing, the standardized tests every year. . . . [My son is] a really good student, well rounded with sports, but it's ridiculous to try to get him into a good school that will foster him.
>
> Moderator: What was frustrating about the enrollment process?
>
> Parent: For Lusher, you invest quite a bit. You do the open house. You talk to teachers and the principal. You do all the research. You apply. You bring your child back for testing, which is a process in itself. You have to involve your kid in the idea of going to the school in order to bring them there to test. It's not like you can keep them sheltered from any of this. . . .
>
> Moderator: Are you satisfied with the options that were available to you? Do you feel like there were options?
>
> Parent: I feel like we really don't have an option. Pretty much it's whatever the system decides is best for your child.

Although its creators argued that OneApp would solve the inequalities in enrollment by replacing a highly discretionary system with a bureaucratic one, parents in both 2012 and 2017 were highly suspicious of the process. Their skepticism was the product of both the city's history of racial exclusion and disinvestment in public education and the lack of transparency in the enrollment process. In other words, parents were primed to distrust the system because of their past experiences, and the contemporary features of public schools contributed to their continued skepticism and frustration. To many parents, OneApp's algorithm was just another way for the relatively well-off and well-connected to maintain their advantages. People filled out their applications and then, somehow, out of a black box came school placements in which those who already had advantages maintained them. As one parent told me:

> There is not a lot of transparency around how schools actually make decisions about what kids get in and what kids don't get in. That is a problem. . . . I think straight-up some schools lie. . . . Also, just some application processes are so complicated. The point system. There's

an entire segment of the point system that could be 100 percent sub-
jective. . . . It made me very suspicious of the process, especially when
you're in an environment that parents are competing with each other
to get spots. . . . I'm also suspicious of how complicated it is. Sometimes I think they make it purposely very complicated so you can't
figure it out. People just give up in frustration or they won't think it's
unfair because they don't really understand.

Nearly every parent seemed to believe that one needs to be well connected
to get into the better schools. One mother stated, "You've got to be special to
get in that school." The policy design of OneApp contributed to these beliefs.
The best schools were not included in OneApp for many years. Even when
their charters were reauthorized and they were added to OneApp, they were
able to maintain control over their application requirements and priority settings. Beyond the applications, the demographic characteristics of the selective-admission schools make it plain that certain types of kids have a better
chance of admission than others.

Lusher Charter School, for example, came up as an example again and
again as a high-performing school that was perceived as off-limits to the poor
African American public school parents in these focus groups. The school
serves about 1,700 students from kindergarten through twelfth grade, of whom
26 percent are Black and 57 percent are white; the city average in public schools
is 81 percent Black and 8.7 percent white. Only 17 percent of Lusher's students
qualify for free or reduced-price lunch, compared with 84 percent citywide,
and only 1.5 percent of students had limited English proficiency, compared
with 6 percent in the rest of the city schools.[51] Parents' beliefs about a rigged
system are not a conspiracy theory. In 2012, parents told moderators:

You're not getting your kid in the same schools [after Katrina] if you
don't know somebody. The top schools, if my kids are straight-A students, they're not getting [into] these schools because we don't know
the movers and shakers of New Orleans. But I know people who
come from out of New Orleans and get in places that our kids are not
allowed to get into. . . . There's no point in applying to [these schools]
because you're not getting in.

When looking for another school, I had my eye on three high-
performing schools: Hynes, Franklin, and Audubon. I went to all of
them. . . . We'd get admitted but never get off the [waiting] list. . . .

Before Katrina, if your child made the grades, like clockwork your child would get into that school because it was just a testing process.

Hynes Elementary—you can forget about it because it's just so sold up with that Lakeview community, and they almost tell you.

You have to know somebody to get into Lusher or McMain.

It's still hard to get into that school. You've got to know somebody.

Lack of Options

As in surveys, nearly all parents in the focus groups agreed that being able to choose schools for their children is very important. Parents also did not seem to have a problem with the idea of a common application; it was the specific mechanics and information about that system that drove parents crazy. Another major area of contention was the lack of real options for their kids. They questioned the value of school choice without decent options with available seats. In 2017, one father stated:

If you only have ninety slots at a school and you already have kids moving up to them [*sic*] grades, what purpose is the OneApp? They say, "Oh, you have a choice," and that was the whole thing they would always push. "You have a choice. Parents have a choice." You don't have a choice if they don't have a place to put you. And if you only have three or four schools that's passing and everything else is failing, so that's ninety times four.

The lack of options made parents feel that they were being sold a bill of goods. The rhetoric suggests parents can apply anywhere, that they have great control over their school choices. The reality, however, is that there are a limited number of seats in desirable schools, and those seats are mostly reserved for folks who are the most advantaged. The average public school parent learns that the rhetoric about choice and opportunity does not match the reality for their children, who are treated in the system as second-class citizens. The new system works well for those kids who already have more advantages, while the majority of New Orleans children continue to be relegated to the lowest-performing schools.

Treatment of Parents and Children within Schools

Parents bring their own experiences in school as they interact with these institutions on behalf of their children. For generations, African American and Latino children have not been treated the same as white children in schools. Black children, for example, are more likely to be suspended than white youth, even though Black children do not commit more or worse offenses than their white peers.[52] Such disparities are often related to differences in how behavior is interpreted and to gaps in cultural knowledge between racial groups. Modern forms of discipline involving zero-tolerance policies and surveillance contribute to a prisonlike experience; these disciplinary tactics are more likely to be used in schools composed predominantly of children of color.[53] Young people may respond to these disparities and "pathologization" of normal behavior with "resistance identities" that actually encourage delinquent behaviors.[54] Scholars have shown that these experiences can depress civic engagement many years later.[55]

As children grow into parents, these identities and experiences also shape how they parent and how they interact with school authorities on behalf of their kids. Many Black parents "cannot presume or trust that their children will be treated fairly in school."[56] On one hand, these parents approach school authorities carefully and tentatively; on the other, they are likely to interpret negative experiences through the lens of the discrimination and racism they have encountered. One mother discussed her treatment by the school board and at least one school in the enrollment process:

> I'd never done this. Where I grew up, you went to school in your neighborhood. So . . . we moved [to the] Uptown [neighborhood] because my husband works at Tulane. We got ourselves a little apartment, and I started calling around, and it's like, "Oh, no. You have to go here to apply and there to apply." So I started doing the applications, and then we missed one of the open houses, so we couldn't go there. And I called the school board. I'm like, "What if we don't get into these schools?" "Oh, it's open, you can apply everywhere." I'm like, "Well, I don't want to apply everywhere." And we got in on the West Bank, and I'm like, "I'm supposed to drive to the West Bank every morning when I'm sitting here between four schools?" There was Lafayette and Audubon, and I'm like, "I can walk to these schools, and you want us to drive to the West Bank?" "Oh, yeah, but you got in."
>
> And . . . they acted like I was really lucky to get in. I sort of felt like I was. OK, good, we can go to school. You know? We moved

because Lusher still had a district, so we just moved. It was pitiful, and I thought, "I can't think of anything else to do." We found out that there were five hundred applications for twenty spots. I'm like, "No, I can't do the lottery." And I was so angry, I thought no child should go through a lottery to go to public school. And I said I should file a suit, a class action suit, I'm being deprived of a public education for my kid. And my husband said, "Just shut up until the kids are in school, and then you can do that." But it's not right.

The mother was upset not just about the injustice in the enrollment system, but also about how she was treated by the officials. Instead of helping her or easing her concerns about her child's education, the person with whom she spoke at the school board gave her the party line: "You can apply everywhere." The school then treated her as if she was lucky to be able to enroll her child there, even though it did not work for her family. Even her husband told her to stay quiet, presumably out of concern for losing their spot or ruining their chance for something better.[57] All these institutions—the school board, the school, and her husband—left her feeling angry and helpless and likely a bit like a victim of gaslighting.

One of the most common problems parents discussed, both in the Cowen Institute focus groups in 2012 and in my discussions in 2017, was with the treatment of their children with special needs. As previously reviewed, the RSD was placed under a consent decree due to a class action lawsuit on the part of parents of children with special needs. Because of their experiences with the schools, parents of these kids were especially frustrated and distrustful of the system. In 2012, parents reported:

I had to search around to schools that can attend to his needs. Every school I went to said they have inclusive [classrooms]. Well, what is that? We're going to see his needs, but you're not putting an aid in the class to see to his needs. . . . I couldn't put him in the school closest to my house because they didn't have the services.

I checked out at least eight schools. I didn't officially apply to all of them because some of them, when I walked in the door, told me they wouldn't take my son.

If you're going to say that you're a public school, public means everybody. So you have to have a system in place that the school is going to be able to provide for those children, to meet their needs and be able to provide them a quality education. . . . I find that schools in New Orleans tend to take the easy way out—suspension and expulsion. They try to keep a child out [rather] than really find out what is it we need to give this child so they can thrive.

My son was at MLK. That was the only school that would accept him because he's dyslexic.

The thing about it is they're not getting the supports they need. Even if your child has an [Individualized Education Program] or 504 [Plan], it's like pulling teeth to get them to honor it. The law says they have to, but they don't always do it.

The other major concern of parents with regard to their treatment in schools is with the teachers. Specifically, in 2017 parents were unhappy about the dearth of experienced Black teachers and linked it with a general undervaluing of them and their children in this system:

> Father: We don't have a lot of older teachers that, like you say, were in the community, you know? I could walk to my school, . . . and all those teachers knew my mother, you know? . . . I don't want to get on the younger teachers, but you kind of need some of that stability, you know, while some of these younger teachers are learning on the job.
> Father: That wisdom.
> Father: You need that familiar face.
> Father: Yeah, and I've seen a guy. . . . He was nicely dressed, with his briefcase sitting on the desk, and the kids were tearing up the classroom, and he just sat there and . . . he was just reading the stock papers. You know, because this is a vacation city and an impoverished city all at once. You know, I don't want to speak bad about Teach for America, because they're so great, but some of them, they just see opportunity and it's like. "I can party here. I can work here, and I can have my student loans paid." That has nothing to do with the long-term—
> Father: [Interrupting] Speak on, man. Speak on. [Laughter]
> Father: You know, the well-being of the education of these kids.

Many respondents had strong, mostly negative opinions about the role of Teach for America (TFA) in the schools. Some doubted the sincerity of the

TFA recruits and strongly believed they were participating in the program only to pay off their student loans, to pad their résumés, or to party in New Orleans. To many parents, TFA seemed to represent the lack of value their children have in the current system. The "kids" who were hired to teach their children had no experience and no intention of staying in New Orleans or even making careers as teachers:

> Mother: The other thing that just turned me off from public school was the amount of people, no offense, coming in from Teach for America.
> Father: Correct.
> Mother: Yes. They're just trying to get their student loans paid off.
> Father: Correct. They're just trying to get them paid.
> Mother: I just, I can't do it. I don't need somebody. . . . I don't need you to babysit.
> Mother: Well, it's not even babysit. There's a tone with that. I don't want you to think that you came into this situation to be the savior for all of these little kids, you know? So I don't need you to be a savior. I need you to teach them and to treat them fairly. When people feel like there's a different economic stance or grouping of the backgrounds of these children, they automatically go in with this whole "feed the children, save the world" type of thing, you know? This type of attitude, and no way was I going to put my child in that type of environment.
> Father: [Nodding] Yes, just because, again, of what the sole mission behind that whole entity is. I've actually sat down and read [TFA's] website, because at one point I didn't know what it was about. But yes, to have my student loans forgiven, teach for five years—I think it is something like that. No. No way. Five years, then they're gone.
> Mother: Right, because that's their motivation. Their motivation is not to come in here and educate these little kids. Their motivation is let me get my student loans paid off.
> Mother: Or let me go ahead and post on my Facebook my class of underserved children.

For others, those who moved into the city through TFA were a part of a mostly negative transformation of their communities by newcomers who sought to come to New Orleans to "help out" but who did not stay and put down roots. For a city with the highest percentage of native-born adult residents, these newcomers had the potential to dramatically change communities in which they had no intention to remain:

> Father: And they wanted to come here and help, and a lot of them have left now because of the frustrations they've dealt with. Did you feel like, or have you felt like in talking to people like that, they sort of come here and . . . they just didn't know what they were getting themselves into? Because when people come here and they tell me, "Oh, I'm coming from out of town. I want to help this. I want to help that," I just think, "Well, good, and I'm glad you're here," but deep down I'm thinking, "I hope you survive, because it's so frustrating to so many of us."
>
> Mother: Right. Yes. I think it was a risk that they just chose to take to see what it was, because they—I mean, like I said—they moved to other states. They didn't just leave the school. They left New Orleans. So, yes, I think they came to see whatever they could just to help, not knowing the outcome of it.
>
> Mother: But when they seen [*sic*] the outcome of it, they got up and went. Like last year the school lost so many teachers that were leaving New Orleans, and it wasn't, like I said, not just leaving the school, but we're leaving here, because the system is just all jacked up and all kinds of sorts of things.
>
> Father: Yes. And you get tired of fighting it.
>
> Mother: Speaking of Teach for America, there's a house on my block, as a matter of fact, and there's a group of Teach for America students. They come. You see them come in when school starts, and you see them leave when the time comes, and then there's another group that comes in. So there's—
>
> Father: [Interrupting] It's a revolving door.
>
> Moderator: So, what potential effect does that have on students?
>
> Father: The lack of consistency.
>
> Mother: Well, I guess it just depends on what level they're teaching on, too, because if they're teaching on the elementary level those kids are not going to remember who that teacher was.
>
> Father: Yes, but they're not giving them what they need, though. But they're not getting what they need.

A recent study of New Orleans youth finds that their ratings of teachers are lower than a national average on factors including the care shown for students' emotional well-being, teachers' ability to spark interest in learning, their ability to manage their classrooms to foster orderly and respectful behavior, and whether teachers value students' ideas.[58] On each of these factors, Black students rated their teachers more poorly than white students. The ratings for school climate are lower among Black students than white kids (bullying, safety, fairness, and equitable treatment).

The Black parents in my study appreciated those who come to serve students and the city more generally. At the same time, however, many were concerned about the motivations and qualifications of the TFA recruits. One mother was very suspicious about these predominantly white college graduates from outside New Orleans who came to "save" children like hers, and others worried about the lack of stability for children when there is such a revolving door for school staff. To the extent that parents believed inexperienced teachers were a manifestation of their children's lack of value, these experiences reinforced other, similar messages about their role in the system. White reformers excluded Black families from the reform planning. Charter boards and school district officials, most of whom are white, continue to ignore their concerns. Schools in which the vast majority of students are Black have many fewer experienced Black teachers who identify with their background, and the young, white teachers who are hired to teach are motivated more by a paternalistic "white savior" mentality than a lifelong desire to teach.

Conclusions

Public opinion about the new system is, at best, mixed. Some evidence indicates that residents believe the schools are better than they used to be and that parents want to have a choice about where their children attend school. However, these attitudes cleave along racial lines. Black parents are much less likely than white parents to believe schools are better, are less satisfied with their choices, and are more likely to believe the system is unfair.

The focus groups illuminate why this might be the case. Black parents are frustrated with enrolling their kids in school. They do not trust the application system and see the unequal enrollments as evidence of inherent unfairness in the system.[59] They want high-quality neighborhood schools and are ambivalent about all the young, inexperienced teachers in the schools. When they have to fight to be treated equitably and fairly, Black parents see how the policy treats them as citizens. At a recent OPSB meeting, the growing Latino population in New Orleans has indicated they also believe the system treats them with disdain. In 2021, parents testified that their children's schools had retaliated against them for asking for information and demanding accommodations for their children.[60]

White kids continue to get into the best schools with experienced teachers. They are the "advantaged," in Schneider and Ingram's typology, positively constructed and powerful.[61] The system continues to be responsive to their needs. In Chapter 3, I show how the district worked behind the scenes so that selective-enrollment schools could maintain their enrollment preferences. Black and Latino parents see how they are blamed for the disparities in outcomes. When they try to get answers, authorities give them only stock replies and tell them they should be happy with whatever they get. When they push back, they fear branding themselves or their kids troublemakers. They are "dependents" in Schneider and Ingram's typology—not exactly negatively constructed, but powerless. They are at the mercy of those with power. White power brokers view Black and Latino children and their parents paternalistically rather than as endowed with valuable experience worth mining to improve the system for everyone.

The exclusion of Black parents and teachers from the start defined them as outside the membership of the community. Without any representation among those who built and maintain the system, these parents continue to be excluded and their experiences, discounted. The next chapter examines the effects of this treatment on political efficacy and trust in local government. Policy feedback theory suggests the effects will be negative, reinforcing Black parents' lower status and perpetuating inequalities.

Trust, Resignation, and Hope for Future

I'm a voter in the city of New Orleans. I'm a voter in the state
of Louisiana. I'm a voter in the United States of America. I
thought I had a say in my children's education, but we found
out really quickly that there were other people and other players
making decisions on the education in my children's lives.

—Harold Bailey, citizen

The experiences with public school enrollment and with teachers and
school officials described in Chapter 5 have the potential to affect not
just parents' attitudes about schools, but also their beliefs about and interaction with other political institutions, in turn influencing the entire political system. Through their design, rules, and practices, public policies define
the membership of the community, assign status to individuals within it, and
thereby affect their perceptions of their roles and positions. The focus groups
showed that for many parents, interactions with the post-Katrina public education system in New Orleans produced frustration, confusion, and resignation. These experiences teach parents such as Harold Bailey that, although
they are citizens and voters, "other players" make the decisions. It would not
be surprising if this belief spills over into parents' attitudes about other public
institutions and actors. Racial disparities in experience with schools in New
Orleans underlies policy feedback. The "other players" are not merely abstract
but, rather, white, affluent, and well-connected reformers who have excluded the experiences and voices of the majority of Black families who interact
with this system day to day. The political effects, then, are almost certainly racialized.

As compared with other public institutions, schools are likely to have pro-
found and lasting impacts. They are the first public institution with which
most Americans interact, a relationship that continues for at least thirteen
years as a student. Political scientists show that higher levels of education
are associated with greater political knowledge, participation, and efficacy.

Most argue that this is largely because individuals pick up skills, information, and "democratic values" within educational institutions.[1] Sarah Bruch and Joe Soss highlight, however, that schools are more than "pre-political" sites where young people pick up civic skills, just as they learn algebra and grammar. Through these early experiences, students learn about power and position, shaping adult political behavior beyond the acquisition of skills and knowledge.

The focus group participants routinely harked back to their experiences in schools as children and young people. This was more than simple nostalgia. Rather, it was in these places that these adults had their first lessons about power and authority and whether their voices mattered. They drew on these experiences as parents, making it clear that all the discussion of "clean slates" and "green fields" after Katrina was a complete misunderstanding of the reality of how individuals interact with systems. As shown in the previous chapter, parents were hopeful about the changes and willing to do the work to enhance their children's opportunities. But they remained skeptical and were not surprised when they continued to encounter a system that excluded their perspectives and blamed them for poor outcomes.

School choice advocates such as John Chubb and Terry Moe claim that when parents choose schools for their children, they learn to engage publicly.[2] The capacity to vote with one's feet if not satisfied, they argue, creates efficacy and empowers parents to engage with greater frequency and with more knowledge and interest. Although participatory democrats such as Benjamin Barber and Carole Pateman suggest that the act of participating in public life whets the appetite for engagement, Barber does *not* believe that school choice is a form of democratic participation, writing:

> Privatization is a kind of reverse social contract: it dissolves the bonds that tie us together into free communities and democratic republics. It puts us back in the state of nature where we possess a natural right to get whatever we can on our own, but at the same time lose any real ability to secure that to which we have a right. . . . [W]hat we experience in the end is an environment in which the strong dominate the weak . . . , the very dilemma which the original social contract was intended to address.[3]

In other words, participating in a private, market-based system that is public only in its source of funding does not engage citizens in the same way that true democratic participation empowers folks to consider the public good through deliberation. Instead, school choice transforms parents into consumers who are competing with other parents for scarce resources. At a minimum, for school choice to contribute to greater trust and efficacy, parents would need to believe in the fairness of the system, and they would need to have positive experiences within these institutions. When these conditions are not met and when parents are frustrated by the process and dissatisfied with the outcomes, as I showed in the previous chapter, they will likely lose efficacy and trust and disengage from the political system. Negative personal experiences depress support for the policies and can deter future involvement and faith in the system.[4]

This chapter examines attitudes and behavior around politics beyond the schools. Policy feedback theory suggests that the negative experiences chronicled in Chapter 5 ought to depress participation, efficacy, and trust. Through the use of survey data, I show how political behavior has changed since Katrina. Given the limits of cross-sectional studies, I also pull from the focus groups I conducted in 2017. In these conversations, it is clear that Black parents see connections between the changes in the schools, particularly the loss of neighborhood schools, and the decline in community since the storm. They connect all this to their attitudes about the reformers' motivations and their lack of faith in elections and government overall.

How Policies Influence Political Efficacy, Trust, and Participation

In their important examination of the effects of policies on democratic citizenship, Suzanne Mettler and Joe Soss argue, "Public policies also may influence the ways individuals understand their rights and responsibilities as members of a political community."[5] Policies convey resources and information about one's status or place, which affect political efficacy and trust. Citizens learn "civic lessons" when they interact with the state. When they perceive that they are treated fairly or that government policies expand their rights, there are positive effects on their support for the public sector and their likelihood of participating.[6] However, when people see government as treating them and other citizens like them arbitrarily and without respect, the opposite occurs.

Studies of police contact, especially among people of color, demonstrate that negative experiences can be damaging for political participation, trust, and efficacy.[7] People of color are less likely to trust the government, especially the police.[8] Amy Lerman and Vesla Weaver find that contact with the criminal justice system, from police questioning to incarceration, depresses political participation. They write, "The racial socialization of the criminal justice system holds little potential for resistance because it regularly conveys to its wards that their fates were due to their choices alone."[9] In other words, because society blames individuals rather than a corrupt or biased system for their negative experiences with police, many African American citizens see little point in voting or getting involved in politics. Further, carceral contact has strong direct effects on factors that influence political participation, including well-being and civic duty.[10]

One's personal experiences certainly matter, but so do those of others with whom they identify. Negative encounters with the criminal justice system can depress participation and efficacy among spouses and children, for example.[11] Studies of health-care and immigration policy show that policy feedback effects can spill over into entire communities.[12] Racial consciousness can mitigate this relationship, such that Black and Latino folks who see public policies as structurally racist and discriminatory may mobilize against them rather than withdraw from public life.[13] However, neoliberal policies, such as the privatization of the governance of New Orleans schools, intentionally foster a sense that one is on one's own and cannot depend on others or the government, disrupting the relationship of the citizen and the state such that people see themselves more as consumers than citizens.[14] Indeed, parents described how they did the best they could for their children and hoped others did, too. These features can diminish a sense of linked fate and weaken spillover effects, which are likely to have both negative and positive repercussions for democratic values.[15] One's political behavior may be less tied to the experiences of others, limiting the effects of one family's negative experiences on system-wide support. However, this atomization also may make folks more resigned and less likely to become active in movements against injustice, contributing to even greater civic withdrawal and cynicism.

Experiences within schools and with school authority figures are unique compared with interactions with other public systems. Schools are where "most individuals have their first, formative experiences of how public institutions and authorities govern putatively equal peer groups. Schools, from this perspective, . . . organize authority relations and position students differently within them; they demonstrate how public institutions work and how authorities can be expected to behave."[16] John Dewey argued that young people learn about citizenship not only from curriculum, but also from the standards of conduct imposed by authority figures.[17] In this way, schools teach lessons about "who matters."[18]

People's experiences as students influence how they interact with schools as parents. Black and Latino students have much more negative experiences with school authorities than do whites, which contribute to later adult political participation. Bruch and Soss show that being suspended or expelled and perceiving unfair treatment in school are independently, negatively related to voting years later. They write, "Young adults may carry their school-based evaluations of authority with them into young adulthood, and generalize them to government as a whole."[19] Similarly, despite all the rhetoric about a "clean slate," their formative experiences with the New Orleans public school system as well as their pre-Katrina experiences as parents likely had significant impacts on parents as they navigated the system when they returned. These early experiences not only influenced which schools the parents selected, but how they interacted with school authorities, and ultimately their orientations about whether it is worthwhile to engage in politics at all.

The political scientist Sally Nuamah introduces the concept of "collective participatory debt" to explain the positive and negative feedback on poor, Black parents who fought school closures in Chicago. This debt is "a type of mobilization fatigue that transpires when citizens engaged in policy processes are met with a lack of democratic transparency and responsiveness despite high levels of repeated participation."[20] She points out that even when parents' activism was successful in "saving" a school from closure, there were significant costs to their views of the policies, the system that created them, and their future participation. In essence, by continually engaging with an unresponsive and opaque system, citizens lose trust and become exhausted and disillusioned. Black activists have fought injustice and inequality in New Orleans schools for generations, but not without significant cost.

When policy feedback contributes to reduced trust, participation, and efficacy among certain groups, it empowers others—a virtuous or vicious cycle, depending on the group. This cycle has important policy implications.[21] If parents of public school children lack trust in school or city authorities, and if they do not believe their voice matters or they have become tired and disillusioned because they consistently lose, many are likely simply to withdraw, enabling elites to continue to ignore their perspectives and to assume that Black folks do not care. Indeed, charter board members expressed these views in Chapter 4. When stakeholders are ignored, there are real political and policy effects that tend to reinforce exclusion.

Trust, Efficacy, and Participation in New Orleans

Before one can examine the potential effects of any policy change, it is important to understand the baseline. In its Quality of Life studies, the University of New Orleans (UNO) asked residents about their trust in local government. A 1997 report on the attitudes of Black residents notes that "between 1985 and 1993 confidence in local government among black voters plummet-

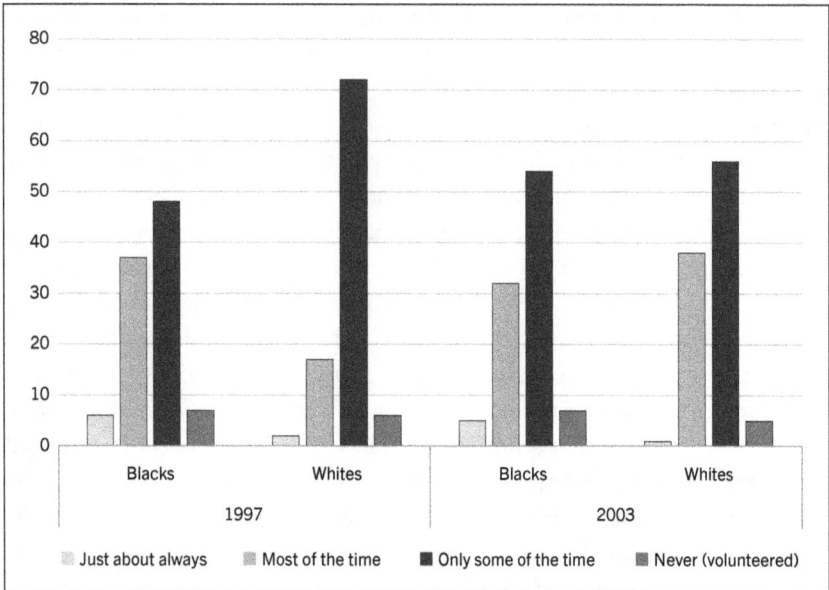

Figure 6.1. New Orleans residents' trust in local government in New Orleans, 1997 and 2003 (*Source:* Author's figure from data in Howell 2003.)

ed, driven by two factors, the allegations of corruption in the [Sidney] Barthelemy administration [1986–1994] and the overall decline in the quality of life in the City. Trust in local government increased considerably after the election of Marc Morial in 1994. This attitude is closely tied to evaluations of an incumbent mayor."[22]

In UNO's 1997 and 2003 surveys of all residents, very few people said they trusted the local government "just about always" (5% in 1997; 4% in 2003). The majority trusted the local government "only some of the time" (55% in 1997; 54% in 2003). The results are similar for white and Black residents (Figure 6.1).[23] A slightly larger proportion of whites trusted the government in 2003 than in 1998, but in general, trust among both groups was very low.

Katrina would have an enormous impact on the city's demography, changes that had the potential to alter these levels of trust in government. Due to both migration out of and into the city, between 2000 and 2014, the percentage of Black residents in New Orleans dropped from 67 percent to 59 percent. In 2014, more than 10 percent of the white and Latino populations were newcomers, compared with only 4 percent of the Black population. Because the African American community has "shaped the city's history and culture enormously, their dwindling numbers and proportions are felt in schools, neighborhoods, churches, and in the city's politics and power structures."[24] Further, the city's average income and education level has risen since Katrina, although these gains are not distributed equally across racial groups. The median income among Black households was lower in 2013 than in 2000, adjusted for inflation, but the median income increased among white households.[25]

Demographic changes, especially rapid changes, often have negative effects on civic engagement, reducing generalized trust in others and in government and depressing support and satisfaction in government performance among some segments of the population.[26] Shifts in the racial or class composition often threaten majority groups and can embolden growing minority groups and create tension and conflict that can result in greater hostility between majority and minority groups.[27] Demographic changes also dampen political efficacy and satisfaction with government performance among those who are losing power and influence. Alongside the decline in their numbers and influence, Alison Blodorn and her colleagues show, Black New Orleanians were more likely than white residents to perceive racism in Katrina-related events, depressing satisfaction in government and willingness to engage in politics.[28]

The 2013 Cowen Institute survey asked a few questions related to trust in government and political efficacy.[29] As seen with earlier studies, there were no racial differences on trust: neither white nor Black residents exhibit substantial trust in the local government (Table 6.1). My colleague and I conducted a poll in advance of the mayoral election in 2017. Controlling for a variety of individual factors, we similarly found no racial differences in trust in local government largely because overall levels of trust in government were very low in 2017.[30] Although there were no racial differences in trust in government in either the 2013 or the 2017 survey, we did find substantial racial differences in generalized trust in others in the 2017 study. As compared with Black residents, whites in New Orleans were more trusting of their neighbors, other white people, Latinos, and newcomers to the city.[31]

The 2013 Cowen Institute survey also asked about internal and external political efficacy. Internal efficacy is the belief that one is capable of understanding politics. Black residents were less likely than whites to believe they were well informed about politics. They were also less likely to believe public officials care what people think, a measure of external efficacy (see Table 6.1). External efficacy is also not extraordinarily high among white New Orleanians; in fact, whites were split evenly in their beliefs about whether politicians

TABLE 6.1. RACIAL DIFFERENCES IN POLITICAL TRUST AND EFFICACY IN NEW ORLEANS, 2013

	White	Black
How much of the time do you think you can trust the local government to do what is right?		
Just about always	2.1	1.6
Most of the time	28.4	24.2
Only some of the time	69.5	74.2
N	95	182
I am as well informed about politics as others.**		
Strongly agree	63.8	37.1
Somewhat agree	28.7	42.5
Somewhat disagree	6.4	14.0
Strongly disagree	1.1	6.5
N	94	186
Public officials don't care about what most people think.*		
Strongly agree	23.3	33.2
Somewhat agree	26.7	35.8
Somewhat disagree	36.7	24.1
Strongly disagree	13.3	7.0
N	90	187

Notes: Numbers in cells represent percentages within categories. Statistical significance determined using Pearson's chi-square.
* $p < .05$
** $p < .01$
Source: Data are from Cowen Institute poll, 2013.

care what people think. However, two-thirds of Black residents believed public officials do not care about what most people think. Given the experience with post-Katrina school reforms, this belief is warranted.

Political Participation

Finally, given the racial differences in efficacy, we should expect racial differences in participation. There is some evidence that charter school enrollment in Ohio is associated with lower turnout in school board elections, primarily in poor and minority districts. Although the mechanism is unclear, the study's authors posit that "charter schools decreased [parents'] stake in school board politics."[32] These politics are likely to play out differently in New Orleans, where all the public schools are charters, and where the elected school board has a limited role. In New Orleans, school board members are elected during presidential election years, making it difficult to use aggregate turnout statistics to make inferences specifically about school board races. Unsurprisingly, there was a substantial drop in turnout in the first post-Katrina presidential election: 61.5 percent of registered voters turned out in 2004, compared with 52.7 percent in 2008. Turnout has since bounced back (63.4% in 2012; 64% in 2016; 65.7% in 2020).

Turnout is always highest in presidential elections, so I also examine voting turnout in mayoral races, beginning with the last pre-Katrina election in 2002. Between 2002 and 2017, overall turnout declined (Figure 6.2), but it declined most precipitously in the two elections immediately following Katrina—in 2006 and 2010. The gap between white and Black turnout was substantial in these years: 21 percentage points in 2006 and 16 points in 2010. White turnout actually increased slightly in 2006. In 2010, Mitch Landrieu became the first white candidate to be elected mayor since his father won in the 1970s. Though he had substantial support from both the white and Black communities, it is important to point out that after Katrina, the African American community declined in numbers and proportion in the electorate. In 2017, there were 38,603 fewer Black registered voters than

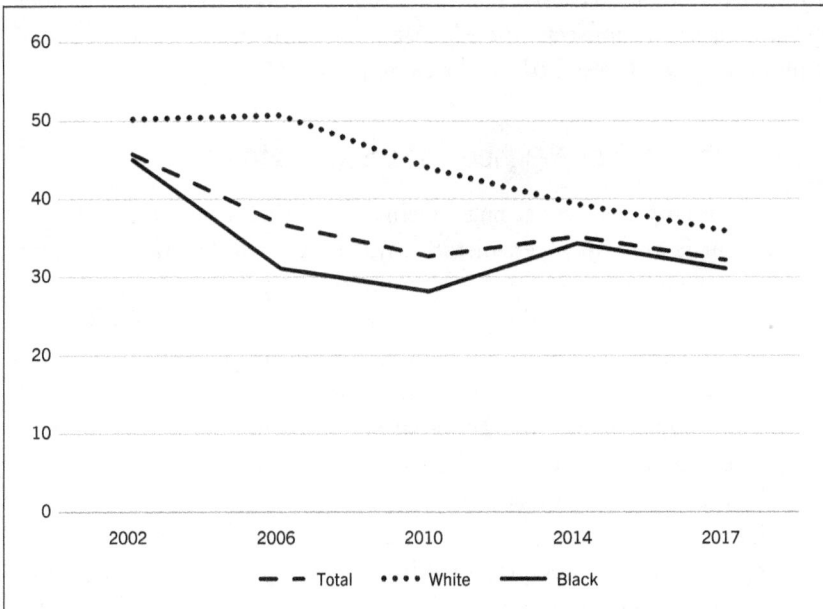

Figure 6.2. Turnout among registered voters in New Orleans mayoral elections, 2002–2017 (*Source:* Louisiana Office of the Secretary of State.)

in 2002 but only 2,597 fewer white registrants and 4,017 *more* "other" registrants, a likely indication of the increasing Latino and mixed-race populations in the city.

The lack of faith in public officials and declines in voting turnout *could* be due to experiences with public systems, but these data do not allow me to test that. Aggregate data such as voter turnout and cross-sectional surveys do not indicate *why* we see lower rates of efficacy and participation among Black residents after Katrina or why trust in local government has remained low. Many factors likely contribute to these patterns. Focus groups allow for deeper questioning about experiences with local public systems and the opportunity to observe how people make connections between issues.

I expected to find that public school parents have more negative attitudes about local politics than those who have not interacted with the public school system. Instead, people were universally negative about politics, regardless of their experiences with the school system. The 2017 flooding event that preceded my study and the city's response to it undoubtedly influenced residents' attitudes, but the responses suggest that their attitudes reflect longstanding beliefs about local politics. These discussions are a window into why we see little change in trust and somewhat reduced levels of efficacy and participation; they also illuminate how attitudes about the schools are connected to opinions about politics. The next section, pulled from a focus group, helps to demonstrate these linkages and, ultimately, why the dramatic policy changes led to so little feedback on political behavior.

Linking the Loss of Neighborhood Schools to Politics

New Orleanians have very strong attachments to their neighborhoods. Place attachment is even stronger, historically, for African American residents, because "attachment to place and community is dependent on social capital embedded in social networks."[33] Before the hurricane, Black New Orleanians had strong social support systems and had learned to rely on one another, largely within the confines of kin and neighborhood-based networks. In Katrina's aftermath, neighborhood-based groups led the city's rebuilding plans, even across racial, class, and geographic lines. Clara Irazábal and Jason Neville argue that the grassroots planning process developed due to lack of an effective governing coalition around land use and that "the widespread 'taste' of autonomous democratic place-making could trigger a wider sociopolitical transformation, resulting in a paradigm shift at other levels of the political process."[34] This participatory democracy did not ultimately come to fruition in part because the governance of public schools was privatized and schools were divorced from the physical spaces in which people lived and were fighting to rebuild.[35]

Many political theorists have emphasized the importance of the neighborhood to education. Barber writes that school choice is "incompatible with the idea of the neighborhood, which is the necessary home of the civic community."[36] Michael Walzer argues that democratic schools should be enclosed within a neighborhood because this is a "known world" for children.[37] Historically, public schools and neighborhoods have a symbiotic relationship, such that schools help maintain community attachments, bring folks together around common goals, and provide physical spaces for community gathering. Of course, school boundaries have also operated as fences that keep people out and maintain segregation. Ryan Coughlan highlights, however, that school choice severs the connections between neighborhoods and schools without increasing racial or economic integration.[38] Thus, removing these boundaries does not, on its own, decrease segregation; however, it does negatively affect collective efficacy and community attachment.

In the focus groups in 2017, nearly all parents lamented the loss of neighborhood schools, and many linked their eradication to the devastating effects on their communities, which they connected to the larger political system. These responses indicate that attitudes about the school system are not independent of beliefs about government and how it operates, whom it serves, and why. These connections are seen most clearly when parents begin to discuss neighborhood schools.

In an especially illuminating exchange, one mother reported the differences between a school one simply attends and a school that is part of a community: "That's how you build those relationships, because this is your neighborhood school and there's an environment, and parents associate. Because now you're just in the carpool lane. You put your kid in the car. You keep going." The parents also believe that, without these community anchors, it is harder for children to be connected to one another and to their communities:

Father: If you're in a neighborhood which is probably, let's say, six to ten blocks, if that child walks in the neighborhood, he tends to know who's on each and every block. Then throughout time you tend to take care of that neighborhood because that's your community. If you wake up and get on a bus and drive across town, you don't know your neighborhood. So then you tend to not care about it because you're not there every day. . . . It all starts at home, but then it starts in the community. Because when I was growing up, everyone walked to school. Like, hey, we're going to walk, the three of us are going to walk to school, we're going to walk home. And then you start knowing your community. But nowadays my daughter doesn't know who's on the next block or the block over.

Mother: Well, that, and if you got up to something, before you got home one of the neighbors would have called your mom and told, "Well, I saw him doing this."

Father: Yeah, I'm saying, like, you knew the neighbors.

Mother: And they knew you.

Father: You know, "Hey, Ms. Such and Such. Hey, Mr. Such and Such." You knew who was out. . . .

Mother: Well, so you knew, yeah, my neighbors are watching and I have to mind myself.

Father: It took a village.

Even if the actual experience was somewhat less idyllic than how these folks remember it, the exchange shows that they linked strong schools with strong neighborhoods and saw them as mutually reinforcing community values and standards. These bonds cannot be forged from a "carpool lane" or when students get on buses to ride across the city. A recent study of New Orleans youth finds that Black children, compared with whites, report significantly higher levels of involvement in religious, cultural, or political groups and greater involvement in community service, providing empirical support for the notion that connections to communities are an important part of life in Black families.[39]

Some parents associated the lack of neighborhood schools with economic decline, as well as the loss of community. One parent said, "Not having schools in those low economic areas creates—I mean, assists in creating—the bleak areas, because you have the school close down, then you don't have anybody move in your neighborhood, because most people like to move in the neighborhood where their school is right there. So it creates even more poverty in those areas." Parents in the focus group saw the destruction of these neighborhoods not as accidental but, rather, as connected to the ill intentions of the reformers and policy makers.

Indeed, research in other cities finds a relationship between development and school siting decisions that often benefits white, affluent families at the expense of poorer, Black families.[40] The siting of school facilities in New Orleans is highly racialized and continues to be a source of major controversy. The Introduction to this book chronicles the system's decision to shutter John Mac High School and give the building to Bricolage Academy, an elementary school founded by a former Teach for America Corps member and Ivy League–educated white reformer. This school serves a much higher proportion of white children than the average public school (46.7% white compared with 8.7% in the city). Like Bricolage, the building that Lusher Charter School High School now occupies had also been a predominantly Black school that today houses a much larger white population than most other schools in the city (56.6% white).[41] Lycée Français de la Nouvelle-Orleans purchased a long-dormant school building in a predominantly Black neighborhood; it, too, serves a predominantly white population (58.7%).

Focus group participants were nearly unanimous in their suspicion of and distrust in the motivations behind the move to the new all-charter model. Parents were quite adamant that white reformers were not truly concerned about the education of Black and Brown children; instead, they thought it was a "big money grab" and noted that chief executives of charter networks were making six-figure salaries. Parents mentioned "out-of-town investors" who profited from taxpayer money, people who briefly or never lived in New Orleans and, in their opinion, had no true concern for the people of the city. Their thoughts about the Teach for America recruits, discussed in Chapter 5, were repeated about charter schools' founders and leaders.

They saw the money grab in schools as attached to gentrification and the demise of neighborhoods as a means for affluent, white residents and out-of-towners to profit from the destruction of Black communities. Black parents talked about how the schools were one of the strengths for communities of color, how they helped to connect people across generations, giving them pride and solidarity. These bonds provided support for families struggling with poverty, crime, and the disinvestment in the public and private sectors. Football games and marching bands brought them together and gave them a shared, positive experience.[42] Public schools also have long been incubators for civic engagement and political mobilization. It is more difficult for communities of color to mobilize to resist the changes in their neighborhoods and schools if they are physically dispersed across town and have limited social ties to those around them. The busing of students across the city is seen as an integral part. One father described this phenomenon by saying:

> Father: [The loss of neighborhood schools] destroys . . . the neighborhoods. It destroys the community. And, to be honest with you, not that that's not probably what it's designed to do, but we're not going to go there.
> Moderator: You can go there.[43]
> Mother: Go ahead.

Moderator: It's OK.

Father: Everyone here has a very valid point. I've sat back, I've listened. You're all right. There's so much wrong that in order for
anything to go right at this point, you have to start on the political level, seriously, and let it work down. Poop runs down. And
that's what we're all dealing with. There's no other way to put it.
I'm not going to sugarcoat it. It's what it is.

Mother: [Laughter] That's trickle down.

Father: You destroy the community, you have nothing left. And that's
what's wrong here. So many communities have been destroyed . . . ,
that the kids coming up now, these kids are walking out their
front door, looking around, going, "Oh, my God, where in the
hell am I?" They don't know. The parents aren't sure themselves,
so how can the kid know? You know? . . . The mom's working.
If the dad is even there, if he's conscious, he's not much help
because, let's face it, he probably doesn't have more than a tenth-
grade education because he's had to work his butt off to support
the family. We're dealing with systematic craziness that has happened over a period of years that, to fix now, how are you going
to fix it? No focus group in the world is going to fix it because it's
too much. It's simply too much.

"Systematic craziness" is how this father describes what has happened not
just since Katrina, but also in the years before. In his eyes, the loss of neighborhood schools was not the catalyst for economic decline but another large factor
that contributed to what has been happening for a long time. The years of disinvestment and neglect, of discrimination and segregation; the destruction of
public housing complexes; and the building of highways through Black neighborhoods were seen as intentional efforts to break bonds among Black community members and divide up their political power.[44] Katrina severed what
was left in many communities, and the institutions that could have helped
them to rebound have been privatized, consolidated, or closed.[45] Individuals
are more disconnected from one another and from their physical spaces. He
was resigned to this "craziness" as "simply too much" to fix.

Another father commented further that this systemic inequality leads
those in power to blame the powerless for their plight. The powerless often
accept the responsibility, which erodes trust in institutions and in one another,
all to the benefit of those in authority. His emotional appeal led others to nod
in agreement:

And if we're talking about resources, and if one neighborhood has a limited amount of resources and another neighborhood keeps taking the resources, [the powerful] can say [to the powerless], "Well, well, you didn't do this, you didn't go out and do this, or you didn't go out and vote." But we're talking about systemic issues. To say that, oh, well, when you get to the voting station and you can't read or you don't understand the language, there's no reason to vote because you don't even know if it's in your best interest.

The distribution of resources has substantial effects on the ability of folks to see their interests and effectively participate. When the decisions of "politicians" create or perpetuate dramatic inequality, this father argues, elites can say whatever they want and, ultimately, do little to make things better for those whose communities have been destroyed by these policies:

> Father: So, for example, if you take a city and let's say you had a hundred resources and you had a hundred police officers, and you put eighty resources on one side with twenty police officers, and you put twenty resources with eighty police officers, what effect are you going to get? You know, and through gerrymandering, through vouchers that take resources out of neighborhoods, and busing kids out of neighborhoods, everything we're talking about here, it is destroying a neighborhood. . . .
>
> Father: Right.
>
> Father: So [they're] not telling us the truth. [They're] not really telling us the truth. [They're] not listening. You know, they're not listening to what people have told them over years and years and years, education-wise, infrastructure-wise. I mean, and they're not hearing it, and then somebody gets on, you know, a news channel or a radio station and they're saying, "Oh, well, these people . . . would be better off if they did X, Y, and Z." But they tried and they've been barred, you know, and that doesn't breed a lot of trust.
>
> Father: That's true.

The group agreed with these sentiments, nodding and mumbling "yes" under their breath. "Politicians" exacerbate long-term racial and economic disparities through policy, then, when there are obvious consequences in depressed turnout and devastated communities, the powerful blame those who are at their mercy for not voting, or having low-performing schools, or living in blighted neighborhoods. "That doesn't breed a lot of trust" would seem to be an understatement.

The racialized aspect of these disparities was left unsaid, probably because these Black parents were uncomfortable sharing their views about this with a white moderator. White reformers and white business leaders have been at the forefront of the policies leading to the devastation of Black communities and Black schools. The Black parents in the focus group saw these policies as purposive actions to weaken their power, blame them for the situation, and rationalize continuing these policies in other domains:

> Moderator: So this leads very naturally to our next question, which I think we probably have a good idea of your answer. How much do you think people in New Orleans generally trust the government?
>
> Father: Depends on their IQ level. The individual's IQ level, I would say. If they're smart, not much. Of course, America is great again. [Group laughter]
>
> Mother: In light of recent experiences, not just, you know— I know we're talking about our city, New Orleans, but there's a culture and a vibe because of things going on all over the nation, and maybe even the world, about allocation of resources and verbiage that makes people just say, "No way. You don't have my best interests in mind." So I've got to build myself up as high as I can to produce what I do have control over and make my life grand. But no, there's— No, there's not a lot of trust.

When the system (or "vibe") is stacked against you, this mother argues, the only thing left is to do what is best for yourself. This set of beliefs was also evident when these parents spoke about schools. When they disagreed with a practice or were upset about how their children were treated, they did not look to the government to devise a better-functioning, more equitable system. In most cases, they also did not look to mutual aid or grassroots organizing. Instead, they decided to fight for their children's opportunities, usually on their own, by using their connections and resources, which were usually limited.

This lack of trust went back years—decades—and had largely taught Black citizens of New Orleans that they were on their own. In this way, as dramatic as the changes were to the school system, the basic structure was unchanged; the well-connected and well-off were able to maneuver effectively, leaving those whose networks lacked powerful players and who could not afford to opt out of the public system stuck with what was left over, just as before the storm. Charter schools or traditional ones, governed by a private board or a public one, selective or open enrollment—none of it mattered because these parents believed that those who were worst off in the old system continue to be worst off today. They had no faith that a different set of elected leaders would change things:

> Moderator: We have an election coming up. So do you think that any of the candidates for any of the positions— Do you think things will get better along these lines? If we change who's the mayor, who's on the City Council, will things change in New Orleans?
>
> Mother: It could, if they did it good. Of course, it could. [Laughter]
>
> Father: That's the problem. But that is the problem. Look, politicians, I've known some good men and good women that became politicians that are not the same people I knew. It's something about that arena. You can take a person with good intentions and a good heart and put them in that arena, and it's like, if they don't play ball, they're unsuccessful. . . .
>
> Father: It's a cult. It's a cult.
>
> Father: Yes, it kind of seems that way, doesn't it? It does seem that way. I mean, to us, the citizens, you have to understand this is how we view it because that's what we're shown. It's a good ol' boy system here in Louisiana. Always has been. I hope to God it won't always be that way, but it probably will be. . . . So do I trust the government? No. Unequivocally no. Not until they clean their act up.
>
> Father: The reason why a lot of people liked [former Governor] Edwin Edwards, right? And we knew he was— But he took care of the people, you know? He took care of people, and people might feel a little bit better about a dirty government if they took care of the people. [Laughter] Because, I mean— If your city is six feet under water, you should be the best at pumping anything they put in there.
>
> Moderator: Did the response to the recent flooding surprise you?
>
> Mother: No.
>
> Moderator: Did your opinion change in any way?
>
> Mother: No. . . . We have, we live in "Stuckville" in New Orleans. Really, it's the same issues, the same problems, the same level of worry. You know, the simple fact that you have to have an evacu-

ation plan always ready—canned goods, batteries, you know? So
it's hard to have a certain quality of life when you have a monkey
on your back. You have the same drama. But I am the flipside of
that coin; I am kind of a Pollyanna sometimes, and I hope that
with youth and enthusiasm and modern concepts and research
of other cities that these young, vibrant candidates can bring a
different vibe and life to our city. But it's going to be a challenge
because we live in Stuckville, so it's going to take a lot for them to
put things on the ballot and people to vote favorably and want to
grow and change and bring a little better vibe to our city.

This sense of resignation mixed with hope and cautious optimism was
common among the focus group respondents. Although some were more
negative and had clearly lost confidence that political officials would listen
and truly represent their interests, many citizens remained hopeful. They
included public school parents, private school parents, and nonparents, indicating that even with all the negative experiences with the school system,
parents of public school children were not more negative or cynical than
anyone else. Also, in spite of theories about positive spillover effects of school
choice, it was very clearly not the case that they had gained efficacy and trust
because of their experience with school choice. In essence, all the changes in governance and in the way that children are assigned to schools and
their experiences within them have had little impact on general political attitudes because the culture of resignation and distrust was so widespread and
ingrained.

A common feature of the focus group conversations was that, after several minutes of cynicism and negativity, respondents inevitably would say
something like this:

Mother: I'll say when we were talking about trusting people and
community, I've lived in a bunch [of places], and . . . I find [New
Orleans to be] a very friendly and accessible city. Right after Katrina, I was standing in the Lowe's [store] and there were some
people, all kinds of people, and we were all just talking about
what we'd all— We've got how much water. And I said something about at least we're not— It was something about Boston.
And the woman behind me said, "Honey, if we were in Boston,
we wouldn't be talking to each other right now." I'm like, that is
the truth.

There is a cliché that even if you leave New Orleans, the city never leaves you. Hurricanes occasionally destroy the infrastructure; politicians steal money and enrich their friends; the pumps do not work to drain even light rainwater from streets and homes; the city tears up the roads all over town, creating traffic jams and parking nightmares; sporadic power outages and boil water advisories make life inconvenient; garbage and recycling pickup is at random; poverty, disinvestment, and gentrification push people out of their neighborhoods; and the public schools fail to provide equitable opportunities. It is not that residents are blind to these phenomena. Rather, in spite of them—indeed, perhaps, because of how these trying life experiences provide solidarity—New Orleanians treasure what they believe is the best place to live in the country.

In this way, the dramatic changes in school governance did not significantly depress efficacy and trust for most longtime residents. Their experiences with schools are largely the same as they had been, and they believe the outcomes are also unchanged. Efficacy and trust were already very low, especially among Black residents. When one has so little faith in the government, additional negative experiences cannot depress one's opinions about public officials or the system any further. Many of even the most cynical respondents remained hopeful and optimistic. Perhaps the next generation would do better, and perhaps the new system—even despite their own experiences with it—would improve the outcomes for their children or grandchildren. They doubted this but saw no reason not to hope for the best anyway.

Conclusions

The findings related to political efficacy, trust, and participation indicate that the new school system has had little impact on general political attitudes or behavior. School choice and privatization certainly have not improved citizens' faith or trust in government, but neither have they depressed them. This is true largely because people had such low levels of trust and external efficacy to start. Although school reform did not set off a negative feedback loop, it also did not improve conditions, as reformers and school choice apostles have argued.

The results from this chapter and the others lead to important questions about school governance, as well as democracy more broadly. One question that many ask with regard to New Orleans is: If the new system is better for the children of the city, should we care about the democratic effects? If test scores have improved and more kids are graduating and going to college, should we care about public engagement and accountability? In the Conclusion, I consider the evidence about the improvements in educational outcomes, then weigh it against what I have found in this book. Ultimately, this discussion leads to an examination of the purpose of public education and how schools are related to broader political and economic phenomena, including the features of democracy that create systems of equality and basic fairness.

Conclusion

So What? What Now?

Whoever decides what the game is about decides
also who gets into the game.

—E. E. Schattschneider

I began this book with the story of John Mac High School, a historic school that by 2005 had educated thousands of students over its nearly one hundred-year history. John Mac pride was legendary, and its students, faculty and alumni continued to "bleed green and gold" even though the school's facilities had been allowed to deteriorate, its performance scores were abysmal, and it was the site of an infamous shooting in 2003. In the years after Hurricane Katrina, the John Mac community fought hard to hang on to the school. They fought against chartering it and then struggled against a charter operator from outside New Orleans who had open disdain for the teachers, students, and families who made up the green and gold. When this failed spectacularly, in spite of continued community activism, the Recovery School District (RSD) gave the facility to an elementary school that attracts white middle- and upper-class residents. After an extensive, multimillion-dollar renovation, the building now has classrooms wired with the latest technology, a library, two science labs, two music rooms, and two art studios. Upon its opening, the school's founder and executive director stated, "The students deserve this."[1] Indeed, all students deserve that type of investment. Only some students get it, and in New Orleans, they have always been more likely to be white and less likely to be poor. Despite the rhetoric about the motivation for the dramatic reforms being to improve education for the predominantly poor, Black school population, these probabilities did not change much after Katrina.

The story of education reform in New Orleans from the mid-1990s to 2020 clearly indicates that a relatively small group of well-connected and powerful folks, most of whom were white, decided that the problem with the schools was not that the city and state had disinvested for decades, or that nearly all white families and many Black middle-class families had pulled their children out of public schools, or that the schools were starved of the multitude of services that would best serve its population. Instead, this group of reformers argued that "public governance was responsible for the low achievement" in New Orleans.[2] As E. E. Schattschneider reminds us, problem definition is so important: defining the problem as one about governance and not lack of investment in schools determined not only the direction of the policies but also who was able to play the game.

This book demonstrates that even before Hurricane Katrina came ashore, this group of elites had worked to dismantle public governance in New Orleans. The policies put in place in the years before the storm enabled them to act quickly afterward and to complete the plan more rapidly and with a wider scope than would have been possible without Katrina. Had the reformers been focused on what decades of education research tells us is most strongly correlated with positive educational outcomes, they would instead have focused on ensuring that schools in the city included a wide array of wraparound services, such as health care, job training for parents, childcare for young children, legal aid, housing assistance, and food programs. Instead, they focused on removing the power of the elected board, stripping teachers of union protections, and placing power in the hands of private individuals who do not see their role as one of service to the public. They strongly believed these reforms would dramatically transform the schools and even save money.

Once we understand that this was what the game was about, then we can understand who was allowed to play. Only those who had been a part of the contemporary reform efforts were able to wield power in the weeks following the storm. They included state officials such as Leslie Jacobs and Cecil Picard; local officials, including some members of the newly elected school board; and other like-minded people in positions of power and influence. This group wrote the law so that only the state board (on which New Orleans has a single member) would have the authority to return schools to the local district. They shaped the narrative to frame Katrina as an opportunity for a "blank slate" and insisted their early maneuvers were being made simply out of necessity, to get schools up and running and to get the city on its feet. If they excluded anyone from this planning, it was only out of the need for expediency—not an intentional maneuver to silence certain perspectives.

Since public governance was *the* problem, they could not allow groups of concerned citizens like those who fought for John Mac to operate schools. Instead, they turned over historic spaces to other true believers in the power of charters and school choice. They ensured that those who were appointed to lead would work to maintain the new system of schools and continue to sideline the folks who make up the schools. These choices told dedicated community members who had fought for social justice for generations that no matter what they did, they could not win even small battles. By excluding and pushing aside the people they claimed to serve, reformers exacerbated already low levels of trust and efficacy and contributed to the intense feelings of resignation and betrayal in the Black community. This has tremendous effects on the system of schools, such that parents of public school children are less likely than those who do not have children in public schools to be satisfied with the reforms and to believe that the system has improved. Black parents are frustrated about the enrollment process and do not believe they have real options or choices, regardless of reformers' spin in the media. These attitudes are reflected when parents make school selections and in how, or whether, they choose to engage with schools. Even if the architects of these school reforms believe that civic outcomes matter little compared with academic performance, research indicates that achievement is positively associated with parental engagement. Thus, the reforms' effects on attitudes and behavior have serious potential to thwart the ultimate goal of the reforms.

Beyond the effects on the schools, the exclusion, disillusionment, alienation, and resignation have a significant impact on democracy. Black parents do not believe the people who said they only wanted what was best for their children and instead see these moves as motivated by greed and racism. They were excluded from the outset and continue to be dismissed, ignored, and even blamed for their lack of engagement, even though reformers make it impossible for alternative voices to be heard. There is no effort to hear from parents; indeed, the system is a take-it-or-leave-it affair. Parents are encouraged to find the "right fit" for their child, as if they are searching for a soulmate instead of a safe and welcoming place to learn long division and sentence structure. Democracy in this system consists only of the occasional ability to ask a question or give a two-minute prepared speech to folks who are under no legal obligation and have no political incentive to respond. There is no accountability, no representation, and no transparency.

At the end of the Conclusion, I present four modest policy recommendations that would enhance the democratic character of the education landscape in New Orleans. But first I consider one of the most common questions I have been asked: *Who cares?* The intensity of focus on educational outcomes in all discussions of education policy leads people to ask why a focus on democratic attitudes and values matters as long as the performance of schools and students is improving. Don't the ends justify the means?

Ends and Means

A common question about the focus on the policies' effects on democratic processes and political behavior is whether we should care, especially in the face of evidence that educational outcomes have improved. In this section, I discuss this evidence about the effects of the reforms on the education of New Orleans children. To start, it is important to remember the reformers' promises about what they expected to happen. Those who put the system in place strongly believed that changing the governance structure and instituting market principles alongside a willingness to close underperforming schools would dramatically—and relatively rapidly—transform education and educational outcomes. It is completely fair to evaluate the results in light of these promises.

As with nearly all the aspects of these reforms, one's beliefs about whether the system has improved outcomes for the city's children depend greatly on which side one is on and the outcomes of interest. The early evidence about test scores and graduation rates was mostly positive, but the analysis was limited and often unsophisticated. Critics often tried unsuccessfully to punch through the cheerleading to point out the folly of simple pre- and post-Katrina comparisons.[3] They would point to the dramatic increase in per-pupil funding, the differences in the pre- and post-Katrina population, and the changes in how success was measured. Researchers also struggled to obtain even public data from the Louisiana Department of Education to do their own analyses.[4] For their part, reformers "create[d] and distribute[d] flyers and brochures with positive messages and news throughout the city, especially during election season and just before key votes in the legislature."[5] Already suspicious of the reformers' motivations, critics argued that Jacobs and other charter leaders manipulated data and omitted negative results to shape public opinion. As I showed in Chapter 3, the local media was a key player in this game, painting a glowing portrait in the first ten years after Katrina.

In his recent book, the economist Douglas Harris conducts more sophisticated statistical analyses that show significant improvement on several educational outcomes: scores on the state exams for elementary- and middle-school students, high school graduation rates, and college entry and persistence rates. He argues that, among the many reforms in the post-Katrina package, the closures of failing schools are primarily responsible for the gains. Although critics are skeptical about these results, the fact that he demonstrates that the reforms have had both positive and negative effects strengthens the study's validity.[6] Accepting the good without bad, or vice versa, is a difficult argument to defend.

One of the chief complaints about much of the work on educational outcomes has been the combining of the results in RSD and Orleans Parish School Board (OPSB) schools into a single district score. There is nothing methodologically incorrect about combining the districts—together they do represent public education in New Orleans. The problem is with the conclusions that combining them allows reformers to make. Test scores and other educational outcomes in RSD schools lagged well behind those in OPSB schools, as would have been expected in the early years, given that only the above-average schools remained under the OPSB. However, reformers had defined the problem as school governance and remained adamant that the only way to improve schools was to remove them from local control. Thus, because they were no longer under local control, we should expect the RSD schools' performance to improve dramatically. That the state-run schools and state-approved charters continued to have such low scores indicated to many critics of reforms that the new system was not working and that the reformers had been wrong when they defined the problems around governance rather than resources. When the scores of the two districts were combined, average scores showed improvement, and reformers used these scores to tout the success of the new system even as they argued the schools simply could not be returned to local control. This hypocrisy has enraged many critics, but politically it was successful in convincing many that the reforms had worked magic. New Orleans cheered as scores went up, and most did not want to hear a counternarrative or delve into nuance.

Much of the focus on educational outcomes is on growth or improvement rather than on absolute scores. As the winner of the "most improved" in riflery award at 4-H camp in 1986, in which I went from not hitting the paper with the target to shooting the paper but still coming nowhere close to the bullseye, I can say that one can still be pretty bad at something and show improvement. Using a complicated set of assumptions, Harris calculates that New Orleans students went from the twenty-second percentile nationally in 2005 to the thirty-seventh percentile in 2015.[7] Though this represents growth, few parents would be thrilled if their child scored in the thirty-seventh percentile on a test, and it is nowhere near the levels of success that reformers had promised. By this estimate, the students are occasionally hitting the paper but are still well outside the bullseye.

An examination of American College Testing (ACT) scores in New Orleans provides an opportunity to compare performance over time on a

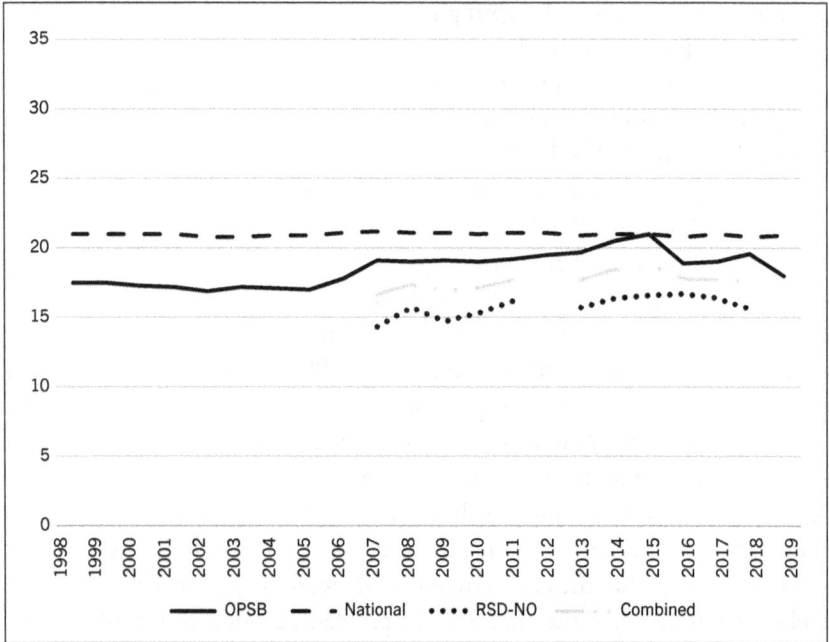

Figure C.1. Average composite American College Test (ACT) scores in the United States and Orleans Parish, 1998–2019 (*Note:* In 2011 and 2013–2018 the Louisiana Department of Education clearly separated the Recovery School District-New Orleans from the OPSB schools. In 2007–2010, the average for the RSD was presented only statewide, so I separated out the scores only for those schools located in New Orleans. The Department of Education gave no ACT score for the RSD in 2012. In 2018, the data for Orleans Parish combined all schools, but since some schools were still authorized by the RSD, I separated the two. By 2019, all schools were under OPSB authorization. *Source:* Louisiana Department of Education website, https://www.louisia nabelieves.com/resources/library/high-school-performance?fbclid=IwAR0Rx-LRBhtmzID14Q50euaxg -WWECvphkc1q7ViC9T9HrNh8T-TqdTJ5fHk. The national figures are from the ACT Profile Reports.)

national test. Louisiana began to require the ACT of all high-school students in 2013, eight years after the reforms were implemented. Although we might expect average scores to be lower with all students taking the test rather than only those intending to go to college, by 2013, nearly a generation of students had gone through the new system. Students taking this test in 2013 would have been in third or fourth grade when Katrina hit. If the reforms have been successful, then there should be no difference between students in RSD and OPSB schools on scores on this national college entry test. As shown in Figure C.1, even as many states began to require the test of all high-school students, ACT scores nationally did not change significantly between 1998 and 2019.[8] Thus, any changes in Louisiana *should* demonstrate real growth (or decline) and are not simply a reflection of an easier test or a reconfiguration of the scoring. The line for OPSB schools includes only those schools that were, in the given year, operated or authorized by the OPSB. The scores in OPSB schools rose from 17.5 in 1998 to 20.5 in 2014, just shy of the national average, and have then dipped down again in recent years, after the RSD and the OPSB merged in 2018.

The OPSB controlled a fraction of the schools in New Orleans after Katrina until 2018, and many of its schools are selective-admissions institutions. Thus, the OPSB line from 2007 to 2018 excludes a lot of schools. Given the expectations that the state takeover would boost educational outcomes in the poorest-performing schools, I include a line for the RSD-NO schools and one for the combined OPSB-RSD averages, which would measure the district as a whole. The average composite score is exceedingly low in the RSD schools in every year. If the takeover had lived up to the hype, the RSD scores would have risen over time, and the gaps between the districts would have begun to narrow, if not disappear. There is some limited improvement in the RSD-NO, but scores peak at 16.7 in 2016—four points below the national average and 2.2 points below the OPSB schools. The gap increased again after 2016.

Despite the rhetoric about how the state takeover would dramatically improve outcomes, there was nothing magical about the RSD. Scores did not improve dramatically over this period, and as the two districts were merged in 2018 and 2019, average scores in the OPSB dropped. The factors affecting ACT scores have little to do with whether the state or local district is the authorizing agency or even whether the schools are traditional neighborhood institutions or charters. Schools that are able to pick their students are, not surprisingly, much more high performing. Finally, though scores "improved" over this period in both school districts, when combined, the average composite scores do not change much from the pre-Katrina period. The gap between the national average and the combined scores in New Orleans was 3.5 points in 1998 and 3.2 points in 2018. There is no wonder, then, that the parents in my focus groups believed little had really changed for their children.

One theory is that the improvements had reached a ceiling. In the decade after the storm, the infusion of cash from private and public sources had upgraded school facilities and classroom resources, which could explain a boost in test scores. However, without continued investment in the lives of these children, it would not be surprising that educational outcomes would plateau. Career educators have argued that without significant efforts to prevent or ease the effects of poverty, schools will only ever be able to do so much. The city, state, and federal government can help to boost achievement by focusing on stable and affordable housing, well-paying jobs for parents, drug and alcohol rehabilitation, counseling support for students who have been exposed to violence and trauma, nutrition assistance, and access to high-quality physical- and mental-health care. Education scholars and practitioners have long argued that educational outcomes are affected primarily by "out of school" factors, especially parental income.[9] Reformers refer to these claims as "excuses," but the early charter schools that got much acclaim, such as the Harlem Children's Zone, did not rely merely on their autonomy for success. They put in mountains of resources to assist the predominantly poor children the schools served.

School performance scores continue to indicate that there are serious barriers to strong academic performance. These scores are one of the most important measures for parents' school decisions and have been touted by reformers as evidence of the system's success. They also carry enormous weight in reauthorization decisions—schools that are failing in the year of their reauthorization are in real peril. Yet rigorous analyses generally do not consider these scores because of the multitude of changes in measures and cut points, and because of so-called charter churn (the number of schools that open, close, or transition from one charter network to another in a given year). Current ratings are largely based on state standardized test scores and for high schools, graduation rates and ACT scores. In 2018, the state added a growth measure to the School Performance Score (SPS), which accounts for 25 percent of an elementary school's grade and 12.5 percent of high schools'. These metrics did not shift between 2018 and 2019, allowing at least one year to be able to make valid comparisons.[10]

In 2019, of the seventy-four schools with full data publicly available, twelve schools (16.2%) earned an F overall. A majority of the seventy-four schools (forty-five) earned an F in their "assessment grade." Thus, without accounting for year-over-year growth, thirty-three more schools would have earned a failing SPS. This measure is not without controversy. Critics claim it provides a way to cover up low test scores, while supporters suggest that we ought to care not only about absolute scores, but also about whether schools are headed in the right direction. We know almost nothing about whether parents understand or are aware of the changes in metrics, or the extent to which parents care about growth versus absolute scores. Only seven schools earned an A in 2019, and two of these schools earned a D and C in assessment; their A grade was due only to this growth metric. Most schools' overall grades did not change between 2018 and 2019, but of those that did, twenty-one schools' grades dropped and six schools' grades rose. In spite of cheerleading and optimism, absolute scores are still quite low.[11]

Another common metric on which to judge the reforms relates to equity and access. Have the reforms improved things for those children who are most in need? And do these kids have the same access as those from more privileged backgrounds? The evidence here is more clearly negative. Harris writes, "If the goal was to give everyone access to the same level of quality, the reforms had failed."[12] Another study shows that, although there was a decline in the share of schools that were concentrated by race or ethnicity, the "average minority student in New Orleans is still highly segregated by race and poverty whereas the typical White student is attending schools with decreasing levels of minority students compared with 10 years ago and lower shares of [students eligible for Free or Reduced price Lunch] from 5 years ago."[13] Similarly, in spite of an increase in the number of racially diverse school options, these schools are almost exclusively located in affluent, predominantly white sections of the city. After all the dramatic changes in educational policy, not much has changed for the vast majority of students in New Orleans public schools.

Educational Outcomes and Democratic Outcomes

It is not realistic to examine the educational outcomes in a vacuum, as if what happens in school each day is the only thing that explains test scores or other outcomes. In addition to the out-of-school factors that education scholars have pointed to for decades, policy feedback theory indicates that democratic outcomes, such as the exclusion and diminution of parents' and community members' voices, have an impact on policy outcomes such as student achievement. There is a positive relationship between trust among teachers, students, and parents and student achievement.[14] Kids are better off when their parents are involved in their schools and when they trust school authorities, but a parent is much less likely to volunteer or engage in a school outside her neighborhood, where she may not know many other parents, where the logistics of participation are a challenge, and where the governing board or staff has made it clear that they do not value her perspective on anything that matters.

Several parents expressed that the education children receive today is worse because there are fewer teachers who are Black native New Orleanians and there is less emphasis on the history and culture that make the city unique and special. Intergenerational ties have been severed due to school closures and takeovers. According to Amanda Walker Johnson, "Losing a school is equivalent to experiencing a 'social' and 'civic death,' characterized by the loss of natality and history, a center for community development and advocacy, as well as the social and economic benefits of a nearby public school."[15]

With the loss of neighborhood schools and as longtime schools have been closed, renamed, or taken over by charter networks, education is increasingly divorced from the communities that help to support and nurture young people. Kids merely *attend* schools and then get in a carpool line or ride the bus across town; they are not *part of* school and neighborhood communities. Given that performance scores continue to be low after all this time, parents remain unconvinced that the reforms have been worthwhile.

The modest improvements in some test scores, the continuing racial disparities in access to high-quality schools, and parents' frustrating experiences cast doubt on the so-called New Orleans miracle.[16] After sixteen years, the children in New Orleans public schools are still performing well below even the state average—a state whose schools are among the lowest-ranked in the nation. Parents spend hours and hours researching schools, only to find that they can count the number of A-rated schools on one hand, and these schools have erected barriers to entry that shut out all but the lucky few. Parents are tired and frustrated and want a simple thing: high-quality schools in their neighborhoods. This all continues to be divided by race, such that Black residents have a distinctly dismal experience with public schools, while white residents largely either opt out or manage to get their children into the top-rated schools. The system teaches Black parents—and their children—that they are not valued, that they must compete with other families for one of the few chances afforded for enrollment in a "high-performing" school, and that there is no use in pushing back against the system. Some parents continue to fight, but most are resigned; they remain cautiously optimistic, but down deep, they seem not to believe things will be better for their kids than it was for them.[17]

Inequality Tied to Undemocratic Features

Democratic theorists suggest that we should not expect a system built on exclusion and inequality to produce anything other than exclusion and inequality. Charles Tilly contends that inequality results from the structure of political relations between "hoarders of opportunity" and those with few chances, rather than market failures or failed policies and procedures.[18] In other words, a system designed to shut out critical perspectives and eliminate democratic deliberation will inherently establish or exacerbate inequality. Rather than move toward greater democratization, privatization initiates "a process of creative destruction that remakes the city physically and discursively. In the process, a different kind of city emerges—a city imagined by someone else, and not for the people that remain there."[19] The privatized system usually retains a veneer of democracy, keeping in place some formal democratic-like institutions and processes, while moving real power into "arenas that are easily accessed and dominated by corporate interests and insulated from the effects of citizen engagement and dissensus."[20] For example, citizens in New Orleans continue to vote for a school board, but this board does not operate any schools, regularly fails to exercise oversight, and has no role in charter boards.[21]

Decision makers often hold community meetings, such as when the Bring New Orleans Back group was developing a plan for schools in 2006, or when the superintendent was tasked with developing a plan to unify the RSD and OPSB, or when the OPSB makes decisions about charter renewals. These are framed as opportunities for the public to give feedback and ask questions. In no case, however, were the views of the community binding, and most times there was no way for voters to hold any of these officials accountable. Public hearings are not discursive; they are monologues. Participation is tightly controlled.[22] In many cases, consultants or attorneys lead these "opportunities" for community input while the actual decision makers are absent.[23] Those who lead the meetings often withhold the full information needed to make informed decisions, and the problems are framed as technical issues best resolved by experts, not deliberative or consensus-building exercises.[24] The processes resemble democracy, but the real decisions are made outside the political arena.[25]

Tilly tells us we should move toward *democratization*, which he defines as policies that are increasingly inclusive of all citizens, where subjects are more equal in their relations with government; that protect subjects from arbitrary state action; and that hold leaders accountable to the public. Movement away from any of these factors is a move against democracy and toward greater inequality. A stakeholder democracy in which people cannot hold policy makers accountable, citizens have grossly unequal access to power, and most voices are excluded is a move away from democracy. If the quality of the democracy affects school performance, then despite the dramatic nature of these changes, very little is likely to be altered in opportunities or outcomes for the vast majority of children. If reformers' goals are to improve schools and increase opportunities for the least advantaged students, then they must take the antidemocratic features of this system seriously. The powerful must give up some of their power and control, which they can do willingly or when the masses demand change through social movements.

A few modest policy prescriptions could increase participation among parents of public school children, improve trust, and strengthen their faith that the system is fair. These changes would make the system more responsive and easier to navigate. Contrary to reformers' rhetoric, a multitude of policy options exist; we are not limited to choosing between what we have now and what we had before. Admittedly, these recommendations will make small improvements in how the existing system operates. If the ultimate goal is to improve educational quality for the least advantaged students and to create a truly equitable system, then my recommendations will fall short. For that, policy makers must decide that a fully funded public education system is a priority, collect the revenue that will make that possible, and distribute it in a truly equitable fashion. Reforms related to governance, curriculum, personnel, and more can succeed only if there is adequate—and equitable—investment in our children. If, however, reformers refuse to make even small adjustments that open up power to those who are directly affected by their policies, then people will demand change in other ways, through social movements and grassroots mobilization.[26]

Recommendation 1: Making NCAP Fairer

Reformers hailed OneApp, now called NOLA-PS Common Application Process (NCAP), as *the* fix for enrollment problems, especially those associated with unfair school practices. The system was supposed to prevent schools from gaming the system and would elicit parents' true preferences. In the first several years, reformers and algorithm fans cheered when findings revealed that the vast majority of children were matched to one of the top three schools their parents had listed. The problems with the system were obvious to parents, however. Chiefly, not all schools were included in the misnamed *One*App. Parents who preferred the schools run or chartered by the Board of Elementary and Secondary Education or OPSB still had to complete separate applications. That problem is nearly fixed: as of 2020, only three schools had a separate application, and all of them were up for charter renewal in 2021. The OPSB has mandated that when schools are reauthorized, they must join NCAP.

However, the rhetoric about how the system operates has never matched reality. Schools can maintain their own preferences for siblings of current children and other selective criteria, such as mandatory meetings, volunteer commitments, entrance exams, early deadlines, and more. So while there may indeed have been a single application as of 2021, children will still have very different probabilities of being matched to their preferred schools for reasons that have nothing to do with their lottery numbers.

Other than eliminating preferences completely, another option is to set up the system so that parents can indicate the intensity of their preferences. At present, parents can only indicate their preference order, and the algorithm assumes that the distance between each preference is the same, such that one prefers *a* over *b* with the same intensity that one prefers *b* over *c*. However, we know this is often not the case. Some parents strongly prefer one school over all the others. Some only have strong preferences among their top three or four options but see all others as the same.

There are a variety of voting systems that allow for the expression of both order and intensity. Although problematic in terms of equity and feasibility, vote selling and vote storing allow some individuals (i.e., parents in this example) to have more votes than others in some elections.[27] Two-stage multivoting systems give all voters the same number of additional votes, which they can distribute as they choose.[28] If parents are asked to rank twelve schools on NCAP, they would be given more than twelve votes and could distribute them in any combination. I encourage the OPSB (now NOLA-PS) to consider alternatives that allow parents to indicate both the order and the intensity of their preferences and to give weight to intense preferences. It is arguable whether one should be matched to one's higher-ranked but weakly preferred school over another with very strong preferences for that school simply because the former draws a better lottery number. If the former parent would be just as satisfied in another school, while the latter parent would be completely dissatisfied, then a system that accounts for intensity will result in fairer outcomes.

I also recommend that the NCAP system include a default option that is within or near the neighborhood in which one lives. This would not go back to neighborhood assignment. Rather, parents would be provided the option of a school near their home that fits their child's needs (grade level, special accommodations). Parents have to enter basic information when they start to complete NCAP—child's name, grade, street address. The system could use this information to identify a default school. Parents could then either select the default—in which case they would be finished—or continue on to the rankings. Perhaps a parent prefers five other schools to the one to which their child matched but would prefer the neighborhood school to all others outside the neighborhood. This parent would then rank their top five schools (ideally indicating their intensity), then list their default school. If the parent did not get their child into any of the top five, the child would be matched automatically to the neighborhood school.

This plan solves two complaints parents have made about the new system of schools. First, they routinely criticize the fact that they have to send their children across town to schools that are no better than the ones near their homes. They believe that if their children cannot get into one of their true top preferences, then they should at least be able to stay close to home.

Second, parents lament the loss of neighborhood schools and the community they help to build. They are not fans of assignment without choice, but parents strongly believe there are numerous benefits of kids going to school with those in their local area. They get to know one another more deeply, as they can play together after school more easily. Parents can rely on a neighbor who has a child in the same school for emergency pickups or after-school care. The school would return as a community center, where neighborhood events beyond just school functions can take place within the school building. The school becomes an anchor for the neighborhood, and residents cheer on the sports teams, listen to the bands practice, and attend concerts and other events. Parents can more easily volunteer and attend conferences and events because they do not have to drive or take public transportation across town. New Orleans can have a semblance of neighborhood schools without taking away parents' choices.[29]

In 2019, the OPSB put in place a new policy that allows applicants who live within a half-mile of an open-enrollment elementary or middle school (those without selective admissions) to receive priority for 25 percent of the open seats. Applicants who live in a school's "geographic zone" receive priority for another 25 percent of open seats. "Open seats" refer to the seats left over *after* those with other priorities have been satisfied, such as siblings. A recent study shows that these geographic priorities largely benefit high-income, white applicants, as opposed to poor, Black and Latino applicants, primarily because the schools that have more demand than seats are located in zip codes with incomes above the city average. The authors note, "There are a small number of students who benefit from this policy, but the benefit to those students is substantial" and is skewed toward the most advantaged children in the city.[30] These "priorities" are limited and primarily benefit those with other advantages. My recommendation would work differently. In conjunction with a ranking system that accounts for intensity as well as preference order, a default option would address the issue parents have expressed about their children being assigned across town when there are similarly ranked schools with seats closer to their residence.

The elimination of neighborhood zones has failed to produce dramatically improved academic achievement, largely because the problem has never been with the neighborhood school model. Rather, the problem is that funding is tied to neighborhoods, and, as in most places, the higher-performing schools are located primarily in upper-income neighborhoods. Neighborhood schools that are equitably funded and do not discriminate in admission should not exacerbate—and could alleviate—inequality.

Recommendation 2: Centralization of Calendars and Transportation

In Fall 2020, as school districts around the country grappled with their COVID-19 plans, *The Lens* ran an ad that read, "Dozens of Charter Schools. Dozens of Reopening Plans. One Place to Keep Track of It." Although the state and the local school board shut schools down or delayed their reopening due to the pandemic, once schools were allowed to reopen, there were literally dozens of different plans. Some schools continued virtually for students in some grades, while those in other grades attended school in-person. Others developed staggered in-person and virtual days, which did not always line up for parents with multiple children. Quarantine requirements varied. The process of returning to school after an exposure varied. For parents of multiple children, this was one more COVID-related struggle.

Parents have complained for years about the varying academic calendars, noting that when they have children in multiple charter schools, it is impossible to juggle different start and end dates, holidays, and early dismissal/late arrival days. In May 2020, charter leaders reported that all but two charter schools or networks had decided on a unified calendar.[31] This was not really a single calendar; rather, they agreed on "common windows" for the start of the year and for other holidays (spring breaks, Mardi Gras, and so on). Schools will continue to schedule their own professional development days and early dismissals or late arrivals.

Although an improvement, this still requires parents with multiple children to juggle multiple calendars. Some kids may have spring break one week, while a sibling has it the next week. For working parents, this presents a child-care nightmare. The vast majority of school districts in the country use a common calendar at the district or state level, and NOLA-PS should insist that New Orleans schools adopt the same start and end dates, holidays, and professional development days. The COVID-19 pandemic has shown the folly of decentralization. It is not just a matter of convenience. There is an economic toll when parents cannot go to work because a child is home from school or they have to hire babysitters. Not everyone can afford to do this. It can also lead to absences from school, which harms the entire educational enterprise in the name of "autonomy." It is another example of a policy pursued in the name of "freedom" that actually creates more constraint for the most vulnerable populations.

Another perennial issue with the decentralized system has been transportation. As discussed in Chapter 3, because of the lack of neighborhood zones, the average length of travel has nearly doubled since before Katrina. In 2018, nearly a quarter of bus rides to schools lasted more than fifty minutes, with some as long as ninety minutes *each way*. Without the economy of scale of a major central bureaucracy, costs for transportation for each charter school that provides transportation have increased substantially. Many schools, however, provide no real transportation options, requiring parents to drop off and pick up their kids. It is past time for this essential service to be centralized. It makes no sense for students to get up before sunrise or spend three hours per day on buses when cities have been busing children to public schools for decades and there are plenty of models for how to do this efficiently and justly. Education reformers often speak about how traditional school systems are set up to work for the adults, while privatization puts the kids first. The decentralized transportation system and academic calendars certainly fail to work for the children or their families. It places the priority again on "autonomy" and on what charter leaders prefer rather than on what children and their families need.

Recommendation 3: Independent Monitor

Chapter 4 detailed charter schools' and networks' lack of compliance with state laws related to public meetings and the provision of public documents. Ironically, charter board members reported that participating in these meetings and reviewing these documents were the best way for the public to get involved. Transparency and public deliberation are simply not priorities for charter boards, and no group has been denied a reauthorization or even had a sanction related to the lack of compliance with these laws. I recommend, then, that the NOLA-PS establish an independent monitor charged with ensuring that charter boards comply with state mandates on public bodies. The monitor would be responsible for collecting and maintaining data on charter boards, including their names and contact information, as well as whether boards are in compliance with all state laws related to public meetings and materials. The monitor would report findings at least once per quarter, and NOLA-PS would be required to establish sanctions for violations. Repeat offenders would risk their reauthorization.

Monitorships are a common feature in the world of compliance. Often under court orders, private and public entities employ monitors after a compliance failure as part of their efforts to remediate and mitigate future failures. According to the legal scholar Veronica Root Martinez, there are five types of monitorship: traditional court-ordered, enforcement, corporate compliance, modern-day court-ordered, and public relations.[32] In 2015, courts ordered that independent monitors oversee the work of the Louisiana Department of Education (LDOE) under a federal consent judgment related to special education services. A private firm, Fluency Plus, LLC, was hired as an independent monitor to ensure that charter schools in New Orleans were providing the special education services to which students have a legal right. Unfortunately, the monitors relied on the LDOE to appropriately select the schools they would monitor, and in 2019 they discovered major errors, resulting in the wrong schools' being selected for targeted monitoring. The independent monitors identified these errors and made the information public.[33] An attorney for the families of students with special needs said the errors show that the LDOE does not have the capacity to oversee the new decentralized school system. The monitors also found that many of the schools they mistakenly monitored were found to have violations, which, they argue, indicates "the level of concerns that continue to exist among [New Orleans]/OPSB schools with regard to [federal] compliance, thus suggesting the continued need for LDOE oversight and support."[34] Without the independent monitors, these errors likely would have required another lawsuit or would have gone unnoticed. Students with special needs would continue to lack the services they need.

I recommend a public relations monitor for the NOLA-PS and LDOE specifically to ensure compliance with state laws on public bodies.[35] Although organizations use these monitors on a voluntary basis (i.e., not ordered by a court or another government body), they are completely independent, as "no regulatory or governing body [should] serve as a countervailing check on the monitorship."[36] Public relations monitorships are usually entered into after there has been a scandal and, according to Martinez, are

> retained by the institution as a service to the public, and accordingly—distinct from the other forms of monitorships—the institution typically distances itself from the monitor once he or she has been selected . . . to assist with remediating the misconduct within the organization without the institution seemingly tainting the process. Although this form of monitorship is clearly about remediation, it is also in large part about rebuilding the public trust that has been lost through the compliance failure or scandal.[37]

Public relations monitors were used to investigate former New Jersey Governor Chris Christie's involvement in the Port Authority scandal; the General Motors scandal related to defects in ignition switches; and Pennsylvania State University senior leaders' knowledge of sexual abuse allegations against Jerry Sandusky, its former assistant football coach. All New Orleans public schools would be required to participate, including those in the city that are authorized by the Board of Elementary and Secondary Education. The results of the investigation must be made public, and ongoing monitoring should continue each year. The monitors would review the availability of meeting agendas before meetings, including committee meetings; the availability of a calendar of meetings, including committee meetings, with times, dates, and locations, and announcements of changes made according to the law; up-to-date information about charter board members' names, biographies, and contact information; the availability of meeting minutes, including committee meeting minutes, and insurance that they include required elements such as dates, attendance, recorded votes of each member, public commentary, and times and rationales for executive sessions; and the availability of budget documents, contracts with vendors, and other potential conflicts of interest of board members with school business. This list may not be all-inclusive of the laws related to public bodies, and the monitor should have wide discretion to evaluate the policies and processes that undergird the charter authorization process and charter boards. Depending on the results of the investigations, the public relations monitor might have other recommendations for remediation and continued monitoring.

Public relations monitors "obtain their legitimacy and power from the extremely transparent manner in which they operate."[38] They assure the public that the organization's misconduct will be discovered and publicly aired; they also ensure that remediation of the harm caused will be monitored. The public benefits from a full accounting and from the organization's efforts to fix the wrongdoing. The organization also benefits from increased public trust, and, in the event that legal proceedings follow, courts often look kindly on organizations that have voluntarily agreed to monitorships. Organizations that make serious attempts to mitigate the behavior that led to a monitorship also reduce the burden on regulatory bodies.

Recommendation 4: Redefine the Membership of Charter Boards

Louisiana laws and NOLA-PS policies govern the membership of charter school boards. Current law prohibits employees from serving on their own governing boards, although other states do allow teachers to be represented. In 2018, Louisiana law was amended to require at least one member who is a parent or guardian of a current student. These members may be appointed or elected, which is determined by the charter boards. The NOLA-PS policy allows this to be satisfied by a parent, a recent graduate (within the previous five years), or parent of a recent graduate (within the previous three years). The state law also mandates that these boards "shall be representative of the community in which the charter school is located by race and gender to ensure diversity, and no fewer than 60 percent of its members shall reside in the parish in which the school is located."[39] The NOLA-PS policy on charter boards requires that they consist of at least seven members and that they represent a "diverse set of professional skills and practical work experience in areas such as education, public/non-profit and/or for-profit administration or operations, community development, finance, and law."[40]

As I showed in Chapter 4, there is great variability in the extent to which charter boards comply with these laws and policies. Charter boards operate primarily as fiduciaries of public funds and set policy indirectly through hiring school leaders. In New Orleans, very few members have educational experience and very few have children in public schools. Most members are selected because of their connections (to the founder, the board chair, or potential donors) or because of their occupation (attorneys and financial professionals).

If the goal of these moves is for boards to be more inclusive and have a greater diversity of voices, they are insufficient. One parent or alumni member, who can be selected by the current board members, is unlikely to offer a different perspective from other board members; if they do, one lone vote has little power. Further, this requirement perpetuates the notion that public schools are private goods and that only parents of current students have a stake in the decisions of the board. Parents in New Orleans expressed a strong desire that schools have strong ties to their neighborhoods, yet there is no inclusion of folks in the surrounding neighborhood in the governance of schools. The "severing [of] communities from their neighborhood public schools [has] consequences for the historic democratic promise of public education."[41]

The state and NOLA-PS should require that *a majority* of each board consist of (1) parents or recent alumni; and (2) residents of the neighborhood in which the school is located.[42] These members should be elected every two to three years by the school community, which consists not only of parents of current students but also of neighborhood residents.[43] As the majority of board members, parents and neighbors would have real power to choose school leaders and determine policies and financial priorities for schools. They also bring valuable experience with public schools that is now missing. Further, each board must include at least one member who has at least five years of K–12 teaching experience. Just as it is critical to have board members with legal or financial expertise, having at least one person with experience in a classroom is essential. Research on site-based management points to the importance of including people with experience and expertise in teaching and learning to improve student performance.[44] These members should be elected every two to three years by the faculty within the school or network.

Reformers are committed to school improvement and accountability but have little experience or expertise in public schools; under this plan, they will be forced to work with those who have the most experience with schools and knowledge about educating young people. With training, parents, neighbors, and teachers who are elected by their peers can exercise the powers of charter boards just like the attorneys, financial professionals, and business owners who serve now. Further, they bring with them their interactions with the enrollment system, their children's experiences with teachers and school officials, their knowledge of teaching and learning, and their desire for *their* kids (their own or those within their neighborhood) to have a high-quality educational experience. Reformers will continue to serve on boards, but they will have to cooperate with parents and neighbors to accomplish their goals instead of paternalistically assuming they know best. A truly child-centered agenda, as reformers claim to have, necessarily involves the communities in which children live and the families in which they are raised. Elections will provide accountability and give constituents a reason to engage with the board.

This composition resembles the Local School Councils (LSCs) that were put in place in Chicago in 1988, which are composed of parents, community representatives, teachers, the principal, and a student (in high schools). The LSCs have power over the selection and evaluation of principals, strategic planning, and the school budget, all powers of charter boards in New Orleans. Studies of Chicago's LSCs show that the parent and community members are relatively well educated and dedicated to their role, spending an average of twenty-eight hours per month involved in aiding their school, including their official duties and volunteering in school.[45] The LSC members take their roles seriously, and the vast majority engage in a thorough process of selecting principals and approving the budget. The LSCs also engage the community as a matter of course, holding community forums around school improvement plans and consulting others in the school community on selection and evaluation of principals.[46] Stefanie Chambers finds that minority residents of Chicago praised LSCs as being open and responsive to their concerns.[47] Further, expanded democratic participation is associated with systemic change centered on school improvement.[48]

Some reformers are skeptical about the participation of parents on charter boards, arguing that parents cannot make decisions in the best interest of the whole school and that restrictions on who serves on these boards interfere with the autonomy of charter schools.[49] Concerns about autonomy, however, ought to be weighed against the many benefits of including parents and educators in school governance. Given that the reform process has always erred more toward exclusion, some course correction is necessary.[50] Further, if we consider the persistently low test scores, the benefits of the tremendous autonomy afforded schools right now are limited.

Skeptics will say that allowing parents, neighbors, and teachers to have so much authority over decisions related to spending and personnel will detract from the mission of academic achievement. School-based councils—and, by extension, a charter governing board with real representation of parents and neighbors—"contribute to high-quality schools by strengthening struggling communities and helping students and families thrive."[51] In other words, a more democratic governance system is not antithetical to a high-quality education. In fact, democracy and education are inextricably linked.[52] When schools help to strengthen the communities in which children are being raised, they serve to help academic achievement *and* impart a sense of responsibility and belonging. Involving all stakeholders in decision making helps to make these connections and build stronger and safer communities. Further, a more deliberative democracy is associated with greater substantive representation: elected officials are better able to represent their constituents' interests when levels of political empowerment are high, racial conflict is low, and "racial and ethnic minorities are equally represented alongside their white counterparts."[53] New Orleans cannot have high-performing schools while its children, their families, and their neighborhoods are struggling and excluded from decision making. The governing bodies are starved of the knowledge and experience of those in the trenches, leading to decisions divorced from the reality of the lives of those who are most affected. Further, those who are excluded have little reason to trust that decision makers have their best interests in mind. They disengage and develop resentment toward the system more generally.

Reformers began their quest by insisting on taking students' achievement seriously and holding schools accountable for performance. Everyone, including the reformers' harshest critics, agreed with the end goal of students' learning more and achieving at higher levels. The folly was that the architects of these reforms believed this could be done on its own, by "fixing" schools without focusing on how privatizing governance affects those who are excluded and how excluding important stakeholders affects the policies by leaving out their experience and knowledge. Allowing parents and neighbors to have a meaningful role in school governance—a chance not simply to be "heard" but to really direct policy—is likely to result in a more holistic look at students' lives from those who understand their experience. Academic achievement and collective efficacy are positively related, indicating the value of a strong bond between schools and their neighborhoods.[54] Further, there may be positive spillover effects on those who serve. As others have proposed about the effects of school choice, the training and experience in governing should increase their civic capacity and skills, and for both these members and the community at large, a governance system in which people like them have real power provides motivation to participate and trust in the institutions, and it might improve satisfaction with the system.[55] Given the participatory debt in which the community is starting, these spillover effects will take some time to bear fruit.[56]

Final Thoughts

The modest reforms I recommend are in no way a real challenge to the post-Katrina system; nor are they likely to dismantle the underlying racist and classist foundation on which public schools in New Orleans are built. They are focused only on one aspect of this system: its lack of democratic representation, accountability, and inclusion. My recommendations should increase engagement—and, potentially, trust—among important stakeholders who have been excluded. Reformers see themselves as acting on behalf of parents, neighbors, and members of the community—such as those who fought for John Mac High School—but they ignore these folks' stated desires. The Black community is right to be frustrated, resigned, and angry and certainly to distrust those who put and keep the reforms in place.

There is an opportunity now to begin to undo some of the damage, but there is no indication that those who govern schools in New Orleans are willing to consider relinquishing their power. In 2020, State Senator Joseph Bouie, of New Orleans, introduced a bill that would have required the elected board to vote on a superintendent's recommendations regarding charter extensions, renewals, and revocations according to normal board policies on vote thresholds, which generally require simple majorities. This would have revoked existing law that allows a board to overrule a superintendent only with a supermajority. It is a perfectly reasonable policy that mirrors the way other cities govern, but when it came to democracy in New Orleans schools, the bill passed unanimously in the Senate but stalled in the House Education Committee, where only five people voted affirmatively. As with the previous state legislation that transformed school governance in New Orleans, the local delegation was split: only one member of the New Orleans delegation on the committee supported the bill, Gary Carter, while the other two voted it down.

The recommendations I make in this conclusion would be only the beginning. Ultimately, a truly democratic system will require reformers to listen and give up some of their control. They should trust the model they put in place and understand that, fundamentally, no undemocratic, exclusionary educational system can have high educational outcomes and real equality of opportunity. The inclusion of alternative perspectives will only strengthen the system and, in turn, contribute to greater student learning. Reformers should be humble about what their reforms have achieved and what is still left to be done and understand after all this time that they do not have all the answers. If they continue to attempt to engineer every outcome so that it is acceptable to the folks who have the most advantages, reformers are asking parents and community members to organize against them. Resistance and social movement organization have increased in New Orleans and other cities with neoliberal reforms. One study finds that in the wake of mass school closures, residents of the predominantly Black neighborhoods in Chicago that bore the brunt of closures, as compared with those in neighborhoods that had fewer closures, increased their attendance at political meetings, mobilized in support of ballot measures to stop future closures, and turned out at higher rates to vote in the subsequent election. In sum, when people felt they had been ignored and their interests were not in the forefront for policy makers, "groups that previously participated at the lowest rates [went] on to participate at the highest rates on community issues that matter to them."[57]

In addition to traditional political participation, citizens can be pushed only so far before they begin to work from the outside. Carrie Sampson and Melanie Bertrand demonstrate that Black community members sometimes find success by subverting the exclusionary rules that govern public bodies, such as refusing to stop talking in the face of short time limits for public comment at school board meetings.[58] These community members referred to their behavior as civil disobedience. Increasingly, grassroots organizations are actively pushing back against these policies. The history of resistance among Black community activists, well before there were charter schools, demonstrates a long-term commitment to racial and social justice in education. Such organizations can be successful in cultivating political power among race-class subjugated communities under certain conditions, such as when people who make up these communities take leading roles; there is adequate funding for resistance-focused organizations; or the media provide a platform for their views.[59]

As other cities look to the New Orleans model, they should recognize that it does not take a man-made or natural disaster to make meaningful reforms to education governance. The sweeping post-Katrina reforms were built on years of incremental change in both policies and rhetoric. Other cities should recognize that the process of excluding the vast majority of the Black community from the planning and execution of such dramatic reform has a serious impact on democracy—without the dramatic improvement in education outcomes that is often promised. Excluding parents, teachers, and community members in favor a privatized system does not—by itself—improve opportunities for most kids. Instead, as educators have argued all along, investments in the whole lives of children is what can move the needle on educational opportunity. Until society decides to make real investments in an equitable education system, there will always be disparities in achievement and weak democratic practices.

Appendix

Information about Data Collection

CHAPTER 2

State Data Collection

These data were retrieved from the Louisiana State Legislature's online archive, which documents the state's legislative history since 1997. For every legislative session, I sorted legislation by the committee in which it was introduced and compiled a data set of every piece of legislation that was referred to the House and Senate committees on K–12 education. I documented the entire legislative history of each bill or resolution, including the timeline of every bill. The data set includes every date indicating when legislation was introduced, referred to a committee, passed or failed during a vote, and passed into law or vetoed by the governor. It also includes the individual votes within the committees and on the floor of the House and Senate and the amendments made to the text of the legislation. In addition, the data include the name, party, and district of every legislator who introduced the bill or resolution, as well as the summaries that accompanied each piece of legislation.

Coding

Every piece of legislation was coded numerically according to its K–12 education topic (1–21). The categories of K–12 education legislation included charter, voucher/choice, Recovery School District (RSD), standards, curriculum, Louisiana Education Assessment Program (LEAP)/student assessment, special education, textbooks/supplies, student behavior/discipline, student health, extracurricular activities, transportation, teachers, local superintendents, school employees (other than teachers), school boards, taxes, the state Department of Education/Board of Elementary and Secondary Education (BESE) and state superintendent, school attendance, and other (i.e., those that do not fit into the categories listed).

I also coded each piece of legislation by type (bill, resolution, and concurrent resolution) and created several dummy variables to indicate whether a piece of legislation was initially referred out of a committee or made it to the House or Senate floor for a vote. There is also a 0–1 variable to indicate whether it became law and a variable (1–3) for the party of each legislator. Legislators were coded according to their party identification at the time the legislation was being introduced to account for party switching when needed. I created a 0–1 variable to denote whether the legislator represented a district that included parts of Orleans Parish.

CHAPTER 3

Content Analysis of the Times-Picayune

I used the online archive of *Times-Picayune* available through the Tulane University library to create a database of every editorial and op-ed about public education in New Orleans, including state policies that were targeted at New Orleans over a ten-year period, from August 29, 2005 (when Katrina struck), to October 4, 2015. I then coded each as positive, negative, neutral, or mixed in tone. A positive editorial was one that promoted the reforms around accountability or school choice or the actors who created or implemented the reforms. A negative editorial criticized the reforms or actors. A neutral editorial merely provided information, with no clear opinion. A mixed editorial provided both negative and positive commentary.

CHAPTER 4

Charter Board Survey

I conducted an online survey of charter board members in late 2015 and early 2016. Because there is no universal list of board members, I relied on the names provided on charter boards' websites to create the list of respondents. Only 7 percent of websites failed to provide the names of their board members, so there were a total of 342 names on my list. Only five of the forty-one boards provided email addresses for each board member; I was ultimately able to find a working email address for 164 board members (48%). Of them, thirty-three people completed the survey—20 percent of those successfully contacted, but only 10 percent of all board members. The response rate of those who were successfully reached is similar to that of the 2009 surveys by the National School Boards Association (23.6% [see Hess and Meeks 2010]) and Michael Ford and Douglas Ihrke (2015, 2016) (18%). Juliet Squire and Allison Crean Davis (2016) had a higher response rate (51%) but were able to offer financial incentives ($150 donations to the ten boards with the highest response rates) that I could not afford. Respondents were contacted first on November 18, 2015, then again on December 8, and finally on January 31, 2016.

The respondents came from each of the main three charter authorizers. The BESE schools were overrepresented with 12 percent of the charter boards authorized by the BESE and 24.4 of respondents on a BESE-authorized board, and Orleans Parish School Board (OPSB) schools were underrepresented, with 39 percent of the charter boards authorized by the OPSB and 26.9 percent of respondents in an OPSB-authorized school or network. The survey exactly represents the RSD, as 48.7 percent of charter boards are

TABLE A.1. DEMOGRAPHIC COMPARISON OF SAMPLE AND ONLINE
INFORMATION OF NEW ORLEANS CHARTER BOARD MEMBERS

	Unweighted Sample	Weighted Sample	Online Photos, Biographies
% White	78.6	59.1	59
% Nonwhite	17.9	40.9	41
% Female	53.6	45.5	46
% Bachelor's degree or higher	82.1	84.8	78*
% Employed in law	26.9	21.2	17.7
% Employed in banking/finance	23.1	18.2	15.8
% Employed in K–12 education	15.4	12.1	8.2

* Based on biographies that explicitly mentioned graduating from a specific college or university. The actual percentage of members with a bachelor's degree is likely higher.

in the state takeover district and 48.8 percent of respondents were on an RSD-authorized board. Given that the BESE and OPSB are quite similar in terms of the types of schools each has authorized, and both are quite different in this respect from the RSD-authorized schools and networks, this over- and underrepresentation is not significantly problematic. For example, schools authorized by the BESE and OPSB tend be higher-performing and have a higher percentage of white students, while those authorized by the RSD are more likely to be predominantly Black and lower-performing.

Given the low response rate, I supplemented the survey with research into the demographic characteristics of charter board members. I coded the race and gender of each member by using photos located on schools' websites or elsewhere. I could not identify the race or ethnicity of only 6.7 percent of the individual members because no picture was available, the picture was indeterminate, or there were multiple people of different races with the same first and last name. I also used the members' biographies provided by charter boards to code their occupation. Nineteen boards (46%) provided short biographies.

Table A.1 compares the demographic profiles of the survey sample and the information from these online sources. In terms of gender, education, and occupation, the sample and the online information are comparable. The survey included a lower percentage of nonwhite respondents than the analysis with online photos. Because the online analysis is as close to a list of the population of charter board members as possible, I use this information to weight the survey data according to the racial composition of this population. The weighted sample also more closely resembles the population on gender and other characteristics. In any case, I caution against making broad conclusions based solely on the survey, which is why other types of data were collected.

Compliance Data
I collected the information related to charter board compliance with public documents from the boards' websites in January 2017. I coded whether charter boards provided the dates, times, and places of all meetings, including committee meetings; whether boards

TABLE A.2. LOUISIANA LEGAL REQUIREMENTS FOR CHARTER BOARD PUBLIC INFORMATION	
Open Meetings La. R.S. 42	All public bodies . . . shall give written public notice of their regular meetings . . . at the beginning of each calendar year. Such notice shall include the dates, times, and places of such meetings. Such notice shall include the agenda, date, time, and place of the meeting. Written public notice given by all public bodies . . . shall include, but need not be limited to: Posting a copy of the notice . . . no less than twenty-four hours . . . before the scheduled time of the meeting. If the public body has a website, additionally by providing notice via the internet on the website of the public body for no less than twenty-four hours . . . immediately preceding the meeting.
Custodian of Records C.B. Forgotson Act La. R.S. 44:33.1	Public bodies shall make the contact information of the custodian available to the public in a manner that will allow a member of the public to quickly determine the appropriate person to whom a public records request should be submitted, including placing this contact information on the internet.
Public Documents La. R.S. 42 And La. R.S. 44	All public bodies shall keep written minutes of all of their open meetings. The minutes shall be public records and shall be available within a reasonable time after the meeting. . . . If the public body has a website, the public body shall post on its website a copy of the minutes made available . . . and shall maintain the copy of those minutes on the website for at least three months after the posting.
Requirements for Meeting Minutes R.S. 42:20	Minutes must include the date, time and location of the meeting; the attendance or absence of each member; the substance of all matters decided; the individual votes of each member; and if applicable, the reason for moving into executive session and the voting records of individual members with respect to moving into executive session.

and their committees provided an agenda for the last scheduled meeting; and whether the previous three months of meeting minutes were posted online. Each board is also required to list the name and contact information for its custodian of public records. Meeting minutes are required to include the time, date, and location of the meeting; the attendance or absence of each member; and the individual votes for each member on each item on which there is a vote. In each case, a board was deemed compliant or noncompliant. Table A.2 lists the text of these Louisiana laws. I created five indexes to indicate each board's level of compliance or transparency: (1) availability of required main meeting information (date, time, location); (2) availability of required main board documents (agenda, minutes, custodian of records); (3) availability of committee meeting and documents information (meeting schedule, agenda, minutes); (4) availability of

TABLE A.3. UNIVERSITY OF NEW ORLEANS QUALITY OF LIFE SURVEYS, 1997–2018

Year	Dates	Number	Margin of Error
1997*	March 11–19	452 Black registered voters in Orleans Parish	4.7%
1998	October 14–27	442 registered voters in Orleans Parish	4.6%
2000	March 17–April 4	425 registered voters in Orleans Parish	4.8%
2002	March 17–April 4	403 registered voters in Orleans Parish	5.0%
2004	March 22–April 1, April 12	400 registered voters in Orleans Parish	5.0%
2012	February 23–29	301 registered voters in Orleans Parish	5.7%
2013	October 19–30	301 registered voters in Orleans Parish	5.7%
2016	March 5–17	403 registered voters in Orleans Parish	4.9%
2018	October 17–November 5	500 registered voters in Orleans Parish	4.4%

* The 1997 survey was "Black Attitudes in New Orleans: Crime, Safety and the Quality of Life." All other surveys were "Quality of Life Surveys."

nonrequired member information (names, emails, photos, biographies); and (5) inclusion of required elements in meeting minutes (time, data, location, attendance).

Meeting Minutes Analysis
In addition to noting whether the minutes complied with state laws, I uploaded meeting minutes for all the main boards (no committees) from July 2016 to January 2017 to the content analysis program Dedoose. There were a total of 249 meeting minutes from thirty-eight boards during this period. I used the minutes to examine the votes held by each board and the items of discussion. I conducted an initial line-by-line coding to identify categories for the items on which boards voted and the issues they discussed. Dedoose then allowed for the use of keywords within each category to organize and determine the board priorities.

CHAPTER 5

University of New Orleans Quality of Life Surveys
I did not have access to raw data files for the University of New Orleans Quality of Life surveys and relied on reports available online, at https://scholarworks.uno.edu/src

_pubs/?utm_source=scholarworks.uno.edu%2Fsrc_pubs%2F24&utm_medium=PDF &utm_campaign=PDFCoverPages. The original reports from 1986, 1992, and 1996 were not available, so I relied on information in other reports. The mode for each survey was a telephone poll (Table A.3).

Kaiser Family Foundation Polls

The Kaiser Family Foundation (KFF) shared its raw data files with me, so the results presented are based on my analyses of these data.

2006: This in-person survey was conducted door to door from September 12 to November 13, 2006. Interviews were conducted in English and Spanish among 1,504 randomly selected adults age eighteen and older residing in Orleans, Jefferson, Plaquemines, and St. Bernard parishes. The sample design was a stratified area probability sample in each of the fourteen census tracts in Orleans Parish, including an oversample in Orleans. The margin of sampling error for the full sample was +/- 5 percent.

2008: The survey was conducted from March 5 to April 28, 2008, among 1,294 randomly selected adults age eighteen and older residing in Orleans Parish. Interviewing was conducted using a mixed-mode design that included by telephone, on the internet, and face to face. Interviews were conducted in English and Spanish. The margin of sampling error for the full sample was +/- 3 percent.

2010: The survey was conducted from May 26 to June 27, 2010, in English and Spanish via landline telephone and cell phone among 1,528 randomly selected adults age eighteen and older residing in Orleans Parish. The margin of sampling error for the full sample was +/- 3 percent.

2015: The survey was conducted from June 2 to July 5, 2015, among 1,517 randomly selected adults age eighteen and older residing in Orleans Parish. Interviews were conducted via landline and cell phone in English and Spanish. The margin of sampling error for the full sample was +/- 3 percent.

Cowen Institute Surveys

I had access to raw files for 2011 and 2013, but the data from other years are based on reports that are available on the Cowen Institute's website.

2009: The Cowen Institute commissioned Market Research Insight to conduct a phone survey of six hundred randomly selected registered voters in Orleans Parish from November 3–14, 2009. It also oversampled three hundred parents with children enrolled in public school. The regular sample had a margin of error of +/- 4.1 percent, and the oversample had a sampling error of +/- 5.7 percent.

2010: Market Research Insight conducted the survey on October 18–21, 2010, by phone among five hundred randomly selected registered voters in Orleans Parish. The margin of sampling error for the full sample was +/- 5 percent.

2011: Market Research Insight conducted the survey. The dates and margin of error are not given in the report. The sample consisted of 349 randomly selected registered voters who were also parents of public school students in Orleans Parish.

2013: Market Research Insight conducted the survey by phone on March 15–25, 2013. It consisted of two surveys, one with 294 randomly selected registered voters in Orleans Parish and another with 250 parents of school-age children enrolled in either public or private schools. No sampling error was given in the report.

2014: The poll was conducted by phone by the firm BDPC on May 1–3, 2014; 602 likely voters responded to the poll (a "likely voter" is a registered voter who voted in four of the previous ten elections or a voter who was newly registered since the November 2012 election). The margin of error was +/- 4 percent.

2015: The poll surveyed a sample of six hundred randomly selected registered voters in New Orleans over landline and cell phones on April 7–14, 2005. The margin of error was +/- 4.1 percent.

2016: Market Research Insight conducted the survey by landline and cell phone from March 21 to April 5, 2016. A sample of six hundred voters was randomly drawn from a list of registered voters. The sampling error was +/- 4 percent.

2017: Market Research Insight conducted the survey by landline and cell phone in April 2017. It had a sample of seven hundred randomly selected registered voters. The sampling error was +/- 4 percent.

2018: Market Research Insight conducted the survey by landline and cell phone in March and April 2018. It had a sample of seven hundred randomly selected registered voters. The sampling error was +/- 4 percent.

2018 Survey

I contracted with a local firm, Focus Group Testing (FGT) to survey the parents of schoolchildren in its database. These respondents had self-selected into this firm's database to be called on to participate in focus groups and surveys. Approximately 180 parents responded to my online survey, conducted on March 13–20, 2018. Thirty-four percent were white and 51.6 percent were Black. Nearly one-third of those surveyed were single parents, most of whom were women: 77.4 percent of those surveyed were mothers or other female caretakers. Two-thirds of the sample had children in public schools, while 37 percent had kids in private school. This does not total 100 percent because there were families in which some children were in public schools and others were in private schools.

Focus Groups

My colleague Mirya Holman and I conducted seven focus groups from August 15 to August 24, 2017, interviewing a total of sixty-one people (eighteen years old or older, nonvulnerable populations). Two groups included only parents of current public school children; one group had children in a private school; and one group had no kids. Other focus groups were mixed in terms of parents: one was composed of first-generation immigrants; another, of folks who lived in New Orleans before Katrina; and the last, of people who had moved to the city after the hurricane.

FGT recruited subjects from its database, then called respondents and invited them to participate in a focus group about New Orleans schools and local politics. We paid each participant $75 at the conclusion of the focus group. Each group met for approximately two hours. Participants completed a survey when they arrived, and when everyone was finished, we began the focus group discussions with the same set of questions for each group. The survey included questions about their demographic characteristics, political interest, trust, voting behavior, and civic engagement. We recorded the discussions and hired a professional transcription service, which provided detailed transcriptions of the conversations.

CHAPTER 6

2017 Survey

Mirya Holman and I conducted a two-wave panel survey during the New Orleans mayoral election in 2017. The survey features two waves of survey participation via FGT, which maintains a database of participants for focus groups that includes such demographic information about participants as their household income, zip code, voter registration status, and home ownership. This is an "opt-in" database: participants registered on their own as potential participants in focus groups in the construction of the database. FGT provided access to its database of participants' email addresses. Benchmarking of the racial and gender breakdown database against the New Orleans voting population demonstrates a close match to the electorate in local elections.

Participants were recruited via a series of short emails asking them for their opinions, with the option of winning one of ten $100 Amazon gift cards. Recruitment for the first wave began eighteen days before the general election and ended as early voting began. In this wave, 525 respondents completed the entirety of the survey. Recruitment for the second wave of the survey started fourteen days before the runoff election, and 483 respondents participated in it. It should be noted that vote choices in this convenience sample were closer to the eventual outcome of both the general and the runoff election than published pre-election polls. While other public polls reported a very close race, this survey indicated in both cases that City Councilor LaToya Cantrell was a solid front-runner in the days just before the elections.

Notes

INTRODUCTION

Epigraph: Altavena et al. 2016.
1. Cook 2015.
2. Flaherty 2008, 30–56.
3. Harris 2020, 6; Moe 2019.
4. Buras 2015; Horowitz 2020; Sanders 2018.
5. Rosario-Moore 2015, 245.
6. Dixson et al. 2015.
7. When John Mac reopened in 2006, students formed the Fyre Youth Squad in response to what they viewed as a prisonlike atmosphere at the school (see Tuzzolo and Hewitt 2006). Beginning in September 2007, members of the Downtown Neighborhood Improvement Association, a community group working with the students and families at John Mac, tried to work with the RSD to apply for private foundation grants to help restore the school.
8. See Buras 2015.
9. Barr had recently left the Green Dot charter schools, the association he founded in Los Angeles, where he had made a name for himself, when Green Dot led a hostile takeover of a high school in the Watts neighborhood.
10. Dreilinger 2013a.
11. Hasselle 2014.
12. Dreilinger 2014c.
13. Stern 2018, 3.
14. Orr 1999, 9.
15. Dixson et al. 2015, 289.
16. McDermott 1999, 6.
17. Rosario-Moore 2015, 245.

18. Mettler and Soss 2004.

19. Skocpol 1992, 58.

20. The racial system of power in New Orleans has a long, complicated history, in which Black elites have worked with white politicians and business elites, largely at the expense of working-class Blacks. One scholar describes the situation this way: "While the vast majority of dispossessed citizens in post-Katrina New Orleans have been black—a clear proof of the racist effects of these policies—the beneficiaries have included a handful of African Americans who embraced their identities as neoliberal politicians or members of the bourgeoisie over that of their blackness" (BondGraham 2011, 287). This book will not delve into these complexities more deeply than to point out that supporters and opponents of the education reforms do not neatly fall on racial lines.

21. Engel 2000, 7.

CHAPTER 1

Epigraph: Quoted in Gewertz 2005b.

1. This is not the royal "we." I watched from my in-laws' living room in New Jersey after evacuating with my flip-flops, wedding photos, and Frito Lay, my little white poofy dog.

2. Rachel Breunlin and Helen A. Regis (2006, 748) describe these days succinctly and accurately: "For displaced New Orleans residents desperately watching television and seeking information, the disaster of the hurricane and the flood was overtopped by the mediated disaster, as we watched and listened to our city being objectified and distorted by journalists, armed with Google Digital Earth, live satellite feeds, and little local knowledge about the people, places, and communities that make New Orleans home."

3. Hoff 2005.

4. Douglas Harris (2020, 54) writes, "Within days of the hurricane, and probably even before the last person evacuated, [Leslie Jacobs] was leading private discussions about a major overhaul of the school system."

5. Cooper 2005.

6. Associated Press 2005, emphasis added.

7. Nobles 2018. The OPSB will phase out the direct-run school until all current students have graduated or transferred, by 2022 at the latest.

8. For an excellent discussion of economic recovery, see Schneider 2018.

9. Ferguson 2018; Harris 2020.

10. Louisiana Department of Education, 2004–2005 Orleans Parish District Accountability Report Card, https://www.louisianabelieves.com/data/reportcards.

11. A parish in Louisiana is the same unit as a county in other states.

12. U.S. Department of Education 2005b.

13. Cowen Institute 2007.

14. Michener 2019, 428.

15. Thevenot 2004a.

16. Burns and Thomas 2015.

17. Robelen 2005.

18. The committee consisted of Assistant Secretary of Education Tom Luce, who left public service to work for the Broad Foundation, a pro-reform private foundation that funds charter schools and alternative teacher certification; Chancellor Alex Johnson of Delgado Community College; the Reverend William Maestri, superintendent of New Orleans archdiocesan schools; Ron Forman, president and chief executive of the Audubon Nature Institute; Mark Granger, president and general manager of the local NBC television affiliate; William Roberti, managing director of Alvarez and Marsal, the "financial development" company that had been hired to review the OPSB's finances prior to Katrina; Mary Garton, the executive director of Teach for America of Greater New Orleans; David Waller, an executive at IBM; Kevin Hall, chief operating officer of the Broad Foundation; James Shelton, education program director at the Bill and Melinda Gates Foundation, which has donated to dozens of pro-charter and anti-teacher causes; Neari Warner, the former president of Grambling State University; Cecil Picard, superintendent of the Louisiana Department of Education (LDOE); Carol Wallin, deputy superintendent of the LDOE; Linda Johnson, a member of BESE; Leslie Jacobs, a member of BESE and architect of state education policies for more than a decade; Phyllis Landrieu, the pro-reform president of the OPSB; and Mary Laurie, principal of O. Perry Walker High School. The committee was headed by Scott Cowen, president of Tulane University (see Torregano and Shannon 2009).

19. Cowen argued that future school boards "should concern themselves solely with oversight and accountability," not involve themselves in battles over contracts and other matters best left to school administrators. The central office should consist of only about "four or five assistants" to the superintendent. Charter schools, the report contended, were a good way to "restart" the system but should not be a long-term solution (Ritea 2006a).

20. U.S. Department of Education 2005a.

21. Darwin BondGraham (2011, 280–281) writes that there was "an interdependent and often cooperative relationship between elites in government and foundations, steered by business leaders, all to carry out a commonly understood reconstruction project . . . to create new opportunities for capitalist accumulation in previously public sectors of the region's political economy." For example, the Heritage Foundation, a conservative think tank in Washington, DC, issued a report that repackaged its longtime education agenda as "disaster recovery." It included portable state, local, and federal funds that would travel with students to any public or private school (i.e., school vouchers); tax incentives for private education service providers; and public-private partnerships to rebuild school facilities (Meese et al. 2005).

22. Ritea 2005a.

23. Gewertz 2005a.

24. Ritea 2005b.

25. Alcée Fortier High School was located in the heart of affluent Uptown and walking distance from Tulane University. Named for a French Creole Tulane University professor of Romance languages who was a known white supremacist, it had been neglected for decades. It lists a former Louisiana governor (David Treen), a U.S. senator (Russell Long), and the acclaimed novelist John Kennedy Toole as alumni. In 2003, it made national headlines when its valedictorian failed to pass the graduation exit exam *five* times. That year, only 125 students graduated of 220 who began the year as seniors;

at least thirty had the grades but failed the graduation exam. Lusher Elementary School, located just a few blocks from Fortier, required students outside its narrowly defined borders to pass an admissions test the school guarded as if it were a crown jewel. Lusher is named for a former Confederate tax collector-turned-state superintendent of education who argued that education was necessary only for whites so they "would be properly prepared to maintain the supremacy of the White race." One hundred years after this statement, Lusher Elementary was one of the few public elementary schools that affluent white families would consider for their children. The OPSB's Vice President Lourdes Moran, coincidentally also a Lusher parent, pushed to allow the school to take over Fortier. Moran noted that she hoped Lusher would not create an application-based high school at the facility, but that she would "have to trust them that they're going to do the right thing" (Anderson 1988, 27; Morris 2017; Rasheed 2003; Ritea 2005f; Robert Mills Lusher Charter School n.d.). In 2021, NOLA Public Schools (the unified district) announced it would rename the buildings that bear the names of Fortier and Lusher because of their actions and writings indicating their clear white supremacy beliefs (NOLA Public Schools 2021). Because NOLA-PS oversees facilities, it has the authority to rename buildings. The charter board, however, has to approve renaming the school, which it has not done.

26. They included provisions that required public schools to have approval from the school's staff and parents before it could convert to a charter and provisions around eligibility for enrollment in charters and timelines for the application and approval of charters.

27. This neighborhood, located in Orleans Parish on the West Bank of the Mississippi River, did not flood and had minimal hurricane damage (see Ritea 2005d).

28. Ritea 2005d.

29. Other OPSB members and Mayor Ray Nagin discussed opening the undamaged East Bank schools as charters (Ritea 2005c).

30. Ritea 2005e.

31. Act No. 35, https://www.legis.la.gov/Legis/BillInfo.aspx?i=103804.

32. Duplessis is now president of the Louisiana Federation for Children, a project of the American Federation for Children, which promotes school choice and the state's voucher program.

33. Research in other cities finds similar opinions on the part of local officials (Morel 2018; Orr 1999).

34. Ritea 2005g.

35. Zanders 2020.

36. Harden 2015b.

37. Lindblom 1959.

38. Schattschneider 1935, 288.

39. Olson 1965.

40. Hill et al. 2000, ix.

41. Rich 1996.

42. Lay and Stokes-Brown 2009.

43. Fairclough 2008; Germany 2007.

44. Stone et al. 2001, 49.

45. Wolbrecht and Hartney 2014.

46. Specifically, the players included conservative foundations such as the Adolph Coors Foundation and John M. Olin Foundation, which promoted many free-market-enterprise causes, including school choice; right-wing and libertarian think tanks such as the Heritage Foundation, the Hudson Institute, the American Enterprise Institute, and the Cato Institute, which sought to break up public school "monopolies"; a growing cohort of young conservative lawmakers such as Newt Gingrich, John Engler, and George W. Bush and "New Democrats" such as Bill Clinton and Mary Landrieu, who sought to use fears about public education to further their political ambitions; the rising Religious Right movement, which believed that public schools had begun to promote "secular humanism"; business entrepreneurs such as William Kolberg of the National Alliance of Business and organizations such as the Business Roundtable and the Business Coalition for Education Reform, which argued that young people were not being appropriately trained for the contemporary economy; and educational conservatives such as Chester Finn, Diane Ravitch, and Lamar Alexander, who argued that excessive federal interventions promoting equity had lowered standards and subverted the educational mission of public schools. Civil rights groups included the Education Trust, the National Association for the Advancement of Colored People, and the National Council of La Raza (see McGuinn 2006; Rhodes 2012).

47. Stone et al. 2001, 13. See also Hess 1999.

48. Moe 2019, 3.

49. Harris 2020, 50.

50. Osborne 2017, 5.

51. Perry and Schwam-Baird 2011.

52. Baumgartner and Jones 1993; Kingdon 1984.

53. Kingdon 1993, 41.

54. Jones 1994.

55. Baumgartner et al. 2014, 64.

56. Schattschneider 1935, 288.

57. Stone 1998, 1.

58. Harris 2020, 60.

59. Patashnik 2008.

60. Baumgartner and Jones 1993, 61.

61. Kingdon 1993, 41.

62. hooks 1989, 113.

CHAPTER 2

Epigraphs: "Was Hurricane Katrina the Best Thing to Happen to New Orleans Schools?" 2010; Ullo 2006.

1. Breunlin and Regis 2006.

2. Stern 2018, 9.

3. Cook and Dixson 2013, 1250.

4. DeVore 2015, 14.

5. Logsdon 2008.

6. DeVore 2015, 123.

7. Baker 1996.

8. Germany 2007.

9. Burns and Thomas 2004.

10. Fairclough 2008.

11. Buras 2015.

12. Morel 2018, 6.

13. Chandler 1989.

14. For more on this school's struggle, see Buras 2013.

15. Thevenot and Rasheed 2004b.

16. For good overviews of these policies, see McGuinn 2006; National Research Council 1996; Rhodes 2012.

17. Mossberger 1999; Shipan and Volden 2006.

18. Hurst et al. 2003.

19. Moe 2012.

20. Burns 2003; Morel 2018.

21. Lipman 2011.

22. Morel 2018, 13.

23. Stone 1998.

24. Mirel 1993; Vander Weele 1994.

25. Kozol 1991; Oakes 1987.

26. Chubb and Moe 1990; Finn 1991.

27. Patashnik 2008, 20.

28. Baumgartner and Jones 1993.

29. Bridges 1984; Erie 1988; Gelfand 1975; Goodnow 1904; Kantor 1988; Riordon 1994, 59–60; Wiebe 1967.

30. Einstein and Glick 2017; Schragger 2016.

31. Dewan 2015.

32. Weir et al. 2005.

33. Burns et al. 2009, 1; Allard et al. 1998.

34. Gamm and Kousser 2013.

35. Morel 2018, chap. 5.

36. I am not the first to point out that the hurricane did not mark the beginning of the reform movement. Peter Burns and Matthew Thomas (2015, 103) write that education policy "did not so much take a new direction after Katrina as Katrina accelerated a change already in motion." Huriya Jabbar (2015a, 756) also writes, "While the post-Katrina reforms dramatically transformed the educational landscape in New Orleans, many of the features we identify as key to the 2005 reforms were actually initiated before the hurricane."

37. Myers 1995. Picard served in both houses of the Louisiana State Legislature from 1975 to 1996, leaving when he was appointed Louisiana state superintendent of education, where he served until his death in 2007. Before entering public service, he was a teacher, a coach, and the principal of Maurice High School.

38. "L[ouisiana] Will Get $336,000 Grant to Support Charters" 1995.

39. "Mike Foster Still Favors Acing BESE" 1995. In 1997, Foster tried again. Republican Representative Bob Barton (Bossier City) wanted to allow the governor to appoint the state superintendent of education and all members of the BESE. The bill passed committee by one vote and over the objections of New Orleans representatives. It failed, however, to pass the full Legislature.

40. Myers 1996a.

41. According to Jacobs, she got involved in education when her family's insurance brokerage company partnered with an elementary school near a now demolished housing project. School administrators told her they needed funds for a kindergarten graduation because it was the only graduation many students would ever have. She later won a seat on the OPSB and became convinced that only the state could turn around the failing New Orleans school system (Ruth 2008).

42. Myers 1996a. According to this report, teachers' unions and school board representatives said that "they ha[d] been excluded from the planning process of the transition team" and "ha[d]n't received copies of reports from the group [and weren't] included in discussions."

43. In the Senate committee that took up the bill, four Republicans voted to approve the plan and two Democrats opposed it. When it failed in the full Senate, the New Orleans delegation was split: two senators (one Democrat and one Republican) voted to approve and four voted to oppose (see Myers 1996b).

44. Myers 1997e.

45. Myers 1997a.

46. Myers 1997d.

47. Schlichtman and McMahon 1997.

48. Myers 1997b, 1997c.

49. After the legislative session, the BESE "revamped" the state's standardized tests, claiming they were not rigorous enough. The governor's education adviser, Louann Bierlein, argued that the new accountability system needed to begin by raising standards. Louisiana's Testing Commission recommended using five "proficiency levels" rather than the existing pass/fail system (Myers 1997f).

50. All information about methodology is in the Appendix.

51. Henig 2013; Mehta 2013; Wolbrecht and Hartney 2014.

52. This law reduced the requirements for charters to serve at-risk students by requiring them to enroll at least 85 percent of the average number of at-risk students from the districts in which the charter school enrolled its students rather than from the district in which the school was located. Because some charters enroll statewide, this means in practice that these schools can be located in places with high numbers of at-risk students but have to ensure only that they serve a similar percentage of these students as are served at the state level.

53. Naomi Favre and Ed Murray opposed the law.

54. The SPS would not be converted to an A–F grading system until 2010, so "failing" schools corresponded to a cut point somewhere along the range. The range and the cut points changed several times over the years, making it difficult to trace changes in performance over time.

55. In 2001, Representative Renee Gill Pratt (New Orleans) introduced a resolution that would have provided that LEAP tests could be used only for diagnostic purposes and that the fourth- and eighth-grade tests would be only one factor in determining advancement to the next grade. It failed.

56. The program offered $3,000 bonuses for the first four years to newly certified teachers in these subjects.

57. Act 9, https://www.legis.la.gov/Legis/BillInfo.aspx?s=03RS&b=ACT9&sbi=y. These conditions were: (1) when the local board fails to present a plan to reconstitute

the failed school; (2) when the local board presents a reconstitution plan that is unacceptable to the state board; (3) when the local board fails to comply with the terms of the approved reconstitution plan; or (4) when the local board has been labeled an academically unacceptable school for four consecutive years. Meeting one of the four conditions sufficed to get the school transferred.

58. Sentell 2003.

59. "Failing Schools Need Makeover" 2003.

60. Burns and Thomas 2015, 69.

61. Cooper 1997.

62. Thevenot and Rasheed 2004a.

63. Nossiter 2004; Thevenot 2004d.

64. Laborde 2004.

65. Thevenot 2004b.

66. Can you imagine his relief, having resigned just four months before Katrina?

67. "Fresh Start for Schools" 2004.

68. Thevenot and Rasheed 2004b.

69. Gail Glapion chose not to run. Cynthia Cade replaced her, defeating a former school board member who had been suspended when he was convicted of tax evasion. In the ever forgiving city, Dwight McKenna was elected coroner in 2017.

70. Board members included Una Anderson, Cynthia Cade, Heidi Lovett Daniels, Jimmy Fahrenholtz, Phyllis Landrieu Lourdes Moran, and Torin Sanders.

71. Thevenot 2004c. Sanders's supporters included Joe Canizaro, Leslie Jacobs, Bob Reily, Gary Solomon, and their family members.

72. Capochina 2005.

73. Burns and Thomas 2015, 75.

74. Bulkley 2010, 23.

CHAPTER 3

Epigraphs: Anderson 2011; Ritea 2007.

1. Patashnik 2008, 23.

2. In 2015, the Choice Foundation honored Huger's "contributions to the charter movement, the school choice movement, and the foundation" with a ribbon cutting at Paul L. Dunbar Charter School's James M. Huger Gymnasium.

3. Waldman 2007.

4. Ritea 2006c. Huger asked, "Did any principal pre-Katrina ever wake up worried about if they were going to meet enrollment or whether their expenses were too high? They were never empowered with consequences. It's that very force that inspires people to strive for excellence. If you have choice and you allow schools to fail, that's not a bad thing because then consumers choose the ones that won't fail."

5. Huger told *The Atlantic* that he would have preferred for his schools to have selective admissions so he could screen applicants for grade point averages and test scores. He did not see these, I suppose, as market distortions.

6. Ritea 2006d. Students at the McDonogh 42 Charter School were told they would have to find another school because the BESE had revoked the Treme Charter School Association's charter two weeks before school started. Special-education and

high school math and science positions were the hardest to fill. RSD officials considered hiring uncertified teachers who had college degrees in the subject in which they would teach.

7. Dunbar 2006; Ritea 2006e. Others delayed their opening by days or weeks due to construction delays, while several pre-Katrina schools opened in alternative locations because their buildings had been destroyed by the flood. Construction delays also led some schools to operate on a "platoon" schedule, in which students from one school would attend from 7 a.m. to 1:15 p.m. and students from another school would begin their day at the site at 1:45 p.m. to 7:30 p.m. School leaders openly worried about "turf battles" in "mixing" students from two different high schools but promised to bring in more security to minimize these problems.

8. Axtman 2006.

9. It took the author a year to replace her Social Security card, birth certificate, marriage certificate, and other essential documents.

10. Ritea 2006b. The parents who were able to return to the city first were doubly advantaged. They not only likely had suffered less damage to their homes or their employment, but they also had the opportunity to enroll their children in the better schools, thus securing the spots of their child and any siblings.

11. Hales 2006. Dr. Hales was my children's pediatrician until he retired.

12. Cowen Institute for Public Education Initiatives 2007, 17.

13. Ibid., 2.

14. Beyond these inequities, many neighborhoods had no public schools in 2007. Schools were initially reopened in the driest parts of the city—a pragmatic decision, perhaps, but not one without serious consequences. The levees along Lake Pontchartrain breached, so those neighborhoods closest to the lake and along the Intracoastal Waterway in eastern New Orleans were the most damaged. The predominantly African American neighborhoods in east New Orleans, in Gentilly, and near the University of New Orleans were heavily damaged and had only a handful of schools in 2007. These neighborhoods remained not only more damaged, but also more affordable than the Uptown and Garden District neighborhoods, where most schools were located. Families were frustrated about the difficulty of getting their children to and from school, as well as about the stalled revitalization more generally in communities that lacked schools.

15. Cowen Institute for Public Education Initiatives 2007, 19.

16. Cowen Institute for Public Education Initiatives 2009.

17. Cowen Institute for Public Education Initiatives 2007, 25. See also Wolf 2011. The OPSB had many fewer schools and students and only those that were higher performing even before Katrina. The OPSB could cap its enrollment, eliminating the overcrowding that was common in RSD schools. It had fewer problems recruiting staff, and its buildings were less damaged. Even RSD charter schools had an easier time recruiting staff, securing better facilities, and earning grants from private foundations than those that were directly run by the RSD.

18. Maloney 2009.

19. McDonogh 35 High School was the last OPSB direct-run school to be chartered. The school opened in 1917 as the first high school for Black youth. Its alumni include the first Black city councilman, the first Black school board member, the first

Black mayor of New Orleans, and the first Black woman elected as a judge in Louisiana. It was a selective high school before Katrina, which helped it maintain higher test scores, and it was not transferred to the RSD. Its building also survived the storm. Even so, it dropped its entrance requirements, and its test scores began to plummet. As one of the last remaining direct-run schools, it suffered dramatic cuts in per pupil spending and routine turnover of school leaders. The OPSB made clear it no longer wanted to operate schools, and in December 2018 the superintendent announced his decision to turn the school over to a charter network (see Clark 2019).

20. Chambers 2006; Fung 2004.

21. Hill et al. 2009, 1.

22. Tyack 1974.

23. There is an inherent tension in contemporary reform rhetoric that seeks simultaneously to highlight the importance of school choice and accountability. The PMM emphasizes accountability, which requires common standards and performance metrics. Free markets for school choice, however, focus on differentiation among options, stressing the idea of parents finding the "best fit" for their child's needs. Governor Jindal commonly stated that "parents are the best accountability system," but in PMM, a district could close popular schools with high enrollment for low performance. Indeed, in New Orleans, the RSD and OPSB have closed several schools over the staunch objections of parents and students.

24. Bulkley 2010, 13.

25. Edward Goetz (2021, 272) is writing about neighborhoods, not schools, but the logic is the same.

26. This is a clear illustration of Campbell's Law, which holds that "the more any quantitative social indicator is used for social decision-making, the more subject it will be to corruption pressures and the more apt it will be to distort and corrupt the social processes it is intended to monitor" (Campbell 1979).

27. Act 9 (2003), https://www.legis.la.gov/Legis/BillInfo.aspx?s=03RS&b=ACT9&sbi =y, reads, "The Recovery School District shall retain jurisdiction over any school transferred to it until the state board, upon the recommendation of the district's administering agency, enters into an agreement with the . . . local public school board . . . from which the school was transferred for its return to the jurisdiction of such school board. . . . When a school in the district is no longer academically unacceptable, the state board shall require the administering agency of the district to seek agreement for the return of the school."

28. Jacobs 2010.

29. Chang 2010.

30. In 2011, State Senator Cynthia Willard-Lewis (New Orleans) sponsored a bill that would have forced the return of the schools to the OPSB, but it failed. Governor Jindal and RSD Superintendent John White argued it was too soon (Vanacore 2011a).

31. Jewson 2014. The RSD had renewed the school's charter for only five years, not seven, and issued the network a notice of breach of contract due to its lack of compliance with OneApp.

32. Vanacore 2011b.

33. Adelson 2015.

34. Robinson 2015.

35. "Few Fireworks in the New Orleans School Board Race" 2020.

36. Ballard 2016.

37. Hertel-Fernandez 2018, 365, emphasis added.

38. Lincove et al. 2018.

39. Patashnik 2008, 30.

40. Strunk et al. 2017.

41. Patashnik 2008, 26. See also McCubbins et al. 1987.

42. New Orleans is not the only city in which charter schools have neglected students with special needs. Early studies that show disparities in charter school enrollment of special needs students include Blackwell 2013; Henig 1999; Ramanathan and Zollers 1999. Kaitlin Anderson's (2017) meta-analysis finds that charter schools serve fewer special needs and English-language learners than traditional public schools, but she concludes there is little evidence that charters are intentionally selecting or pushing out these students. Julian Vasquez Heilig and his colleagues (2016) find that, although there are only modest disparities in segregation statewide in Texas, a local-level descriptive and geospatial analysis shows there are large disparities within large metropolitan areas.

43. Carr 2010a.

44. Vanacore 2014.

45. Dreilinger 2015b.

46. Harden 2015.

47. Dreilinger 2016. The flagged schools were Algiers Technology Academy, Carver Prep, Cohen College Prep, Crescent Leadership Academy, International High, Joseph Craig, Lake Area, Landry-Walker High, Mildred Osborne, and Sophie B. Wright. In 2017, the OPSB warned Robert Russa Moton Charter School twice in one year for failing to identify and serve special needs students, threatening to pull its charter if the issue was not fixed (see Jewson 2017b).

48. Henry 2019; Henry and Dixson 2016.

49. Harris 2020, 190.

50. Henry 2021.

51. Carr 2010b.

52. Hernandez 2019.

53. Barrett et al. 2017.

54. Southern Poverty Law Center 2010.

55. The OPSB and BESE charter schools eventually signed on to use the same policies. In 2013, the schools collectively recommended 451 students for expulsion; about forty cases were disqualified by the screening expert, and the rest went to an expulsion hearing. Sixty-seven percent of those resulted in removing the students from the school. According to Education Research Alliance reports, suspensions and expulsions declined substantially between 2008 and 2013, but significant racial disparities remained. Black students are more likely to be suspended for longer periods of time and across all grades, including kindergarten (see Hernandez 2019; Vanacore 2012b).

56. Vanacore 2012a.

57. Vanacore 2011c.

58. The system was developed by the Stanford University economist Al Roth. The RSD contracted with Roth's Institute for Innovation in Public School Choice to create a

"strategy-proof design" that would elicit only true preferences on the part of parents. The machinery relies on "deferred placements" to prevent families whose first-choice schools are filled from being prevented from enrolling in their second- or third-choice schools. "If the school cannot accommodate all families applying for that grade, then the algorithm makes tentative assignments based on the school's priority groupings and students' lottery numbers. At this point, students who were not assigned to their first-choice school are rejected from that school. Importantly, however, the algorithm leaves all assignment tentative until the final step. This means that students tentatively assigned to their first-choice school might later lose their seats to students who ranked that school lower than first but were rejected from all higher-ranked schools" (Harris et al. 2015).

59. Harris et al. 2015, 19.

60. In 2014, in a debacle that has gone down in the collective memory, about eight hundred parents showed up as instructed on a day in July at an RSD Family Resource Center because their children had not been assigned a school or they were dissatisfied with the placement. The facility was expecting only about one hundred people and ran out of applications almost immediately. These parents—mostly Black mothers and grandmothers—took time off work and maneuvered a poor public transportation system to wait outside in the July heat, only to be told they would have to go to a different facility the next day (Higgins 2014).

61. Dreilinger 2013b.

62. Jabbar 2015b.

63. Jewson 2018a.

64. "Recovery School District and Orleans Parish School Board OneApp Year 4 Main Round Summary" n.d.

65. Williams 2018. The match rates for those outside the transition years are not provided. This rate is not due to a greater number of children applying: although the number of students enrolled in public schools grew 6.7 percent between 2014 and 2018, the number of kindergarten applicants fell 15 percent in that time. Growth has been confined to high schools, where there are too few schools, especially those that are highly rated. See also Hasselle 2019.

66. Schattschneider 1960, 7.

67. Bachrach and Baratz 1962.

68. Charters did not want to share these services with other schools in part to preserve their school cultures (Cowen Institute 2010).

69. Those attending schools outside their neighborhood were given tickets to ride city buses.

70. Dreilinger 2014a.

71. Zimmerman and Vaughan 2013. They also show that the poorest children traveled slightly less than the most affluent kids.

72. Lincove and Valant 2018.

73. Jewson 2017c.

74. Williams and Hasselle 2014.

75. Cowen Institute for Public Education Initiatives 2010. In 2008–2009, the OPSB paid $947 per student on transportation for its direct-run schools; this rose to $1,061 in 2010–2011 and to $1,106 in 2012–2013 (Hasselle and Jewson 2013).

76. Hasselle 2013.

77. Morris 2015b.

78. Lewis 2015.

79. Morris 2015a, emphasis added.

80. The neighborhood preference applied only to kindergarten. Students who moved across the street from the school in fourth grade, for example, did not have priority.

81. Kreitzer and Smith 2018; Schneider and Ingram 1993.

82. Strauss 2013.

83. Graber 1980; Iyengar 1992; Lippmann 1984.

84. Gamson and Modigliani 1989.

85. Chong and Druckman 2007; Iyengar and Kinder 1987.

86. Gilens 1999.

87. Goldstein 2011, 543. See also Malin et al. 2020.

88. Druckman 2001.

89. Entman 1989.

90. Chong and Druckman 2007, 111.

91. Iyengar and Kinder 1987, 63.

92. Malin et al. 2020.

93. Dautrich and Hartley 1999.

94. Gerstl-Pepin 2002.

95. Tamir and Davidson 2011.

96. Wong and Jain 1999.

97. Gerstl-Pepin 2007, 4.

98. See, e.g., Fishman 1980; Johnson et al. 1971; Martindale 1986; Tuchman and Tuchman 1978.

99. On welfare beneficiaries, see Gilens 1999; van Doorn 2015. On immigrants, see Farris and Silber Mohamed 2018.

100. Torin Sanders and Ora Watson said that no schools on the East Bank would likely open that year. Schools in Orleans Parish on the West Bank wanted to open as charter schools with their own district, and these two OPSB members stood in the way (the West Bank refers to an area across the Mississippi River from the city of New Orleans; a small portion of this area is in Orleans Parish).

101. "Time to Make a Move" 2005.

102. They included James Gill, John Maginnis, and Stephanie Grace.

103. Sanders 2005.

104. "Stop Posturing on Schools" 2005.

105. See the Appendix for information about methodology.

106. Three critical editorials in 2010 criticized an employee at Langston Hughes Elementary for stealing from the school. In contrast, in the face of a 2010 lawsuit that provided evidence that charter schools were discriminating against students with special needs, the *Times-Picayune* published a single editorial. And, while it did criticize schools for their treatment of these children, the editors also chose to simultaneously highlight improvements in test scores ("Do Right by Special Ed Kids" 2010).

107. After Paul Vallas was appointed to lead the RSD in 2007, the criticisms largely stopped, even though the problems in the RSD around performance, facilities, and oversight continued for many years.

108. "Unfulfilled Promise for Parents" 2011.

109. "Improve Charter Oversight" 2011.

110. "Better, but Far from Done" 2011.

111. An especially illustrative editorial in December 2014 shows the editors' efforts to temper a critical report about the system. The Center for Reinventing Public Education found that 44 percent of parents in New Orleans said they had difficulty finding a school that fit their needs and one-third said they were confused about which schools their children were able to attend. The editors acknowledged the real deficiency in the system: "The breakup of the old Orleans Parish school system after Hurricane Katrina allowed the creation of dozens of charter schools tailored to students' needs, but it also made choosing a school confusing and chaotic for families." The editorial went on, however, to note that the district's performance is better than it was before Katrina and that even though a substantial portion of parents are confused and had problems choosing a school, there is really a lot of information out there: "To be fair to school officials, there is a great deal of information available about the array of options in New Orleans." In other words, it's a problem that so many parents are confused about the enrollment process and can't find a school, but really, what else is the system supposed to do? ("Demystifying New Orleans School Options" 2014).

112. In August 2009, "The awful old Orleans Parish school system was dismantled . . . and four years after the storm, the charter and state-run schools that largely replace it are worlds better in many cases" ("A Dream Takes Wing" 2009). In supporting Governor Jindal's plans to expand charter schools, the paper said, "Before Katrina, the vast majority of public schools in New Orleans were absolutely dreadful" ("Nurturing New Schools" 2009).

113. In 2007, the theology professor Michael Homan claimed, "Charter schools have given new impetus to our two-tier system of education in New Orleans. . . . The RSD has become a dumping ground for students without resources to break into more elite schools" (Homan 2007, 7). As with the aforementioned piece by OPSB member in 2005, another op-ed cheering the reforms ran in close proximity. Leslie Jacobs wrote a few days later in direct response to Homan, "Charters are not 'elite.' One does not need connections or to 'know someone' to attend. It is true that once charters hit their enrollment cap, they do not have to enroll additional students, while the RSD operated schools must. The answer is to open more schools" (Jacobs 2007). A *Times-Picayune* columnist, Jarvis DeBerry, published three critical pieces, one each in 2009, 2010, and 2011, in which he criticized unfair enrollment practices and the lack of Black teachers in charter schools. However, his pieces often made reference to improvements and the terrible bad old days.

CHAPTER 4

Portions of this chapter were originally published in Lay and Bauman 2019.
Epigraphs: Johnson 2006; response to the author's survey.

1. Baumgartner and Jones 1993, 42.

2. Many scholars and activists have questioned the motivations of the reformers, especially given that the political dynamics often pitted white, upper-class "reformers," who were neither in nor of the neighborhoods and schools they sought to transform, against Black, poor community residents. For example, Kristen Buras (2015, 39) writes

that what happened in New Orleans was "a feeding frenzy, a revivified Reconstruction-era blueprint for how to capitalize on public education and line the pockets of white entrepreneurs (and their black allies) who care less about working-class schoolchildren and their grandmothers and much more about obtaining public and private monies and an array of lucrative contracts." Although money may have been one motivation, it is just as likely that many, if not most, of the reformers were true believers. Both because of their own personal experience and their underlying ideologies, the white business elite were very enamored with the market model. Like the majority of New Orleans residents, they were frustrated and angry about the quality of the schools and the corruption among those chosen to lead. There are easier ways to make money than opening charter schools. This is meant not to excuse the prejudices and paternalism inherent in much of their rhetoric and ideology but, rather, to cast doubt on the idea that we can understand individual motivations on the basis of outcomes. Regardless of their intentions, we can now, after fifteen years of experience, consider the effects.

3. Henig and Rich 2003; Morel 2018; Wong and Farris 2011.

4. Lay and Tyburski 2017.

5. Glickman 1993; Kirst 1984; Wirt and Kirst 1997.

6. Feuerstein 2002; Iannaconne and Lutz 1994.

7. On community service, see Burns et al. 2001. On progressive ambition, see Sweet-Cushman 2020.

8. McDonnell 2000, 4.

9. Strike 1993, 267.

10. Collins 2021.

11. Marsh 2007.

12. Gay 2002; Leighley 2001.

13. Chubb and Moe 1990; Finn 1992; Maeroff 2010; McDermott 1999.

14. Feuerstein 2002, 18.

15. Hochschild and Scovronick 2003, 5.

16. Allen and Plank 2005; Hess and Leal 2005.

17. Campbell 2005.

18. Smith 2001. See also Smith et al. 2007, 22. Critics of elected boards claim both that they are hostage to special interests and that they marginalize minorities because they work to appeal to the majority. They apparently do not understand contradiction.

19. Smith 2001, 31. Yet she also notes that charter proponents "stress goods such as productivity and efficiency, spurred by competition, rather than goods like collective debate within democratic decision-making processes" (ibid., 21).

20. Wells et al. 2002.

21. Schneider et al. 2000.

22. Mansbridge 1999.

23. Pitkin 1967. On the empirical link, see Holman 2014, 2015; Schwindt-Bayer and Mishler 2005.

24. Bratton and Haynie 1999; Bullock and MacManus 1981; Hero and Tolbert 1995; Lublin 1999.

25. Berkman and Plutzer 2010; Leal et al. 2004; Meier and England 1984; Robinson et al. 1985.

26. Meier et al. 1989.

27. Bobo and Gilliam 1990; Mansbridge 1999.

28. Campbell 2003; Mettler 2005; Michener 2018; Weaver and Lerman 2010.

29. Hess and Meeks 2010.

30. Marschall 2005; Robinson et al. 1985.

31. Shober and Hartney 2014.

32. Butler et al. 2008.

33. Miron and Nelson 2001, 33.

34. Ford 2017; Ford and Ihrke 2015, 2016; Nelson 2015; Squire and Davis 2016.

35. Squire and Davis 2016.

36. Louisiana law gives responsibility for choosing and maintaining board members to the boards themselves, and though the law states that appointing authorities to boards and commissions "shall give due consideration to the demographics of the population of the state, including but not limited to geography, gender, and race," it does not require boards to take these characteristics into account (*Louisiana Charter School Board Legal Handbook* 2014, 17).

37. Men continued to make up the majority after the 2017 elections.

38. David 1993; Reay 1998; Scarborough 2019.

39. Lay 2019.

40. The same is true in other states, such as Massachusetts (see Dingerson and Ross 2016).

41. Jewson 2018b.

42. The schools in which these comments were discussed were Benjamin Franklin High School, Lusher Charter School, Einstein Charter Schools, and International High School.

43. Donors outside the city and state have increasingly become the primary funders of school board races in New Orleans (and other cities). In 2020, the largest campaign contributor was Democrats for Education Reform (DFER), a national advocacy group that endorses candidates who support contemporary reforms, including charter schools and school choice. The DFER's Louisiana affiliate raised nearly all its contributions from Education Reform Now Advocacy, which is funded by privatization supporters such as Jim Walton. The second-largest contributor was Stephen Rosenthal, who is Leslie Jacobs's brother and who sits on multiple charter boards (Jewson 2020). My students calculated in 2015 that the Rosenthal family had contributed 10 percent of all the donations to OPSB and BESE candidates in the previous elections.

44. Hess and Meeks 2010.

45. Ibid., 7.

46. Vergari 2007.

47. Burns 2003.

48. Jewson 2016a.

49. Vargas 2010.

50. Williams 2012.

51. Dreilinger 2014b, 2015c.

52. Jewson 2021.

53. As ESPN's *College GameDay* segment goes, "You Had One Job!"

54. Although voluntary contributions typically make up a small percentage of revenue for public schools (Brunner and Sonstelie 2003), they tend to exacerbate inequi-

ties between economically advantaged parents and their counterparts (Posey-Maddox 2016).

55. Allen and Robinson 2006, 3

56. Fiske and Ladd 2000; Miron and Nelson 2001.

57. Williams 2010.

58. Williams 2011.

59. Gamard 2016.

60. Louisiana's Revised Statute 42:13 (Definitions) includes "any committee or subcommittee of any" public body in the definition of a "public body."

61. The Appendix lists the text of the Louisiana laws that apply.

62. I have revised this section since it was published in SAGE's *Urban Affairs Review* in 2018. That article included information about the compliance with two other state-mandated pieces of information: the posting of the name of the school or network's data director and a list of private vendors with whom schools and networks contracted. In 2017, when these data were collected, charters were no longer required to provide this information online; rather, they had to provide it at the "main office of the governing authority." Of course, there is also confusion about the "governing authority." Is that the charter authorizer? Or the charter board? Charter boards do not have "main offices," for the most part. Where, exactly, would one find this information? The law is intended to prevent conflicts of interests; board members must recuse themselves when making decisions about vendors that may create a conflict of interest with their occupation/business or personal relationships. Besides self-reporting of members, the only way for the media or the public to ensure there is no conflict of interest is to have access to a list of vendors.

63. Hess and Meeks 2010.

64. Gamard 2016.

65. Most of the boards studied in Minnesota have active finance committees, while fewer than half have committees for human resources or fundraising and development (see Stone et al. 2012).

66. Foster 2012.

67. Jewson 2016d.

68. Jewson 2016c. Many other schools had similar stories. Warren Easton High School had four public meeting violations in 2012 alone. The Lycée Français de la Nouvelle-Orléans repeatedly shut out the press from its controversial meetings in 2012 and 2013 in which decisions about leadership and the future of the school were made. The Friends of King board routinely refused to fully comply with public notices of meetings.

69. Jewson 2016b.

70. Jewson 2017a.

71. Williams 2013.

72. Allen and Robinson 2006.

73. Ford and Ihrke 2015, 2016.

74. Stone et al. 2012.

75. Anecdotally, this notion means that parents are always looking around for a better deal, and at the first sign of a problem, many start looking for the exits. As a mother to two school-age children, I can attest to the annual conversations with other parents

about whether they will apply to other schools. If a mother does not like a school's principal, she looks for another school. If a father feels that a school is not assigning enough homework or is not rigorous enough, he tries to find one that is. Few decide to get involved and make change within their current institutions.

76. Cucchiara 2013; Useem et al. 2006.

77. Williams 2013.

78. Ibid.

79. Dreilinger 2015a. Further, when this reporter for *The Lens* requested the score sheets the RSD used in its decision making, she was told they were not public documents, even though the RSD is a public body.

80. Huff 2015.

81. Dreilinger 2013c.

82. Atkeson 2003; Atkeson and Carillo 2007; Barreto 2010; Gay 2002; Merolla et al. 2013; Sanchez and Morin 2011.

83. Research on corporate boards shows that diversity is associated with performance: Erhardt et al. 2003; Green and Cassell 1996; Miller and Triana 2009.

84. Michener 2019, 428.

CHAPTER 5

Epigraph: Focus group respondent, 2017.

1. "Support for Schools" 2009. The title of this chapter, "They Choose, We Lose," is adapted from the "Harry and Louise" ads from the 1993 debate on health-care reform.

2. Thevenot 2009.

3. Mettler and Soss 2004.

4. Campbell et al. 1960.

5. For a selection of political socialization literature, see Gimpel et al. 2003; Jennings and Niemi 1974; Lay 2012; Oxley et al. 2020; Sapiro 2004.

6. Fiorina 1981; Key 1966; Kramer 1971; Lay and Tyburski 2017; Popkin 1991.

7. Lerman and McCabe 2017.

8. Pierson 1992; Campbell 2012.

9. Brady et al. 1995. An especially illustrative summary of this research is, "To give a reductionist version of our findings—political interest is especially important for turnout; civic skills, for acts requiring an investment of time; and money, for acts involving an investment of money. To the extent that money is the least equally distributed resource and to the extent that making contributions has become in recent decades an increasingly important citizen activity, the character of American politics is profoundly altered" (ibid., 285).

10. Pierson 1992.

11. Schneider and Ingram 1993.

12. Schneider and Ingram 1990.

13. Campbell 2003; Mettler 2005.

14. Campbell 2011, 963. See also Soss 1999, 2005. Similarly, encounters with the criminal justice system also tend to depress participation because people receive negative citizenship messages (see Weaver et al. 2014; Weaver and Lerman 2010; White 2019a).

15. Henry Brady and his colleagues (1995) find that participants in means-tested programs are less likely to vote or engage in other types of electoral behavior.

16. White 2019b.

17. Gilens 1999; van Doorn 2015.

18. Bruch et al. 2010, 208.

19. Ibid.; Mettler 1998; Soss 1999.

20. Gustafson 2009; Morgan 2009; Reich 1963.

21. Campbell 2012. For example, programs that are "submerged," such that even recipients do not recognize themselves as beneficiaries, are less likely to have feedback effects than those that are highly visible and traceable to the government (Mettler 2011). When benefits or burdens are limited, as with the Medicare Modernization Act of 2003, policies may not lead to significant feedback effects (Morgan and Campbell 2011).

22. Patashnik 2008, 29–30. He defines "general-interest" policy reform as a "conscious, non-incremental shift in a preexisting line of policymaking intended to produce general benefits" (ibid., 16).

23. For more about the polls referenced in this chapter, see the Appendix.

24. I am grateful to the KFF for sharing its data with me.

25. Domingo Morel and Sally Nuamah (2020) attribute the positive attitudes about pre-Katrina schools among Black residents of New Orleans to the shifts in power from local control, which was seen as Black-led, to a white-led school governance structure. Likewise, my theory suggests that governance is a key to understanding how attitudes about school reform are divided along racial lines. However, I argue that Black families' experiences with the school system are an integral component of their dissatisfaction.

26. A 2009 poll by Democracy Corps similarly showed substantial racial differences on the question of direction of schools. A majority of whites (66%) said schools were getting better since Katrina, but only 46 percent of Blacks agreed. About 22 percent of Black residents said schools were getting worse compared with only 14 percent of white residents ($p < .01$). At the same time, Black New Orleanians reported warmer feelings toward public schools in New Orleans: a mean of 44.6 on a scale of 1–100 compared with a mean of 39 for white residents ($p < .05$).

27. Cowen Institute for Public Education Initiatives 2007, 36.

28. Cowen Institute for Public Education Initiatives 2019.

29. These differences were not reported or were not statistically significant differences in other years.

30. Cowen Institute for Public Education Initiatives 2017.

31. Nuamah 2020b.

32. Soss and Schram 2007.

33. Vladimir Kogan and his colleagues (2021) find that in majority-nonwhite jurisdictions, there are significant demographic differences between voters in school board elections and the students who attend the schools the boards oversee. Public opinion surveys that sample on these voters are unlikely to adequately represent the views of the students or their parents.

34. Thevenot 2009.

35. I also interviewed one group of nonparents but do not use their responses here because the group was not aware of the education landscape in New Orleans and had very few opinions.

36. For more about the methodology, see the Appendix. I focus on parents' opinions about the school enrollment process and their treatment in schools because these were the areas about which parents were most passionate. When I asked the parents general questions about the schools, their responses nearly always revolved around enrollment and school options or how they and their children were treated in schools and by school officials.

37. See, e.g., Bruch et al. 2010; Kumlin and Rothstein 2005; Michener 2018; Soss et al. 2011; Tyler 1998.

38. Some schools required proof of citizenship; others did not. Some required report cards or standardized test scores; others did not. A few required essays, tryouts, or examples of artwork. Some allowed applications to be mailed, while many required them to be dropped off in person, often during limited hours.

39. BESE-authorized, OPSB-authorized, and direct-run schools were added later.

40. Originally, the maximum was eight.

41. Truman 1951.

42. Abrams and Gibbs 2002; Allen and White-Smith 2018; Diamond and Gomez 2004; Lareau and Horvat 1999.

43. Lightfoot 2004; Lott 2001.

44. Ingram 2007, 245.

45. Gaventa 1982, vii.

46. Lipman 2011, 14–15.

47. Engel 2000.

48. Ingram 2007, 249.

49. Thaler and Sunstein 2008.

50. Osborne and Sibley 2013; Osborne et al. 2015.

51. Orleans Public Education Network and Louisiana Center for Children's Rights 2019.

52. Kupchik and Ward 2014; Ramey 2015; Skiba et al. 2016; Welch and Payne 2010.

53. Kupchik 2010.

54. Gibson et al. 2014.

55. Bruch and Soss 2018; Kupchik and Catlaw 2015; Lyons and Drew 2006.

56. Lareau and Horvat 1999, 42.

57. Anecdotally, I can attest to many of my friends saying something similar about problems they have with their schools. No one really complains or works to improve things at their schools; they simply move the kids to another place, hoping for a better experience. When one's children are in a "good" school, there is serious reluctance to do anything that might jeopardize their placement. Parents put up with all sorts of things rather than work to change the situation because they fear their children will be kicked out and they will have to find another, presumably worse option.

58. Weixler et al. 2020.

59. These findings mirror those in other cities, such as in Chicago, around school closings (see Vaughan and Gutierrez 2017).

60. Desselle 2021.

61. Schneider and Ingram 1993.

CHAPTER 6

Epigraph: Quoted in Altavena et al. 2016.

1. Galston 2001; Nie et al. 1996; Verba et al. 1995.

2. Chubb and Moe 1990.

3. Barber 1984, 2007, 143–144; Pateman 1970.

4. See, e.g., individuals who lost their health insurance as a result of new mandates in the Affordable Care Act (Jacobs and Mettler 2018).

5. Mettler and Soss 2004, 61.

6. Druckman et al. 2018.

7. Lerman and Weaver 2014; White 2019.

8. Policy design can mitigate this, at least in part (see Marschall and Shah 2007).

9. Lerman and Weaver 2014, 198.

10. Davis 2020a, 2020b.

11. Lee et al. 2014; White 2019a.

12. Aranda et al. 2014; Michener 2017.

13. Cho et al. 2006; Merolla et al. 2013; Walker 2019; Zepeda-Millan 2017. For more on racial consciousness, see Dawson 1991; Shingles 1981.

14. Neoliberalism is a philosophy "predicated on the abatement of labor rights, social provision, public amenities, environmental regulation, and other artifacts of social democracy deemed impediments to capital accumulation. . . . Neoliberals do not really embrace classic laissez-faire ideas in a strict sense, but instead favor opportunistic use of the state to colonize all spheres of human activity under market logic" (Johnson 2011, xxi). The important term here is "market logic." Some scholars have criticized those who characterize the New Orleans school system as a market system, largely because the government is involved in authorizing charters. Even with this minor bit of government oversight, the *logic* of the system is certainly neoliberal in character—parental choice (even if options are limited), competition among schools (even if is distorted by the supply), and site-based management of the most important and expensive aspects of schooling (personnel, curriculum, and transportation).

15. Soss and Jacobs 2009.

16. Bruch and Soss 2018, 37.

17. Dewey 1916.

18. Justice and Meares 2014; Levin 1986.

19. Bruch and Soss 2018, 48.

20. Nuamah 2020a, 1.

21. Einstein et al. 2019.

22. Howell and Lee 1997, 5. The authors measure "trust in local government" as an index of four items: belief that the city wastes money, trust in city decisions, perception of corruption, and perceived power of big interests.

23. White residents were much more supportive than Black residents of the new mayor, Ray Nagin, and had been much less approving of the previous mayor, Marc Morial. In 1996, 23 percent of whites "strongly approved" of Morial, while 58 percent of Blacks did so; in 2003, this flipped, with 60 percent of whites strongly approving of Nagin compared with 37 percent of Blacks. White voters played a decisive role Nagin's

first election. Most mayoral elections over the previous twenty years had been racially polarized. In 2002, two African American candidates faced off, splitting the Black vote and giving white voters the opportunity to select their preferred Black candidate (Lay 2009).

24. Holman and Lay 2020, 119.

25. Casselman 2015.

26. Putnam 2007.

27. Citrin et al. 1997; Green et al. 1998; Kalmoe and Piston 2013; Key 1949.

28. Blodorn et al. 2016.

29. The sample included only forty-four parents (of 294 total respondents), only thirty of whom had children in the public schools. This does not allow for a reliable statistical analysis based on interaction with public schools.

30. We believe these finding may have captured the residents' frustration with the outgoing mayor. Our survey was fielded just after a(nother) flood event, in which a major portion of the city flooded due to insufficient city pump capacity. Mayor Mitch Landrieu misled the city about many aspects of the response to this crisis.

31. Holman and Lay 2020.

32. Cook et al. 2019.

33. Li et al. 2010, 106.

34. Irazábal and Neville 2007, 131.

35. Cynics would argue that one of the unstated goals of school privateers was to interrupt a burgeoning grassroots democratic movement in the aftermath of Katrina.

36. Barber 1984, 297.

37. Walzer 1983, 225.

38. Coughlan 2017.

39. Weixler et al. 2020.

40. See Makris and Brown 2020. Pauline Lipman (2011, 67) also notes a link between school closures in Chicago and the neighborhoods selected for housing development. Some neighborhoods that had been neglected for decades were identified for the building of new homes at the same time that the schools in these neighborhoods were closed for "poor performance." The new neighborhoods ultimately price out the long-term residents, leaving residents to contend that the new schools are not designed for them.

41. These figures are from the New Orleans Equity Index, accessed August 26, 2021, http://neworleansequityindex.org/schools.

42. Sakakeeny 2015.

43. Respondents in several focus groups told me they were reluctant to say something because of my affiliation with Tulane University. The university is seen not as a neutral arbiter in the community but, rather, as a bastion of white supremacy. It often took some persuasion to assure them that they could trust me as a white professor at the institution.

44. Rose 2012; Trounstine 2018.

45. In addition to schools and public housing projects, thirty-three Catholic churches were closed after Katrina, even before the sexual abuse scandals that have also devastated this institution. In 2019, the Archdiocese of New Orleans closed five schools due to low enrollment.

CONCLUSION

Epigraph: Schattschneider 1960, 107.

1. Langenhennig 2018.

2. Ferguson 2018, 8.

3. Some of these folks include the educators Mercedes Schneider (see https://deutsch29 .wordpress.com) and Michael Deshotels (see http://louisianaeducator.blogspot.com) and Jason France, a former Louisiana Department of Education data analyst (see https://cra zycrawfish.wordpress.com/author/crazycrawfish).

4. Michael Deshotels had to sue the state to obtain access to data that should have been publicly available.

5. Harris 2020, 174.

6. For example, Harris (2020, 264) omits high schools from his analysis because of changes and variations in the testing regime and because the composition of the test takers before and after Katrina likely affects the results. He argues that the rising graduation rate means some students take the high school exams who would have dropped out prior to Katrina. But he also points out the many problems that likely lead to the inflation of the high school graduation rate, such as schools' tendency to eliminate some dropouts through creative coding of students as transfers rather than dropouts. So it is very hard to know whether the population of test takers is significantly different and why it would be different only in high schools. High schools have seen the least improvement in test scores, leading critics to argue that their omission from Harris's study allows for a much rosier conclusion than would be shown if they were included. Critics have also pointed to the many changes in tests and in the composition of the students in the pre-Katrina and post-Katrina population as reasons that nearly any pre- and post-hurricane analysis is flawed. Harris attempts to control for these changes with a difference-in-difference research design. He attempts to compare the Orleans district's scores and outcomes to those of similar districts that did not undergo the same reforms. However, there are many methodological assumptions that require many schools to be excluded from the analysis and require that the control districts, which are other "hurricane-affected districts," are indeed similar to Orleans Parish in every way except the reforms. The potential for an omitted variable is a common problem in natural experiments.

7. Ibid., 93. Harris explains in the endnotes that he calculated this via a conversion based on Louisiana's performance on the National Assessment of Educational Progress (NAEP). He writes, "I determined, first, how far Louisiana was below the national average (in standard deviation units) [on the NAEP,] then how far New Orleans was from the state average (at baseline) [on the state LEAP test]. This is where the 22nd percentile figure comes from. Next, I added the reform effect size (again, in standard deviation units) [a figure based on his complicated formula that is based on state tests that exclude high-school students] to obtain the shift to the 37th percentile. I describe this as a 'rough' estimate because it requires assumptions, such as that New Orleans was just as far below the state average on the NAEP as the state test" (ibid., 280). This estimate also requires that scores on one test (NAEP) that is given to a random sample of schools across the state are comparable to scores on another (LEAP) and that the effect size, which is calculated from scores on the state tests for all elementary- and

middle-school children, is the same as would be the case on the NAEP, which is given only to fourth and eighth graders.

8. The state data did not have scores for RSD-NO in 2012.

9. Berliner 2013; Coleman 1966.

10. Jewson 2019b.

11. It is also essential to highlight that test scores are contentious beyond methodological debates, because they are a tool in a much larger exercise in the privatization of public services. Neoliberal policies "narrowly define the purpose of school as private, and in service to individual rather than societal needs" (Vaughan and Gutierrez 2017, 6). Black parents are especially likely to understand that schools do more than teach math and reading and to see these institutions as critical anchors of stability in communities that are devastated by poverty, disinvestment, gentrification, and aggressive policing (see Noguera 2003). My results in Chapter 6 show that parents connect education reform with these other arenas of housing, economic development, and disenfranchisement.

12. Harris 2020, 134. Harris argues that he and his colleagues found that achievement gaps between Black and white students narrowed (ibid., 88), but the book does not present the figures associated with the gaps.

13. Kotok et al. 2018, 828.

14. Bryk and Schneider 2002; Goddard et al. 2009.

15. Johnson 2012, 246.

16. John White, Louisiana's former superintendent of education, and many others have referred to the reforms as a miracle (see White 2016).

17. Nuamah 2020b.

18. Tilly 1999.

19. Pedroni 2011, 206.

20. Huff 2015, 90.

21. And increasingly, reformers from within and outside the city fund these school board campaigns as a mechanism to ensure that these officials do nothing to disrupt the reforms.

22. Baker et al. 2005; Freelon 2018.

23. Nuamah 2020b.

24. Lipman 2011, 62.

25. Swyngedouw and Wilson 2014.

26. Anderson and Dixson 2016; Buras 2011; Ferman 2017; Scott 2011.

27. Buchanan and Lee 2000; Casella 2005; Hasen 2000.

28. Suggs 2020.

29. The plan works only if charters are not allowed to cap their enrollments. Like all other public schools, charter schools should have to accept everyone. Caps are a mechanism to exclude, especially at selective schools. Reasonable maximums related to space constraints can be made, but the school should not be able to determine this number without central oversight.

30. Gerry et al. 2020. This study looks only at kindergarten applicants in high-demand schools.

31. Hasselle 2020.

32. Martinez 2021.

33. The independent monitors' report is available at https://www.document cloud.org/documents/6444342-IMreportSchoolSelection2019.html#document/p14 /a528255.

34. Jewson 2019a.

35. For the sake of consistency, I have referred to the Orleans Parish School Board (OPSB) throughout this volume. When the RSD and OPSB merged in 2019, the OPSB rebranded itself NOLA-PS.

36. Root 2016, 137.

37. Martinez 2021, 14–15.

38. Root 2016, 150.

39. Louisiana Revised Statute 17:3991 (Charter Schools, Requirements, Limitations, Renewal, Amendment, Revocation), pt. IVA(1c).

40. See "School Board Chartering Authority" 2020.

41. Vaughan and Gutierrez 2017, 7.

42. At least one member from each category should be required, and together this group should compose the majority of the board. For networks with multiple schools, the group should include at least one member from each school or neighborhood in which a school within their network is located.

43. The board should draw the neighborhood lines along the same lines as transportation policy, which requires the district to provide transportation to all students who live more than one mile from the school's physical location. In accordance, the neighborhood should include all residences that are within and inclusive of one mile of the school's physical location.

44. Wohlstetter et al. 1994.

45. Moore 2002.

46. There is an extensive literature on the opportunities and challenges of school councils, with best practices that include consistent engagement among council members, a shared vision, data-informed decision making, shared responsibility, and school leadership focused on improving school performance *and* involving the entire community (see Biag and Castrechini 2014; Epstein 2009, 8–12).

47. Chambers 2006.

48. Bryk et al. 1998.

49. The executive director of the Louisiana Association of Public Charter Schools has stated that elections "bring politics to the table" (while presumably the current system is apolitical) (Williams 2014; see also Jewson 2018b).

50. Of interest to New Orleans, before he was appointed as the superintendent of the Recovery School District, Paul Vallas served as the chief executive of Chicago Public Schools, where he criticized LSCs, claiming some members were felons and "homeless people." He tried unsuccessfully to eviscerate their powers. His experience there undoubtedly affected his support for parental involvement in New Orleans.

51. Medina et al. 2020.

52. Dewey 1916.

53. Collins 2018, 965.

54. Coughlan 2017.

55. Edward Lawler (1986) contends that involving those lower in the organizational hierarchy improves the effectiveness of the organization when they are adequate-

ly trained, have the information they need, and are rewarded for high performance. Kenneth Leithwood and his colleagues argue that school councils in Ontario, which have limited decision-making authority, have a "mildly positive" effect on school and classroom practices, and they are not particularly effective at empowering parents or improving schools (Leithwood et al. 1999).

56. Nuamah 2020a.

57. Nuamah and Ogorzalek 2021, 757.

58. Sampson and Bertrand 2020.

59. Danley and Rubin 2020; Glazer and Egan 2018; Lipman 2017; Michener 2020; Simon et al. 2017.

References

Abrams, Laura S., and Jewelle Taylor Gibbs. 2002. "Disrupting the Logic of Home-School Relations: Parent Involvement Strategies and Practices of Inclusion and Exclusion." *Urban Education* 37:384–407.

Adelson, Jeff. 2015. "In Visit to New Orleans School, Jindal Urges Support for Program Deemed One of His Defining Legacies." *The Advocate*, December 15.

Allard, Scott, Nancy Burns, and Gerald Gamm. 1998. "Representing Urban Interests: The Local Politics of State Legislatures." *Studies in American Political Development* 12:267–302.

Allen, Ann, and David N. Plank. 2005. "School Board Election Structure and Democratic Representation." *Educational Policy* 19:510–527.

Allen, Ann, and Dwan Robinson. 2006. "Weighing the Public-Private Balance of Charter School Governance." Policy brief, Ohio Collaborative: Research and Policy for Schools, Children, and Families. Accessed November 17, 2017. http://citeseerx.ist.psu.edu/viewdoc/download?doi=10.1.1.604.9015&rep=rep1&type=pdf.

Allen, Quaylan, and Kimberly White-Smith. 2018. "'That's Why I Stay in School': Black Mothers' Parental Involvement, Cultural Wealth, and Exclusion in Their Son's Schooling." *Urban Education* 53:409–435.

Altavena, Lily, Rose Velazquez, and Natalie Griffin. 2016. "School Takeovers Leave Parents without a Voice in Education." *News21*, August 20. Accessed May 29, 2018. https://votingwars.news21.com/school-takeovers-leave-parents-without-a-voice-in-education.

Anderson, Celia Rousseau, and Adrienne D. Dixson. 2016. "Down by the Riverside: A CRT Perspective on Education Reform in Two River Cities." *Urban Education* 51:363–389.

Anderson, Ed. 2011. "Better Teachers Should Earn More, Gov. Bobby Jindal Says." *Times-Picayune*, December 9.

Anderson, J. D. 1988. *The Education of Blacks in the South, 1860–1935*. Chapel Hill: University of North Carolina Press.

Anderson, Kaitlin. 2017. "Evidence on Charter School Practices Related to Student Enrollment and Retention." *Journal of School Choice* 11:527–545.

Aranda, Elizabeth, Cecelia Menjivar, and Katharine M. Donato. 2014. "The Spillover Consequences of an Enforcement-First U.S. Immigration Regime." *American Behavioral Scientist* 58:1687–1695.

Associated Press. 2005. "New Orleans' Public School Opens Its Doors." November 28. Accessed April 18, 2018. http://www.nbcnews.com/id/10238526/ns/us_news-katrina _the_long_road_back/t/new-orleans-public-school-opens-its-doors/#.WtdnP4gbNaQ.

Atkeson, Lonna Rae. 2003. "Not All Cues Are Created Equal: The Conditional Impact of Female Candidates on Political Engagement." *Journal of Politics* 65:1040–1061.

Atkeson, Lonna Rae, and Nancy Carillo. 2007. "More Is Better: The Influence of Collective Female Descriptive Representation on External Efficacy." *Politics and Gender* 3:79–101.

Axtman, Madeline. 2006. "School Situation Seems No Better than Before." Letter to the editor, *Times-Picayune*, July 31.

Bachrach, Peter, and Morton Baratz. 1962. "The Two Faces of Power." *American Political Science Review* 56:947–952.

Baker, Liva. 1996. *The Second Battle of New Orleans: The Hundred-Year Struggle to Integrate Schools*. New York: HarperCollins.

Baker, William H., H. Lon Addams, and Brian Davis. 2005. "Critical Factors for Enhancing Municipal Public Hearings." *Public Administration Review* 65:490–499.

Ballard, Mark. 2016. "Louisiana Senate Panel OKs Bill to Return New Orleans Schools to Local Control." *The Advocate*, April 14.

Barber, Benjamin. 1984. *Strong Democracy: Participatory Politics for a New Age*. Berkeley: University of California Press.

———. 2007. *Consumed: How Markets Corrupt Children, Infantilize Adults, and Swallow Citizens Whole*. New York: W. W. Norton.

Barreto, Matt. 2010. *Ethnic Cues: The Role of Shared Ethnicity in Latino Political Participation*. Ann Arbor: University of Michigan Press.

Barrett, Nathan, Andrew McEachin, Jonathan N. Mills, and Jon Valant. 2017. *What Are the Sources of School Discipline by Student Race and Family Income?* Report, Education Research Alliance, November 20.

Baumgartner, Frank R., and Bryan D. Jones. 1993. *Agendas and Instability in American Politics*. Chicago: University of Chicago Press.

Baumgartner, Frank R., Bryan D. Jones, and Peter B. Mortensen. 2014. "Punctuated Equilibrium Theory: Explaining Stability and Change in Public Policymaking." In *Theories of the Policy Process*, edited by Paul A. Sabatier and Christopher M. Weible, 59–104. Boulder, CO: Westview.

Berkman, Michael B., and Eric Plutzer. 2010. *Ten Thousand Democracies: Politics and Public Opinion in America's School Districts*. Washington, DC: Georgetown University Press.

Berliner, David C. 2013. "Effects of Inequality and Poverty versus Teachers and Schooling on America's Youth." *Teachers College Record* 115:1–26.

"Better, but Far from Done." 2011. Editorial, *Times-Picayune*, November 6.

Biag, Manuelito, and Sebastian Castrechini. 2014. *The Links between Program Participation and Students' Outcomes: The Redwood City Community Schools Project.* Stanford, CA: John W. Gardner Center for Youth and Their Communities.

Blackwell, William H. 2013. "An Era of Charter School Expansion: An Examination of Special Education in Massachusetts' Charter Schools." *Journal of Disability Studies* 24:75–87.

Blodorn, Alison, Laurie T. O'Brien, Sapna Cheryan, and S. Brooke Vick. 2016. "Understanding Perceptions of Racism in the Aftermath of Hurricane Katrina: The Roles of System and Group Justification." *Social Justice Research* 29:139–158.

Bobo, Lawrence, and Franklin Gilliam. 1990. "Race, Sociopolitical Representation, and Black Empowerment." *American Political Science Review* 84:377–393.

BondGraham, Darwin. 2011. "Building the New New Orleans: Foundation and NGO Power." *Review of Black Political Economy* 38:279–309.

Brady, Henry E., Sidney Verba, and Kay Lehman Schlozman. 1995. "Beyond SES: A Resource Model of Political Participation." *American Political Science Review* 89:271–294.

Bratton, Kathleen A., and Kerry L. Haynie. 1999. "Agenda Setting and Legislative Success in State Legislatures: The Effects of Gender and Race." *Journal of Politics* 61:658–679.

Breunlin, Rachel, and Helen A. Regis. 2006. "Putting the Ninth Ward on the Map: Race, Place, and Transformation in Desire, New Orleans." *American Anthropologist* 108:744–764.

Bridges, Amy. 1984. *A City in the Republic.* Cambridge: Cambridge University Press.

Bruch, Sarah K., Myra Marx Ferree, and Joe Soss. 2010. "From Policy to Polity: Democracy, Paternalism, and the Incorporation of Disadvantaged Citizens." *American Sociological Review* 75:205–226.

Bruch, Sarah K., and Joe Soss. 2018. "Schooling as a Formative Political Experience: Authority Relations and the Education of Citizens." *Perspectives on Politics* 16:36–57.

Brunner, Eric, and Jon Sonstelie. 2003. "School Finance Reform and Voluntary Fiscal Federalism." *Journal of Public Economics* 87:2157–2185.

Bryk, Anthony S., and Barbara Schneider. 2002. *Trust in Schools: A Core Resource for Improvement.* New York: Russell Sage.

Bryk, Anthony S., Penny Bender Sebring, David Kerbow, Sharon Rollow, and John Q. Easton. 1998. *Charting Chicago School Reform: Democratic Localism as a Lever for Change.* Boulder, CO: Westview.

Buchanan, James M., and Dwight R. Lee. 1986. "Vote Buying in a Stylized Setting." *Public Choice* 65:3–15.

Bulkley, Katrina. 2010. "Introduction: Portfolio Management Models in Urban School Reform." In *Between Public and Private: Politics, Governance and the New Portfolio Models of Urban School Reform*, edited by Katrina Bulkley, Jeffrey R. Henig, and Henry Levin, 3–26. Cambridge, MA: Harvard Education Press.

Bullock, Charles S., III, and Susan MacManus. 1981. "Policy Responsiveness to the Black Electorate: Programmatic versus Symbolic Representation." *American Politics Research* 9:357–368.

Buras, Kristen L. 2011. "Race, Charter Schools, and Conscious Capitalism: On the Spatial Politics of Whiteness as Property (and the Unconscionable Assault on Black New Orleans)." *Harvard Educational Review* 81:296–331.

————. 2013. "'We're Not Going Nowhere': Race, Urban Space, and the Struggle for King Elementary School in New Orleans." *Critical Studies in Education* 54:19–32.

————. 2015. *Charter Schools, Race, and Urban Space: Where the Market Meets Grassroots Resistance*. New York: Routledge.

Burns, Nancy, Laura Evans, Gerald Gamm, and Corrine McConnaughy. 2009. "Urban Politics in the State Arena." *Studies in American Political Development* 23:1–22.

Burns, Nancy, Kay L. Schlozman, and Sidney Verba. 2001. *The Private Roots of Public Action*. Boston: Harvard University Press.

Burns, Peter F. 2003. "Regime Theory, State Government, and a Takeover of Urban Education." *Journal of Urban Affairs* 25:285–303.

Burns, Peter F., and Matthew O. Thomas. 2004. "Governors and the Development Regime in New Orleans." *Urban Affairs Review* 39:791–812.

————. 2015. *Reforming New Orleans: The Contentious Politics of Change in the Big Easy*. Ithaca, NY: Cornell University Press.

Butler, Elizabeth A., Joanna Smith, and Priscilla Wohlstetter. 2008. *Creating and Sustaining High-Quality Charter School Governing Boards: A Guide for State Policymakers*. Report, National Resource Center on Charter School Finance and Governance. Accessed November 17, 2017. https://charterschoolcenter.ed.gov/sites/default/files /files/field_publication_attachment/Governing_Board_v3_0.pdf.

Campbell, Andrea L. 2003. *How Policies Make Citizens: Senior Political Activism and the American Welfare State*. Princeton, NJ: Princeton University Press.

————. 2011. "Policy Feedbacks and the Impact of Policy Designs on Public Opinion." *Journal of Health Politics, Policy and Law* 36:961–973.

————. 2012. "Policy Makes Mass Politics." *Annual Review of Political Science* 15:333–351.

Campbell, Angus, Philip E. Converse, Warren Miller, and Donald E. Stokes. 1960. *The American Voter*. Chicago: University of Chicago Press.

Campbell, David E. 2005. "Contextual Influences on Participation in School Governance." In *Besieged: School Boards and the Future of Education Politics*, edited by William G. Howell, 288–307. Washington, DC: Brookings Institution Press.

Campbell, Donald. 1979. "Assessing the Impact of Planned Social Change." *Evaluation and Program Planning* 2:67–90.

Capochina, April. 2005. "Orleans Parish School Board Moves Forward with Hiring of N[ew] Y[ork] Accounting Firm." *New Orleans City Business*, June 13.

Carr, Sarah. 2010a. "Special Needs Students Aren't in Charters." *Times-Picayune*, February 1.

————. 2010b. "Report: Expulsions Soar in Louisiana, Suspensions Higher than Most States." *Times-Picayune*, April 21.

Casella, Alessandra. 2005. "Storable Votes." *Games and Economic Behavior* 51:391–419.

Casselman, Ben. 2015. "Katrina Washed Away New Orleans's Black Middle Class." *FiveThirtyEight* (blog), August 24. Accessed October 2, 2020. https://fivethirtyeight .com/features/katrina-washed-away-new-orleanss-black-middle-class.

Chambers, Stefanie. 2006. *Mayors and Schools: Minority Voices and Democratic Tensions in Urban Education*. Philadelphia: Temple University Press.

Chandler, Diana. 1989. "Ninth Ward Cheers Martin Luther King Jr. School." *Times-Picayune*, January 12.

Chang, Cindy. 2010. "BESE OKs Plan for Local Control—But Some Schools May Choose to Stay in RSD." *Times-Picayune*, December 10, A01.

Cho, Wendy K. Tam, James G. Gimpel, and Tony Wu. 2006. "Clarifying the Role of SES in Political Participation: Policy Threat and Arab American Mobilization." *Journal of Politics* 68:977–991.

Chong, Dennis, and James N. Druckman. 2007. "Framing Theory." *Annual Review of Political Science* 10:103–126.

Chubb, John E., and Terry M. Moe. 1990. *Politics, Markets, and America's Schools.* Washington, DC: Brookings Institution Press.

Citrin, Jack D., Donald P. Green, Christopher Muste, and Cara D. Wong. 1997. "Public Opinion toward Immigration Reform: The Role of Economic Motivations." *Journal of Politics* 59:858–881.

Clark, Jess. 2019. "Charter Schools Nearly Destroyed this New Orleans School. Now It Will Become One." *Hechinger Report*, April 29. Accessed August 22, 2021. https://hechingerreport.org/charter-schools-nearly-destroyed-this-new-orleans-school-now-it-will-become-one.

Coleman, James S. 1966. *Equality of Educational Opportunity.* Summary report, Office of Education, U.S. Department of Health, Education, and Welfare, Washington, DC.

Collins, Jonathan. 2018. "Urban Representation through Deliberation: A Theory and Test of Deliberative Democracy at the Local Level." *Journal of Urban Affairs* 40:952–973.

———. 2021. "Does the Meeting Style Matter? The Effects of Exposure to Participatory and Deliberative School Board Meetings." *American Political Science Review* 115:790–804.

Cook, Daniella Ann, and Adrienne D. Dixson. 2013. "Writing Critical Race Theory and Method: A Composite Counterstory on the Experiences of Black Teachers in New Orleans Post-Katrina." *Journal of Qualitative Studies in Education* 26:1238–1258.

Cook, Jason B., Vladimir Kogan, Stephane Lavertu, and Zachary Peskowitz. 2019. "Government Privatization and Political Participation: The Case of Charter Schools." *Journal of Politics* 82:300–314.

Cook, Peter. 2015. "Going Backward: A Year in the Old New Orleans Schools." *PE+CO* (blog), n.d. Accessed April 9, 2018. https://peterccook.com/2015/08/18/going-backwards.

Cooper, Christopher. 1997. "Strong Role in Schools Planned by Morial—Maybe Mayoral Control Is the Way to Go, He Says." *Times-Picayune*, December 24, A1.

———. 2005. "Old-Line Families Escape Worst of Flood and Plot the Future." *Wall Street Journal*, September 8.

Coughlan, Ryan William. 2007. *Schools Un/bounded: The Utility of School Zone Boundaries.* Ph.D. diss. Rutgers University and New Jersey Institute of Technology, Newark.

Cowen Institute for Public Education Initiatives, Tulane University. 2007. *The State of Public Education in New Orleans.* Report, June.

———. 2009. *Creating a Governing Framework for Public Education in New Orleans.* Report, November.

———. 2010. *The State of Public Education in New Orleans.* Report.

———. 2017. *Perceptions of Public Education in New Orleans.* Report, February.

————. 2019. *What Do Parents Think?* Report, October.

Cucchiara, Maia Bloomfield. 2013. *Marketing Schools, Marketing Cities: Who Wins and Who Loses When Schools Become Urban Amenities.* Chicago: University of Chicago Press.

Danley, Stephen, and Julia Sass Rubin. 2020. "What Enables Communities to Resist Neoliberal Education Reforms? Lessons from Newark and Camden, New Jersey." *Journal of Urban Affairs* 42:663–684.

Dautrich, Kenneth, and Thomas H. Hartley. 1999. *How the News Media Fail American Voters: Causes, Consequences and Remedies.* New York: Columbia University Press.

David, Miriam. 1993. *Parents, Gender and Education Reform.* Cambridge: Polity.

Davis, Brandon Rudolph. 2020a. "Feeling Politics: Carceral Contact, Well-being and Participation." *Policy Studies Journal* 49:591–615.

————. 2020b. "Testing Mechanisms: Carceral Contact and Political Participation." *Social Science Quarterly* 101:909–924.

Dawson, Michael. 1991. *Behind the Mule: Race and Class in African-American Politics.* Princeton, NJ: Princeton University Press.

"Demystifying New Orleans School Options." 2014. Editorial, *Times-Picayune*, December 28, E02.

Desselle, Sherman. 2021. "Parents Express Communication Concerns with NOLA Public Schools." *WDSU News*, February 26. Accessed August 25, 2021. https://www.wdsu.com/article/parents-express-communication-concerns-with-nola-public-schools/35638487.

DeVore, Donald E. 2015. *Defying Jim Crow: African American Community Development and the Struggle for Racial Equality in New Orleans, 1900–1960.* Baton Rouge: Louisiana State University Press.

Dewan, Shaila. 2015. "States Are Blocking Local Regulations, Often at Industry's Behest." *New York Times*, February 23.

Dewey, John. 1916. *Democracy and Education.* New York: Free Press.

Diamond, John B., and Kimberley Gomez. 2004. "African American Parents' Educational Orientations: The Importance of Social Class and Parents' Perceptions of Schools." *Education and Urban Society* 36:383–427.

Dingerson, Leigh, and Clayton Ross. 2016. *Whose Schools? Charter School Governance in Massachusetts.* Providence: Annenberg Institute for School Reform, Brown University.

Dixson, Adrienne D., Kristen L. Buras, and Elizabeth K. Jeffers. 2015. "The Color of Reform: Race, Education Reform, and Charter Schools in Post–Katrina New Orleans." *Qualitative Inquiry* 2:288–299.

"Do Right by Special Ed Kids." 2010. Editorial, *Times-Picayune*, April 21, B6.

"A Dream Takes Wing." 2009. Editorial, *Times-Picayune*, August 26, 4.

Dreilinger, Danielle. 2013a. "John McDonogh CEO Defends Decision to Let in 'Blackboard Wars' Cameras." *Times-Picayune*, March 5.

————. 2013b. "Two New Orleans High Schools Said They Were 'Full'—Then Enrolled More Students." *Times-Picayune*, November 22.

————. 2013c. "Community Rallies to Keep Sarah T. Reed High School Open—But with a Twist." *Times-Picayune*, December 10.

————. 2014a. "Traveling Farther to School, but Choice was in New Orleans Before." *Times-Picayune*, January 18.

———. 2014b. "KIPP New Orleans Charter School Employee Embezzled $70,000, Audit Says." *Times-Picayune*, February 10.

———. 2014c. "BESE Takes John McDonough Decision Out of Orleans Parish School Board's Hands." *Times-Picayune*, November 12.

———. 2015a. "Did the Community Get a Voice in Recent New Orleans School Decisions? Attendees Tell BESE Yes, No." *Times-Picayune*, February 26.

———. 2015b. "Flagrant Special Ed Violations, Cover-up Alleged at New Orleans Charter Lagniappe." *Times-Picayune*, March 3.

———. 2015c. "$26,000 Theft at New Orleans High School Remains Unsolved." *Times-Picayune*, April 27.

———. 2016. "Special Education Shortcomings Found at New Orleans Schools." *Times-Picayune*, December 21.

Druckman, James N. 2001. "On the Limits of Framing Effects: Who Can Frame?" *Journal of Politics* 63:1041–1066.

Druckman, James N., Jacob E. Rothschild, and Elizabeth A. Sharrow. 2018. "Gender Policy Feedback: Perceptions of Sex Equity, Title IX, and Political Mobilization among College Athletes." *Political Research Quarterly* 71:642–653.

Dunbar, Folwell. 2006. "500 Lose Their Schools." Letter to the editor, *Times-Picayune*, August 18.

Einstein, Katherine Levine, and David M. Glick. 2017. "Cities in American Federalism: Evidence on State-Local Government Conflict from a Survey of Mayors." *Publius* 47:599–621.

Einstein, Katherine Levine, Maxwell Palmer, and David M. Glick. 2019. "Who Participates in Local Government? Evidence from Meeting Minutes." *Perspectives on Politics* 17:28–46.

Engel, Michael. 2000. *The Struggle for Control of Public Education: Market Ideology versus Democratic Values*. Philadelphia: Temple University Press.

Entman, Robert M. 1989. "How the Media Affect What People Think: An Information Processing Approach." *Journal of Politics* 51:347–370.

Epstein, Joyce L. 2009. *School, Family and Community Partnerships: Caring for the Children We Share*, 3d ed. Thousand Oaks, CA: Corwin.

Erhardt, Niclas L., James D. Werbel, and Charles B. Shrader. 2003. "Board of Director Diversity and Firm Financial Performance." *Corporate Governance* 11, no. 2: 102–111.

Erie, Steven P. 1988. *Rainbow's End: Irish-Americans and the Dilemmas of Urban Machine Politics, 1840–1985*. Berkeley: University of California Press.

"Failing Schools Need Makeover." 2003. *The Advocate*, September 14.

Fairclough, Adam. 2008. *Race and Democracy: The Civil Rights Struggle in Louisiana, 1915–1972*. Athens: University of Georgia Press.

Farris, Emily M., and Heather Silber Mohamed. 2018. "Picturing Immigration: How the Media Criminalizes Immigrants." *Politics, Groups and Identities* 6:814–824.

Ferguson, Barbara. 2018. *Outcomes of the State Takeover of New Orleans Schools*. Pittsburgh: Dorrance.

Ferman, Barbara, ed. 2017. *The fight for America's schools: Grassroots organizing in education*. Cambridge, MA: Harvard Education Press.

Feuerstein, Abe. 2002. "Elections, Voting, and Democracy in Local School District Governance." *Educational Policy* 16:15–36.

"Few Fireworks in the New Orleans School Board Race—but That Doesn't Mean All Is Well." 2020. The74million.org, n.d. Accessed January 18, 2020. https://www.the74million.org/article/new-orleans-school-board-election.

Finn, Chester. 1991. *We Must Take Charge.* New York: Free Press.

———. 1992. "Reinventing Local Control." In *School Boards: Changing Local Control,* edited by Patricia F. First and Herbert J. Walberg, 21–25. San Pablo, CA: McCutchan.

Fiorina, Morris P. 1981. *Retrospective Voting in American National Elections.* New Haven, CT: Yale University Press.

Fishman, Mark. 1980. *Manufacturing the News.* Austin: University of Texas Press.

Fiske, Edward B., and Helen F. Ladd. 2000. *When Schools Compete: A Cautionary Tale.* Washington, DC: Brookings Institution Press.

Flaherty, Jordan. 2008. "New Orleans Culture of Resistance." In *What Is a City? Rethinking the Urban after Hurricane Katrina,* edited by Philip E. Steinberg and Rob Shields, 30–56. Athens: University of Georgia Press.

Ford, Michael R. 2017. *The Consequences of Governance Fragmentation: Milwaukee's School Voucher Legacy.* Lanham, MD: Lexington.

Ford, Michael R., and Douglas M. Ihrke. 2015. "A Comparison of Public and Charter School Board Governance in Three States." *Nonprofit Management and Leadership* 25:403–416.

———. 2016. "Comparing Nonprofit Charter and Traditional Public School Member Perceptions of the Public, Conflict, and Financial Responsibility." *Public Management Review* 18:972–992.

Foster, Kelsey. 2012. "Concerned about Personnel Issues, Protesters Mass at Closed Board Meeting," *The Lens,* July 15. Accessed January 28, 2019. https://thelensnola.org/2012/07/16/algiers-charter-school-association-meets-2.

Freelon, Rhoda. 2018. "Transformational Resistance and Parent Leadership: Black Parents in a School District Decision-making Process." *Urban Education* (September). https://doi.org/10.1177/0042085918801886.

"Fresh Start for Schools." 2004. Editorial, *Times-Picayune,* November 8.

Fung, Archon. 2004. *Empowered Participation: Reinventing Urban Democracy.* Princeton, NJ: Princeton University Press.

Galston, William A. 2001. "Political Knowledge, Political Engagement, and Civic Education." *Annual Review of Political Science* 4:217–234.

Gamard, Sarah. 2016. "Most Charter Boards Didn't Comply with or Know about Open-Meetings Law." *The Lens,* August 19. Accessed January 28, 2019. https://thelensnola.org/2016/08/19/most-charter-schools-unaware-or-noncompliant-with-transparency-law.

Gamm, Gerald, and Thad Kousser. 2013. "No Strength in Numbers: The Failure of Big-City Bills in American State Legislatures." *American Political Science Review* 107:663–678.

Gamson, William A., and Andre Modigliani. 1989. "Media Discourse and Public Opinion on Nuclear Power: A Constructionist Approach." *American Journal of Sociology* 95:1–37.

Gaventa, John. 1982. *Power and Powerlessness: Quiescence and Rebellion in an Appalachian Valley.* Urbana: University of Illinois Press.

Gay, Claudine. 2002. "Spirals of Trust? The Effect of Descriptive Representation on the Relationship between Citizens and Their Government." *American Journal of Political Science* 46:717–733.

Gelfand, Mark I. 1975. *A Nation of Cities: The Federal Government and Urban America, 1933–1965*. New York: Oxford University Press.

Germany, Kent B. 2007. *New Orleans after the Promises: Poverty, Citizenship, and the Search for the Great Society*. Athens: University of Georgia Press.

Gerry, Alica, Cathy Balfe, and Lindsay Bell Weixler. 2020. *White and Higher Income Students Are More Likely to Benefit from OneApp's Half-Mile Admissions Priority*. Report, Education Research Alliance, December.

Gerstl-Pepin, Cynthia I. 2002. "Media (Mis)representations of Education in the 2000 Presidential Election." *Educational Policy* 16:37–55.

———. 2007. "Introduction to the Special Issue on the Media, Democracy, and the Politics of Education." *Peabody Journal of Education* 82:1–9.

Gewertz, Catherine. 2005a. "Divided New Orleans Board Debates Reopening Schools." *Education Week*, September 23.

———. 2005b. "Judge Calls Halt to New Orleans' Charter School Plan." *Education Week*, October 25.

Gibson, Priscilla A., Robert Wilson, Wendy Haight, Misa Kayama, and Jane M. Marshall. 2014. "The Role of Race in the Out-of-School Suspensions of Black Students: The Perspectives of Students with Suspensions, Their Parents and Educators." *Children and Youth Services Review* 47:274–282.

Gilens, Martin. 1999. *Why Americans Hate Welfare: Race, Media, and the Politics of Antipoverty Policy*. Chicago: University of Chicago Press.

Gimpel, James, J. Celeste Lay, and Jason Schuknecht. 2003. *Cultivating Democracy: Civic Environments and Political Socialization in America*. Washington, DC: Brookings Institution Press.

Glazer, Joshua L., and Cori Egan. 2016. *The Tennessee Achievement School District: Race, History, and the Dilemma of Public Engagement*. Report, Tennessee Consortium on Research, Evaluation and Development, Peabody College, Vanderbilt University, Nashville, February.

Glickman, Carl D. 1993. *Renewing America's Schools: A Guide to School-based Action*. San Francisco: Jossey-Bass.

Goddard, Roger D., Serena J. Salloum, and Dan Berebitsky. 2009. "Trust as a Mediator of the Relationships between Poverty, Racial Composition, and Academic Achievement." *Educational Administration Quarterly* 45:292–311.

Goetz, Edward G. 2021. "Democracy, Exclusion, and White Supremacy: How Should We Think about Exclusionary Zooming?" *Urban Affairs Review* 57:269–283.

Goldstein, Rebecca A. 2011. "Imaging the Frame: Media Representations of Teachers, Their Unions, NCLB, and Education Reform." *Educational Policy* 25:543–576.

Goodnow, Frank Johnson. 1904. *City Government in the United States*. New York: Century.

Graber, Doris. 1980. *Mass Media and American Politics*. Washington, DC: CQ Press.

Green, Donald P., Dara Z. Strolovitch, and Janelle Wong. 1998. "Defended Neighborhoods, Integration, and Racially Motivated Crime." *American Journal of Sociology* 104:372–403.

Green, Eileen, and Catherine Cassell. 1996. "Women Managers, Gendered Cultural Processes and Organizational Change." *Gender, Work and Organization* 3:168–178.

Gustafson, Kaaryn. 2009. "Criminal Law: The Criminalization of Poverty." *Journal of Criminal Law and Criminology* 99:643–716.

Hales, Stephen W. 2006. "Start-ups Are Messy, but Schools Have Promise." Letter to the editor, *Times-Picayune*, August 10

Harden, Kari. 2015a. "Lagniappe Academies Tenures as Charter School Ends." *Louisiana Weekly*, May 18. Accessed March 18, 2021. http://www.louisianaweekly.com/lagniappe-academies-tenure-as-charter-school-ends.

———. 2015b. "A Look Back in Time at Decades of Fighting for Education Equity in New Orleans." *Louisiana Weekly*, September 22.

Harris, Douglas N. 2020. *Charter School City: What the End of Traditional Public Schools in New Orleans Means for American Education*. Chicago: University of Chicago Press.

Harris, Douglas N., Jon Valant, and Betheny Gross. 2015. "The New Orleans One-App." *Education Next*, Fall, 17–22.

Hasen, Richard L. 2000. "Vote Buying." *California Law Review* 88:1323–1372.

Hasselle, Della. 2013. "For Some Students Attending 'A' Schools, Transportation Gets an 'F.'" November 15. Accessed May 1, 2018. http://wwno.org/post/some-students-attending-schools-transportation-gets-f.

———. 2014. "As Officials Debate Governance, John Mac Community Members Seek Orleans Parish School Board Oversight." *The Lens*, July 2.

———. 2019. "Fewer Kindergarteners Signing Up for New Orleans Public Schools; Percentage of Black Students Falling." *The Advocate*, January 29.

———. 2020. "For the First Time, Most New Orleans Charter Schools to Follow Unified Calendar in the Fall." *Times Picayune/New Orleans Advocate*, May 5.

Hasselle, Della, and Marta Jewson. 2013. "Cost of Busing Students in New Orleans Rises as Parents Exercise School Choice." *The Lens*, September 12.

Henig, Jeffrey R. 1999. "School Choice Outcomes." In *School Choice and Social Controversy: Politics, Policy, and Law*, edited by Stephen D. Sugarman and Frank R. Kemerer, 68–110. Washington, DC: Brookings Institution Press.

———. 2013. *The End of Exceptionalism in American Education: The Changing Politics of School Reform*. Cambridge, MA: Harvard Education Press.

Henig, Jeffrey R., and Wilbur C. Rich. 2003. *Mayors in the Middle: Politics, Race and Mayoral Control of Urban Schools*. Princeton, NJ: Princeton University Press.

Henry, Kevin Lawrence, Jr. 2019. "Heretical Discourses in Post-Katrina Charter School Applications." *American Educational Research Journal* 56:2609–2643.

———. 2021. "'The Price of Disaster': The Charter School Authorization Process in Post-Katrina New Orleans." *Educational Policy* 35:235–258.

Henry, Kevin Lawrence, Jr., and Adrienne D. Dixson. 2016. "'Locking the Door before We Got the Keys': Racial Realities of the Charter School Authorization Process in Post-Katrina New Orleans." *Educational Policy* 30:218–240.

Hernandez, Monica. 2019. "The Effects of the New Orleans School Reforms on Exclusionary Discipline Practices." Policy brief, Education Research Alliance, March 19.

Hero, Rodney E., and Caroline Tolbert. 1995. "Latinos and Substantive Representation in the U.S. House of Representative: Direct, Indirect or Nonexistent?" *American Journal of Political Science* 39:640–652.

Hertel-Fernandez, Alexander. 2018. "Policy Feedback as Political Weapon: Conservative Advocacy and the Demobilization of the Public Sector Labor Movement." *Perspectives on Politics* 16:364–379.

Hess, Frederick M. 1999. *Spinning Wheels: The Politics of Urban School Reform*. Washington, DC: Brookings Institution Press.

Hess, Frederick M., and David Leal. 2005. "School House Politics: Expenditures, Interests, and Competition in School Board Elections." In *Besieged: School Boards and the Future of Education Politics*, edited by William G. Howell, 228–253. Washington, DC: Brookings Institution Press.

Hess, Frederick M., and Olivia Meeks. 2010. *Governance in the Accountability Era: School Boards circa 2010*. Report, National School Boards Association, Thomas B. Fordham Institute, and Iowa School Boards Foundation. Accessed November 17, 2017. https://www.nsba.org/school-boards-circa-2010-governance-accountability-era.

Higgins, Matt. 2014. "Frustrated Parents Wait to Enroll Children in Schools, Only to Be Turned Away." *The Lens*, July 9.

Hill, Paul T., Christina Campbell, and James Harvey. 2000. *It Takes a City: Getting Serious about Urban School Reform*. Washington, DC: Brooking Institution Press.

Hill, Paul T., Christine Campbell, David Menefee-Libey, Brianna Dussealt, Michael DeArmond, and Betheny Gross. 2009. *Portfolio School Districts for Big Cities: An Interim Report*. Seattle: Center on Reinventing Public Education, University of Washington.

Hochschild, Jennifer, and Nathan Scovronick. 2003. *The American Dream and the Public Schools*. Oxford: Oxford University Press.

Hoff, David J. 2005. "More Openings Scheduled for School Districts Hit by Storm." *Education Week*, September 16. Accessed April 18, 2018. https://www.edweek.org/ew/articles/2005/09/21/04katstatus.h25.html?r=1935608527.

Holman, Mirya R. 2014. "Sex and the City: Female Leaders and Spending on Social Welfare Programs in U.S. Municipalities." *Journal of Urban Affairs* 36:701–715.

———. 2015. *Women in Politics in the American City*. Philadelphia: Temple University Press.

Holman, Mirya R., and J. Celeste Lay. 2020. "How Katrina Shaped Trust and Efficacy in New Orleans." *The Forum* 18:117–130.

Homan, Michael. 2007. "Nation Watching Our Education Lab." *Times-Picayune*, March 31, 7.

hooks, bell. 1989. *Talking Back: Thinking Feminist, Thinking Black*. Boston: South End.

Horowitz, Andy. 2020. *Katrina: A History, 1915–2015*. Cambridge, MA: Harvard University Press.

Howell, Susan E. 2003. *A First Look at the Nagin Administration*. Paper no. 17, University of New Orleans Survey Research Center Publications.

Howell, Susan E., and Silas Lee. 1997. "Black Attitudes in New Orleans: Crime, Safety and the Quality of Life." Paper no. 27, University of New Orleans Survey Research Center Publications.

Huff, Alice. 2015. "Re-forming the Post-political City? Public School Reform and Democratic Practice in Post-Katrina New Orleans." In *Only in New Orleans: School Choice and Equity Post–Hurricane Katrina*, edited by Luis Miron, Brian R. Beabout, and Joseph L. Boselovic, 87–102. Rotterdam: Sense.

Hurst, David, Alexandra Tan, Anne Meek, and Jason Sellers. 2003. *Overview and Inventory of State Education Reforms: 1990–2000*. Report, National Center for Education Statistics, July.

Iannaconne, Laurence, and Frank W. Lutz. 1994. "The Crucible of Democracy: The Local Arena." In *The Study of Educational Politics*, edited by Jay D. Scribner and Donald H. Layton, 39–52. Washington, DC: Falmer.

"Improve Charter Oversight." 2011. Editorial, *Times-Picayune*, September 21, B4.

Ingram, Helen. 2007. "Poverty, Policy, and the Social Construction of Target Groups." In *Remaking America: Democracy and Public Policy in an Age of Inequality*, edited by Joe Soss, Jacob S. Hacker, and Suzanne Mettler, 245–253. New York: Russell Sage Foundation.

Irazábal, Clara, and Jason Neville. 2007. "Neighborhoods in the Lead: Grassroots Planning for Social Transformation in Post-Katrina New Orleans?" *Planning, Practice and Research* 22:131–153.

Iyengar, Shanto. 1992. "The Accessibility Bias in Politics: Television News and Public Opinion." In *The Mass Media in Liberal Democratic Societies*, edited by Stanley Rothman, 85–102. New York: Paragon.

Iyengar, Shanto, and Donald R. Kinder. 1987. *News That Matters: Television and American Opinion*. Chicago: University of Chicago Press.

Jabbar, Huriya. 2015a. "'Drenched in the Past:' The Evolution of Market-Oriented Reform in New Orleans." *Journal of Education Policy* 30:751–772.

———. 2015b. "'Every Kid Is Money': Market-like Competition and School Leader Strategies in New Orleans." *Educational Evaluation and Policy Analysis* 37:638–659.

Jacobs, Lawrence R., and Suzanne Mettler. 2018. "When and How New Policy Creates New Politics: Examining the Feedback Effects of the Affordable Care Act on Public Opinion." *Perspectives on Politics* 16:345–363.

Jacobs, Leslie. 2007. "In City Nowadays, Charter Schools Are the Norm." *Times-Picayune*, April 4, 6.

———. 2010. "Bold Gamble Transforming Schools." *Times-Picayune*, August 10.

Jennings, M. Kent, and Richard G. Niemi. 1974. *The Political Character of Adolescence: The Influence of Families and Schools*. Princeton, NJ: Princeton University Press.

Jewson, Marta. 2014. "Dr. King School Becomes First RSD Charter to Seek Return to School Board Oversight." *The Lens*, December 9.

———. 2016a. "ReNEW Sci Tech Used Special-Ed Designation for Cash, State Report Finds." *The Lens*, January 29. Accessed January 28, 2019. https://thelensnola .org/2016/01/29/renew-sci-tech-used-special-ed-designation-for-cash-state-report-finds.

———. 2016b. "How Lusher's School Board Shut Out the Public in Dealing with Teachers' Union Drive." *The Lens*, August 4. Accessed January 28, 2019. https:// thelensnola.org/2016/08/04/how-lushers-school-board-shut-out-the-public-in-deal ing-with-teachers-union-drive.

———. 2016c. "Twenty-four Hours after CEO Floats Idea, New Beginnings Board Votes to Close Gentilly Terrace Charter School." *The Lens*, October 20. Accessed January 28, 2019. https://thelensnola.org/2016/10/20/24-hours-after-ceo-floats -idea-new-beginnings-board-votes-to-close-gentilly-terrace-charter-school.

———. 2016d. "If You Saw this Meeting Agenda, You'd Never Guess this Charter Board Was Going to Close a School." *The Lens*, October 26. Accessed January 28, 2019. https://bit.ly/2MzTy0J.

———. 2017a. "School District Took No Action Regarding Lusher Board's Circumvention of Public Meetings Law." *The Lens*, May 26. Accessed January 28, 2019.

https://thelensnola.org/2016/08/04/how-lushers-school-board-shut-out-the-public-in-dealing-with-teachers-union-drive.

———. 2017b. "Moton Charter School Is in Trouble Again for Failing to Serve Its Special-Ed Students." *The Lens*, September 7.

———. 2017c. "Orleans Parish School Board to Study Long Bus Rides, Early Pickups." *The Lens*, December 13.

———. 2018a. "School District Reprimands Einstein Charter Schools for Enrolling Students outside OneApp." *The Lens*, January 3.

———. 2018b. "New Orleans Charter Schools Add Parents to Boards to Increase Parent Involvement." *The Lens*, July 5.

———. 2019a. "Court-Appointed Special Education Monitors Detail How the State Picked Wrong New Orleans Schools for Federal Consent Decree Scrutiny." *The Lens*, October 2.

———. 2019b. "Compare 2019 New Orleans School Ratings." *The Lens*, November 6.

———. 2020. "Brown, Parker Win OPSB Seats, and Five Other Races Head to Runoff." *The Lens*, November 4.

———. 2021. "Police Investigating Alleged Embezzlement at Warren Easton Charter High School." *The Lens*, February 24.

Johnson, Amanda Walker. 2012. "'Turnaround' as Shock Therapy: Race, Neoliberalism and School Reform." *Urban Education* 48:232–256.

Johnson, Cedric. 2011. "Introduction." In *The Neoliberal Deluge: Hurricane Katrina, Late Capitalism, and the Remaking of New Orleans*. Minneapolis: University of Minnesota Press.

Johnson, Linda. 2006. "Prepared Statement of Linda Johnson." In *A Fresh Start for New Orleans' Children: Improving Education after Katrina*. Hearing before the Subcommittee on Education and Early Childhood Development of the Committee on Health, Education, Labor, and Pensions, U.S. Senate. 109th Cong., 2d sess., July 14.

Johnson, Paula B., David O. Sears, and John B. McConahay. 1971. "Black Invisibility, the Press, and the Los Angeles Riots." *American Journal of Sociology* 76:698–721.

Jones, Bryan D. 1994. *Reconceiving Decision-making in Democratic Politics: Attention, Choice, and Public Policy*. Chicago: University of Chicago Press.

Justice, Benjamin, and Tracey L. Meares. 2014. "How the Criminal Justice System Educates Citizens." *Annals of the American Academy of Political and Social Science* 651:159–177.

Kahne, Joseph, Bernadette Chi, and Ellen Middaugh. 2006. "Building Social Capital for Civic and Political Engagement: The Potential of High School Civics Courses." *Canadian Journal of Education* 29:387–409.

Kalmoe, Nathan P., and Spencer Piston. 2013. "Is Implicit Prejudice against Blacks Politically Consequential? Evidence from the AMP." *Public Opinion Quarterly* 77:305–322.

Kantor, Paul. 1988. *The Dependent City*. Glenview, IL: Scott, Foresman.

Key, V. O. 1949. *Southern Politics in State and Nation*. New York: Alfred A. Knopf.

———. 1966. *The Responsible Electorate: Rationality in Presidential Voting, 1936–1960*. Cambridge, MA: Harvard University Press.

Kingdon, John W. 1984. *Agendas, Alternatives and Public Policies*. Boston: Little, Brown.

———. 1993. "How Do Issues Get on the Public Policy Agenda?" In *Sociology and the Public Agenda*, edited by William Julius Wilson, 40–50. Newbury Park, CA: Sage.

Kirst, Michael W. 1984. *Who Controls Our Schools? American Values in Conflict*. New York: Freeman.

Kogan, Vladimir, Stephane Lavertu, and Zachary Peskowitz. 2021. "The Democratic Deficit in U.S. Education Governance." *American Political Science Review* 115:1082–1089.

Kotok, Stephen, Brian Beabout, Steven L. Nelson, and Luis E. Rivera. 2018. "A Demographic Paradox: How Public School Students in New Orleans Have Become More Racially Integrated and Isolated since Hurricane Katrina." *Education and Urban Society* 50:818–838.

Kozol, Jonathan. 1991. *Savage Inequalities: Children in America's Schools*. New York: Harper Perennial.

Kramer, Gerald. 1971. "Short-Term Fluctuations in U.S. Voting Behavior." *American Political Science Review* 71:131–143.

Kreitzer, Rebecca J., and Candis Watts Smith. 2018. "Reproducible and Replicable: An Empirical Assessment of the Social Construction of Politically Relevant Target Groups." *PS: Political Science and Politics* 51:768–774.

Kumlin, Staffan, and Bo Rothstein. 2005. "Making and Breaking Social Capital: The Impact of Welfare-State Institutions." *Comparative Politics Studies* 38:339–365.

Kupchik, Aaron. 2010. *Homeroom Security: School Discipline in an Age of Fear*. New York: New York University Press.

Kupchik, Aaron, and Thomas J. Catlaw. 2015. "Discipline and Participation: The Long-Term Effects of Suspension and School Security on the Political and Civic Engagement of Youth." *Youth and Society* 47:95–124.

Kupchik, Aaron, and Geoff Ward. 2014. "Race, Poverty, and Exclusionary School Security: An Empirical Analysis of U.S. Elementary, Middle and High School." *Youth Violence and Juvenile Justice* 12:332–354.

Laborde, Errol. 2004. "New Orleanian of the Year: Anthony Amato, Orleans Parish School Superintendent." *New Orleans Magazine*, November 1.

Langenhennig, Susan. 2018. "Now Home to Bricolage Academy, Historic John McDonogh High School Building Gleams after Extensive Renovation." *Preservation in Print*, Preservation Resource Center of New Orleans, November 7. Accessed November 29, 2020. https://prcno.org/now-home-bricolage-academy-historic-john -mcdonogh-high-school-building-gleams-extensive-renovation.

Lareau, Annette, and Erin McNamara Horvat. 1999. "Moments of Social Inclusion and Exclusion: Race, Class, and Cultural Capital in Family-School Relationships." *Sociology of Education* 72:37–53.

Lawler, Edward E., III. 1986. *High-Involvement Management*. San Francisco: Jossey-Bass.

Lay, J. Celeste. 2009. "Race, Retrospective Voting, and Disasters: The Re-election of C. Ray Nagin after Hurricane Katrina." *Urban Affairs Review* 44:645–662.

———. 2012. *A Midwestern Mosaic: Immigration and Political Socialization in Rural America*. Philadelphia: Temple University Press.

———. 2019. "Choosy Moms Choose Schools: Gender and School Choice in an All-Charter System." Paper presented at the Southern Political Science Association meetings, January.

Lay, J. Celeste, and Anna Bauman. 2019. "Private Governance of Public Schools: Representation, Priorities and Compliance in New Orleans Charter School Boards." *Urban Affairs Review* 55:1006–1034.

Lay, J. Celeste, and Atiya Kai Stokes-Brown. 2009. "Put to the Test: Understanding Differences in Support for High-Stakes Testing." *American Politics Research* 37:429–448.

Lay, J. Celeste, and Michael Tyburski. 2017. "The Buck Stops with the Education Mayor: Mayoral Control and Local Test Scores in U.S. Urban Mayoral Elections." *Politics and Policy* 45:964–1002.

Leal, David L., Valerie Martinez-Ebers, and Kenneth J. Meier. 2004. "The Politics of Latino Education: The Biases of At-Large Elections." *Journal of Politics* 66:1224–1244.

Lee, Hedwig, Lauren C. Porter, and Megan Comfort. 2014. "Consequences of Family Member Incarceration: Impacts on Civic Participation and Perceptions of the Legitimacy and Fairness of Government." *Annals of the American Academy of Political and Social Science* 651:44–73.

Leighley, Janet. 2001. *Strength in Numbers: The Political Mobilization of Racial and Ethnic Minorities*. Princeton, NJ: Princeton University Press.

Leithwood, Kenneth, Doris Jantzi, and Rosanne Steinbach. 1999. "Do School Councils Matter?" *Educational Policy* 13:467–493.

Lerman, Amy E., and Katherine T. McCabe. 2017. "Personal Experience and Public Opinion: A Theory and Test of Conditional Policy Feedback." *Journal of Politics* 79:624–641.

Lerman, Amy E., and Vesla M. Weaver. 2014. *Arresting Citizenship: The Democratic Consequences of American Crime Control*. Chicago: University of Chicago Press.

Levin, Betsy. 1986. "Educating Youth for Citizenship: The Conflict between Authority and Individual Rights in the Public School." *Yale Law Review* 95:1647–1680.

Lewis, Henderson, Jr. 2015. "OPSB Policy Changes Will Help in Unifying Schools." *Times-Picayune*, October 2.

Li, Wei, Christopher A. Airriess, Angela Chia-Chen Chen, Karen J. Leong, and Verna Keith. 2010. "Katrina and Migration: Evacuation and Return by African Americans and Vietnamese Americans in an Eastern New Orleans Suburb." *Professional Geographer* 62:103–118.

Lightfoot, Dory. 2004. "'Some Parents Just Don't Care': Decoding the Meanings of Parental Involvement in Urban Schools." *Urban Education* 39:91–107.

Lincove, Jane Arnold, Nathan Barrett, and Katharine O. Strunk. 2018. "Lessons from Hurricane Katrina: The Employment Effects of the Mass Dismissal of New Orleans Teachers." *Educational Researcher* 47:193–203.

Lincove, Jane Arnold, and Jon Valant. 2018. *New Orleans Students' Commute Times by Car, Public Transit, and School Bus*. Report, Urban Institute, September.

Lindblom, Charles. 1959. "The Science of 'Muddling Through.'" *Public Administration Review* 19:78–88.

Lipman, Pauline. 2011. *The New Political Economy of Urban Education: Neoliberalism, Race, and the Right to the City*. New York: Routledge.

———. 2017. "The Landscape of Education 'Reform' in Chicago: Neoliberalism Meets a Grassroots Movement." *Education Policy Analysis Archives* 25:1–28.

Lippmann, Walter. 1984. "Newspapers." In *Media Power in Politics*, edited by Doris Graber, 73–80. Washington, DC: CQ.

Logsdon, Dawn, dir. 2008. *Faubourg Tremé: The Untold Story of Black New Orleans*. Serendipity Films, San Francisco.

Lott, Bernice. 2001. "Low-Income Parents and the Public Schools." *Social Issues* 57:247–259.

Louisiana Charter School Board Legal Handbook. 2014. https://vdocument.in/louisiana-charter-school-board-legal-handbook-louisiana-charter-school-board.html.

"L[ouisiana] Will Get $336,000 Grant to Support Charters." 1995. *The Advocate*, September 23, 8-A.

Lublin, David. 1999. "Racial Redistricting and African-American Representation." *American Political Science Review* 93:183–186.

Lyons, William, and Julie Drew. 2006. *Punishing Schools: Fear and Citizenship in American Public Education*. Ann Arbor: University of Michigan Press.

Maeroff, Gene I. 2010. *School Boards in America: A Flawed Exercise in Democracy*. New York: Palgrave Macmillan.

Makris, Molly Vollman, and Elizabeth Brown. 2020. "School Development in Urban Gentrifying Spaces: Developers Supporting Schools or Schools Supporting Developers?" *Journal of Urban Affairs* 42:571–594.

Malin, Joel R., Christopher Lubienski, and Queenstar Mensa-Bonsu. 2020. "Media Strategies in Policy Advocacy: Tracing the Justifications for Indiana's School Choice Reforms." *Educational Policy* 34:118–143.

Maloney, Stephen. 2009. "Momentum Continues for Switch to Charters." *New Orleans CityBusiness*, January 12.

Mansbridge, Jane. 1999. "Should Blacks Represent Blacks and Women Represent Women? A Contingent 'Yes.'" *Journal of Politics* 61:628–657.

Marschall, Melissa. 2005. "Minority Incorporation and Local School Boards." In *Besieged: School Boards and the Future of Education Politics*, edited by William G. Howell, 173–198. Washington, DC: Brookings Institution Press.

Marschall, Melissa, and Paru R. Shah. 2007. "The Attitudinal Effects of Minority Incorporation: Examining the Racial Dimensions of Trust in Urban America." *Urban Affairs Review* 42:629–658.

Marsh, Julie A. 2007. *Democratic Dilemmas: Joint Work, Education Politics, and Community*. Albany: State University of New York Press.

Martindale, Carolyn. 1986. *The White Press and Black America*. New York: Greenwood.

Martinez, Veronica Root. 2021. "Third Party and Appointed Monitorships." In *Cambridge Handbook on Compliance*, edited by Daniel Sokol and Benjamin van Rooij, 600–615. Cambridge: Cambridge University Press.

McBride, Allan, and Joseph B. Parker. 2008. "'Chocolate City' Politics: Race and Empowerment in the First Post-Katrina New Orleans Mayoral Election." *Politics and Policy* 36:350–374.

McCubbins, Mathew, Roger Noll, and Barry Weingast. 1987. "Administrative Procedures as Instruments of Political Control." *Journal of Law, Economics, and Organization* 3:243–278.

McDermott, Kathryn A. 1999. *Controlling Public Education: Localism versus Equality*. Lawrence: University Press of Kansas.

McDonnell, Lorraine. 2000. "Defining Democratic Purposes." In *Rediscovering the Democratic Purposes of Education*, edited by Lorraine McDonnell, P. Michael Timpane, and Roger Benjamin, 1–20. Lawrence: University Press of Kansas.

McGuinn, Patrick J. 2006. *No Child Left Behind and the Transformation of Federal Education Policy, 1965–2005*. Lawrence: University Press of Kansas.

Medina, Monica A., Jim Grim, Gayle Cosby, and Rita Brodnax. 2020. "The Power of Community School Councils in Urban Schools." *Peabody Journal of Education* 95:73–89.

Meese, Edwin, III, Stuart M. Butler, and Kim R. Holmes. 2005. *From Tragedy to Triumph: Principled Solutions for Rebuilding Lives and Communities*. Special report, Heritage Foundation, September 12. Accessed April 19, 2018. https://www.heritage.org/homeland-security/report/tragedy-triumph-principled-solutions-rebuilding-lives-and-communities.

Mehta, Jal David. 2013. "How Paradigms Create Politics: The Transformation of American Educational Policy, 1980–2001." *American Educational Research Journal* 50:285–324.

Meier, Kenneth J., and Robert E. England. 1984. "Black Representation and Educational Policy: Are They Related?" *American Political Science Review* 78:392–403.

Meier, Kenneth J., Robert E. England, and Joseph Stewart. 1989. *Race, Class, and Education: The Politics of Second-Generation Educational Discrimination*. Madison: University of Wisconsin Press.

Merolla, Jennifer L., Adrian D. Pantoja, Ivy A. M. Cargile, and Juana Mora. 2013. "From Coverage to Action: The Immigration Debate and Its Effects on Participation." *Political Research Quarterly* 66:322–335.

Merolla, Jennifer L., Abbylin H. Sellers, and Derek J. Fowler. 2013. "Descriptive Representation, Political Efficacy, and African Americans in the 2008 Presidential Election." *Political Psychology* 34:863–875.

Mettler, Suzanne. 1998. *Dividing Citizens: Gender and Federalism in New Deal Public Policy*. Ithaca, NY: Cornell University Press.

———. 2005. *Soldiers to Citizens: The G.I. Bill and the Making of the Greatest Generation*. New York: Oxford University Press.

———. 2011. *The Submerged State: How Invisible Government Policies Undermine American Democracy*. Chicago: University of Chicago Press.

Mettler, Suzanne, and Joe Soss. 2004. "The Consequences of Public Policy for Democratic Citizenship: Bridging Policy Studies and Mass Politics." *Perspectives on Politics* 2:5–73.

Michener, Jamila D. 2017. "People, Places, Power: Medicaid Concentration and Local Political Participation." *Journal of Health Politics, Policy and Law* 42:856–900.

———. 2018. *Fragmented Democracy: Medicaid, Federalism, and Unequal Politics*. Cambridge: Cambridge University Press.

———. 2019. "Policy Feedback in a Racialized Polity." *Policy Studies Journal* 47:423–450.

———. 2020. "Power from the Margins: Grassroots Mobilization and Urban Expansions of Civil Legal Rights." *Urban Affairs Review* 56:1390–1422.

"Mike Foster Still Favors Acing BESE." 1995. *The Advocate*, October 3, 5-A.

Miller, Toyah, and María del Carmen Triana. 2009. "Demographic Diversity in the Boardroom: Mediators of the Board Diversity-Firm Performance Relationship." *Journal of Management Studies* 46:755–786.

Mirel, Jeffrey. 1993. *The Rise and Fall of an Urban School System: Detroit 1901–81*. Ann Arbor: University of Michigan Press.

Miron, Gary, and Christopher Nelson. 2001. *What's Public about Public Schools: Lessons Learned about Choice and Accountability*. Thousand Oaks, CA: Corwin.

Moe, Terry M. 2012. "Teachers Unions and American Education Reform: The Politics of Blocking." *The Forum* 10:art. 4.

———. 2019. *The Politics of Institutional Reform: Katrina, Education and the Second Face of Power*. Cambridge: Cambridge University Press.

Moore, Donald R. 2002. *Chicago's Local School Councils: What the Research Says*. Report, Designs for Change.

Morel, Domingo. 2018. *Takeover: Race, Education and American Democracy*. Oxford: Oxford University Press.

Morel, Domingo, and Sally A. Nuamah. 2020. "Who Governs? How Shifts in Political Power Shape Perceptions of Local Government Services." *Urban Affairs Review* 56:1503–1528.

Morgan, Kimberly J., and Andrea L. Campbell. 2011. *The Delegated Welfare State: Medicare, Markets, and the Governance of Social Policy*. Oxford: Oxford University Press.

Morgan, Preston L., 2009. "Public Assistance for the Price of Privacy: Leaving the Door Open on Welfare Home Searches." *McGeorge Law Review* 227:227–260.

Morris, Robert. 2015a. "Lusher School Leaders Express Concern about OPSB Rewrite of Charter Requirements." *Uptown Messenger*, August 22.

———. 2015b. "New Policy Could Spell an End to Lusher Neighborhood Admissions." *Uptown Messenger*, September 11.

———. 2017. "Amid National Furor over Monuments, White-Supremacist Namesake of Lusher School Draws New Scrutiny." *Uptown Messenger*, August 18. Accessed May 1, 2018. http://uptownmessenger.com/2017/08/amid-national-furor-over-mon uments-white-supremacist-namesake-of-lusher-school-draws-new-scrutiny.

Mossberger, Karen. 1999. "State-Federal Diffusion and Policy Learning: From Enterprise Zones to Empowerment Zones." *Publius* 29:31–50.

Myers, Doug. 1995. "Senate Approves 'Charter Schools' Proposal." *The Advocate*, May 4, 1-B.

———. 1996a. "Foster Era May Alter Education in Louisiana." *The Advocate*, January 11, 7-B.

———. 1996b. "Senate Rejects Charter Schools Expansion Plan." *The Advocate*, April 11, 9-A.

———. 1997a. "Panel Wants Accountability Tied to Education Package." *The Advocate*, February 1, 2-B.

———. 1997b. "Bill to Amend Charter School Rule Approved." *The Advocate*, April 18, 14-A.

———. 1997c. "Bill Increases the Number of Charter Schools." *The Advocate*, May 1, 18-A.

———. 1997d. "BESE Releases Timetables for Education Projects." *The Advocate*, June 27, 2-B.

———. 1997e. "Rating Session '97: Legislators Say Time at Capitol Was Well-Spent." *The Advocate*, June 29, 1-A.

———. 1997f. "State Officials Consider Toughening LEAP Tests." *The Advocate*, September 20, 1-A.

National Alliance for Public Charter Schools. 2016. *A Growing Movement: America's Largest Charter Public School Communities and Their Impact on Student Outcomes*, 11th ed. Report, November.

National Research Council. 1996. *Improving America's Schools: The Role of Incentives*. Washington, DC: National Academies Press. https://doi.org/10.17226/5143.

Nelson, Steven L. 2015. "Gaining 'Choice' and Losing Voice: Is the New Orleans Charter School Takeover a Case of the Emperor's New Clothes?" In *Only in New Orleans: School Choice and Equity Post–Hurricane Katrina*, edited by Luis Miron, Brian R. Beabout, and Joseph L. Boselovic, 237–265. Rotterdam: Sense.

Nie, Norman, Jane Junn, and Kenneth Stehlik-Barry. 1996. *Education and Democratic Citizenship in America*. Chicago: University of Chicago Press.

Nobles, Wilborn P., III. 2018. "McDonogh 35 Handoff to Make New Orleans First All-Charter School System by 2022." *Times-Picayune*, December 21. Accessed February 1, 2019. https://www.nola.com/education/2018/12/new-orleans-set-to-be-1st-all-char ter-school-system-in-us-by-2022-despite-outcry.html.

Noguera, Pedro. 2003. *City Schools and the American Dream: Reclaiming the Promise of Public Education*. New York: Teachers College Press.

NOLA Public Schools. 2021. "Facilities Renaming Initiative Update." April 20. Accessed August 28, 2021. https://go.boarddocs.com/la/nops/Board.nsf/files/C25Q9H 67E137/%24file/Facilities%20Renaming%20Initiative%20Board%20Update%20 42021.pdf.

Nossiter, Adam. 2004. "School Chief Given Power through Bill." *The Advocate*, June 10.

Nuamah, Sally A. 2020a. "The Cost of Participating while Poor and Black: Toward a Theory of Collective Participatory Debt." *Perspective on Politics*. https://doi.org/10.1017 /S1537592720003576.

———. 2020b. "The Paradox of Educational Attitudes: Racial Differences in Public Opinion on School Closure." *Journal of Urban Affairs* 42:554–570.

Nuamah, Sally A., and Thomas Ogorzalek. 2021. "Close to Home: Place-based Mobilization in Racialized Contexts." *American Political Science Review* 115:757–773.

"Nurturing New Schools." 2009. Editorial, *Times-Picayune*, February 15, 6.

Oakes, Jeannie. 1987. *Improving Inner-City Schools*. Santa Monica, CA: Rand Corporation and Center for Policy Research in Education.

Olson, Mancur, Jr. 1965. *The Logic of Collective Action: Public Goods and the Theory of Groups*. Cambridge, MA: Harvard University Press.

Orleans Public Education Network and Louisiana Center for Children's Rights. 2019. "New Orleans Equity Index." Accessed June 24, 2019. http://neworleansequityindex .org/schools/lusher-charter-school-1#student-characteristics.

Orr, Marion. 1999. *Black Social Capital: The Politics of School Reform in Baltimore*. Lawrence: University of Kansas Press.

Osborne, Danny, and Chris G. Sibley. 2013. "Through Rose-Colored Glasses: System-Justifying Beliefs Dampen the Effects of Relative Deprivation on Well-being and Political Motivation." *Personality and Social Psychology Bulletin* 39:991–1004.

Osborne, Danny, Kumar Yogeeswaran, and Chris G. Sibley. 2015. "Hidden Consequences of Political Efficacy: Testing an Efficacy-Apathy Model of Political Mobilization." *Cultural Diversity and Ethnic Minority Psychology* 21:533–540.

Osborne, David. 2017. *Reinventing America's Schools*. New York: Bloomsbury.

Oxley, Zoe M., Mirya R. Holman, Jill S. Greenlee, Angela L. Bos, and J. Celeste Lay. 2020. "Kids' Views of the President: Replicating Early Political Socialization Scholarship." *Public Opinion Quarterly* 84:141–157.

Patashnik, Eric. 2008. *Reforms at Risk: What Happens after Major Policy Changes Are Enacted*. Princeton, NJ: Princeton University Press.

Pateman, Carole. 1970. *Participation and Democratic Theory*. Cambridge: Cambridge University Press.

Pedroni, Thomas. 2011. "Urban Shrinkage as a Performance of Whiteness: Neoliberal Urban Restructuring, Education, and Racial Containment in the Post-industrial, Global Niche City." *Discourse: Studies in the Cultural Politics of Education* 32:203–215.

Perry, Andre, and Michael Schwam-Baird. 2011. "School by School: The Transformation of New Orleans Public Education." In *Resilience and Opportunity: Lessons from the U.S. Gulf Coast after Katrina and Rita*, edited by Amy Liu, Roland V. Anglin, Richard M. Mizelle Jr., and Allison Plyer, 31–44. Washington, DC: Brookings Institution Press.

Pierson, Paul. 1992. "When Effect Becomes Cause: Policy Feedback and Political Change." *World Politics* 45:595–628.

Pitkin, Hanna Fenichel. 1967. *The Concept of Representation*. Berkeley: University of California Press.

Popkin, Samuel. 1991. *The Reasoning Voter*. Chicago: University of Chicago Press.

Posey-Maddox, Linn. 2016. "Beyond the Consumer: Parents, Privatization, and Fundraising in US Urban Public Schools." *Journal of Education Policy* 31:178–197.

Putnam, Robert D. 2007. "*E Pluribus Unum:* Diversity and Community in the Twenty-First Century, the 2006 Johan Skytte Prize Lecture." *Scandinavian Political Studies* 30:137–174.

Ramanathan, Arun K., and Nancy J. Zollers. 1999. "For-profit Schools Continue to Skimp on Special Education: A Response to Naomi Zigmond." *Phi Delta Kappan* 81:284–290.

Ramey, David M. 2015. "The Social Structure of Criminalized and Medicalized School Discipline." *Sociology of Education* 88:181–201.

Rasheed, Aesha. 2003. "Falling Short: The Graduate Exit Exam Stopped Bridget Green from Being Valedictorian." *Times-Picayune*, August 10.

Reay, Diane. 1998. "Engendering Social Reproduction: Mothers in the Educational Marketplace." *British Journal of Sociology of Education* 19:195–209.

"Recovery School District and Orleans Parish School Board OneApp Year Four Main Round Summary." N.d. Accessed May 3, 2018. https://www.documentcloud.org/documents/2070410-oneapp2015-0428-mr-summary.html#document/p2/a215814.

Reich, Charles A. 1963. "Midnight Welfare Searches and the Social Security Act." *Yale Law Journal* 72:1347–1360.

Rhodes, Jesse H. 2012. *An Education in Politics: The Origins and Evolution of No Child Left Behind*. Ithaca, NY: Cornell University Press.

Rich, Wilbur C. 1996. *Black Mayors and School Politics*. New York: Garland.

Riordon, William L. 1994. *Plunkitt of Tammany Hall: A Series of Very Plain Talks on Very Practical Politics*, edited by Terrance J. McDonald. Boston: Bedford.

Ritea, Steve. 2005a. "School Board Politics Emerge Intact, Division May Hamper Rebuilding Opportunity." *Times-Picayune*, October 3.

———. 2005b. "State Gets Grant for Charter Schools." *Times-Picayune*, October 6.

———. 2005c. "Algiers Charter School Plan Gets Good Grades." *Times-Picayune*, October 7.

———. 2005d. "Orleans Board Makes 13 Schools Charters." *Times-Picayune*, October 8.

———. 2005e. "Charter Schools Urged for N.O. District." *Times-Picayune*, October 25.

———. 2005f. "Lusher Middle to Move into Fortier High." *Times-Picayune*, November 3.

———. 2005g. "Absent School Employees Face Ax." *Times-Picayune*, December 1.

———. 2006a. "Nagin's Schools Panel Issues Reforms." *Times-Picayune*, January 18.

———. 2006b. "Many Students Must Register in Person, 1,900 Face Being Dropped from Rolls." *Times-Picayune*, August 11.

———. 2006c. "Public Schools Compete for Kids; New Array of Choices Gives Parents Power." *Times-Picayune*, August 12.

———. 2006d. "L[ouisian]a-Run School District Lacking Teachers." *Times-Picayune*, August 16.

———. 2006e. "Three Schools Can't Reopen in September, Students Will Need to Register Elsewhere." *Times-Picayune*, August 22.

———. 2007. "School Leader Reveals Ideas." *Times-Picayune*, May 9.

Robelen, Erik W. 2005. "New Orleans Eyed as Clean Educational Slate." *Education Week*, September 16.

Robert Mills Lusher Charter School. N.d. "Partnering with Tulane University." Accessed May 1, 2018. http://www.lusherschool.org/partnerships.

Robinson, Gerard. 2015. "Preserving School Choice in the Pelican State." *U.S. News and World Report*, December 1. Accessed January 18, 2020. https://www.usnews.com/opinion/knowledge-bank/2015/12/01/john-bel-edwards-wont-end-school-choice-in-louisiana.

Robinson, Ted P., Robert E. England, and Kenneth J. Meier. 1985. "Black Resources and Black School Board Representation: Does Political Structure Matter?" *Social Science Quarterly* 66:976–982.

Root, Veronica. 2016. "Modern-Day Monitorships." *Yale Journal on Regulation* 33:109–164.

Rosario-Moore, Alexios. 2015. "OneApp, Many Considerations: Black Social Capital and School Choice in New Orleans." *Souls* 17:231–247.

Rose, Mark H. 2012. *Interstate: Highway Politics and Policy since 1939*, 3d ed. Knoxville: University of Tennessee Press.

Ruth, Dawn. 2018. "Leslie Jacobs." *New Orleans Magazine*, December. Accessed April 18, 2018. http://www.myneworleans.com/New-Orleans-Magazine/December-2008/Leslie-Jacobs.

Sakakeeny, Matt. 2015. "Music Lessons as Life Lessons in New Orleans Marching Bands." *Souls* 17:279–302.

Sampson, Carrie, and Melanie Bertrand. 2020. "'This Is Civil Disobedience. I'll Continue': The Racialization of School Board Meeting Rules." *Journal of Education Policy*. https://doi.org/10.1080/02680939.2020.1778795.

Sanchez, Gabriel, and Jason L. Morin. 2011. "The Effect of Descriptive Representation on Latinos' Views of Government and Themselves." *Social Science Quarterly* 45:483–508.

Sanders, Raynard. 2018. *The Coup d'État of the New Orleans Public Schools: Money, Power, and the Illegal Takeover of a Public School System*. New York: Peter Lang.

Sanders, Torin. 2005. "Katrina Wipes Slate Clean for City's Schools." *Times-Picayune*, November 10.

Sapiro, Virginia. 2004. "Not Your Parents' Political Socialization: Introduction to a New Generation." *Annual Review of Political Science* 7:1–23.

Scarborough, William J. 2019. "Choosing Schools, Reproducing Family Inequality? Race, Gender and the Negotiation of a New Domestic Task." *Sociological Quarterly* 60:46–70.

Schattschneider, E. E. 1935. *Politics, Pressure and the Tariff*. New York: Prentice-Hall.

———. 1960. *Semi-sovereign People: A Realist's View of Democracy in America*. New York: Holt.

Schlichtman, Barbara, and Bill McMahon. 1997. "Governor Lays Out His Plan to Reform State." *The Advocate*, March 14, 1-A.

Schneider, Aaron. 2018. *Renew New Orleans? Globalized Development and Worker Resistance after Katrina*. Minneapolis: University of Minnesota Press.

Schneider, Anne, and Helen M. Ingram. 1990. "Behavioral Assumptions of Policy Tools." *Journal of Politics* 52:510–529.

———. 1993. "Social Constructions of Target Populations: Implications for Politics and Policy." *American Political Science Review* 87:334–347.

Schneider, Mark, Paul Teske, and Melissa Marschall. 2000. *Choosing Schools: Consumer Choice and the Quality of American Schools*. Princeton, NJ: Princeton University Press.

"School Board Chartering Authority." 2020. NOLA Public Schools website, revised November 19. Accessed September 4, 2021. https://nolapublicschools.com/CAPS /Policies/HA-20_(School_Board_Chartering_Authority).htm.

Schragger, Richard. 2016. *City Power: Urban Governance in a Global Age*. New York: Oxford University Press.

Schwindt-Bayer, Leslie A., and William Mishler. 2005. "An Integrated Model of Women's Representation." *Journal of Politics* 67:407–428.

Scott, Janelle. 2011. "Market-driven Education Reform and the Racial Politics of Advocacy." *Peabody Journal of Education* 86:580–599.

Sentell, Will. 2003. "Committee OKs Plan to Let BESE Take Over Schools." *The Advocate*, April 10.

Shingles, Richard D. 1981. "Black Consciousness and Political Participation: The Missing Link." *American Political Science Review* 75:76–91.

Shipan, Charles R., and Craig Volden. 2006. "Bottom-up Federalism: The Diffusion of Antismoking Policies from U.S. Cities to States." *American Journal of Political Science* 50:825–843.

Shober, Arnold F., and Michael T. Hartney. 2014. "Does School Board Leadership Matter?" Report, Thomas B. Fordham Institute. Accessed November 17, 2017. https://edexcellence.net/publications/does-school-board-leadership-matter.

Simon, Elaine, Rand Quinn, Marissa Martino Golden, and Jody Cohen. 2017. "With Our Powers Combined: Grassroots Activism in Philadelphia." In *The Fight for*

America's Schools, edited by Barbara Ferman, 55–74. Cambridge, MA: Harvard Education Press.

Skiba, Russell J., Kavitha Mediratta, and M. Karega Rausch, eds. 2016. *Inequality in School Discipline: Research and Practice to Reduce Disparities*. New York: Palgrave Macmillan.

Skocpol, Theda. 1992. *Protecting Soldiers and Mothers: The Political Origins of Social Policy in the United States*. Cambridge, MA: Harvard University Press.

Smith, Joanna, Priscilla Wohlstetter, and Dominic J. Brewer. 2007. "Under New Management: Are Charter Schools Making the Most of New Governance Options?" In *Hopes, Fear, and Reality: A Balanced Look at American Charter Schools*, edited by Robin J. Lake, 17–28. Seattle: National Charter School Research Project.

Smith, Stacy. 2001. *The Democratic Potential of Charter Schools*. Bern, Switzerland: Peter Lang.

Soss, Joe. 1999. "Lessons of Welfare: Policy Design, Political Learning, and Political Action." *American Political Science Review* 93:363–380.

———. 2005. "Making Clients and Citizens: Welfare Policy as a Source of Status, Belief, and Action." In *Deserving and Entitled: Social Constructions and Public Policy*, edited by Anne L. Schneider and Helen M. Ingram, 291–328. Albany: State University of New York Press.

Soss, Joe, Richard C. Fording, and Sanford F. Schram. 2011. *Disciplining the Poor: Neoliberal Paternalism and the Persistent Power of Race*. Chicago: University of Chicago Press.

Soss, Joe, and Lawrence R. Jacobs. 2009. "The Place of Inequality: Non-participation in the American Polity." *Political Science Quarterly* 124:95–125.

Soss, Joe, and Sanford F. Schram. 2007. "A Public Transformed? Welfare Reform as Policy Feedback." *American Political Science Review* 17:111–127.

Southern Poverty Law Center. 2010. "Lawsuit Changes New Orleans Schools Security Policies." November 9. Accessed May 2, 2018. https://www.splcenter.org/news/2010/11/10/lawsuit-changes-new-orleans-schools-security-policies.

Squire, Juliet, and Allison Crean Davis. 2016. "Charter School Boards in the Nation's Capital." Report, Thomas B. Fordham Institute and Bellwether Education Partners. Accessed November 17, 2017. https://edexcellence.net/publications/charter-school-boards-in-the-nations-capital.

Stern, Walter C. 2018. *Race and Education in New Orleans: Creating the Segregated City, 1764–1960*. Baton Rouge: Louisiana State University Press.

Stone, Clarence N., ed. 1998. "Introduction: Urban Education in Political Context." In *Changing Urban Education*, edited by Clarence N. Stone, 1–20. Lawrence: University Press of Kansas.

Stone, Clarence N., Jeffrey R. Henig, Bryan D. Jones, and Carol Pierannunzi. 2001. *Building Civic Capacity: The New Politics of Urban School Reform*. Lawrence: University Press of Kansas.

Stone, Melissa M., Jerry Zhao, and Colin Cureton. 2012. "Toward Understanding Governance in Hybrid Organizations: The Case of Minnesota's Charter Schools." Paper presented at the ARNOVA Conference, Indianapolis, November 15–17. Accessed November 17, 2017. https://repositories.lib.utexas.edu/bitstream/handle/2152/61794/Melissa%20Stone_ARNOVA_RGK.pdf?sequence=2.

"Stop Posturing on Schools." 2005. *Times-Picayune*, November 10.

Strauss, Valerie. 2013. "Reformers: Stop Accusing Critics of Wanting to 'Defend the Status Quo.'" *Washington Post*, May 3.

Strike, Kenneth A. 1993. "Professionalism, Democracy, and Discursive Communities: Normative Reflections on Restructuring." *American Educational Research Journal* 30:255–275.

Strunk, Katharine O., Nathan Barrett, and Jane Arnold Lincove. 2017. *When Tenure Ends: Teacher Turnover in Response to Policy Changes in Louisiana*. Report, Education Research Alliance, February 22.

Suggs, Emilia J. 2020. "Identifying Voter Preferences through Two-Stage Multivoting Elections: Experiments in the Preface of the 2020 Democratic Primaries." SSRN, September 24. https://ssrn.com/abstract=3337158 or http://dx.doi.org/10.2139/ssrn.3337158.

"Support for Schools." 2009. Editorial, *Times-Picayune*, December 17, B-6.

Sweet-Cushman, Jennie. 2020. "Where Does the Pipeline Get Leaky? The Progressive Ambition of School Board Members and Personal and Political Network Recruitment." *Politics, Groups, and Identities* 8:762–785.

Swyngedouw, Erik, and Japhy Wilson, eds. 2014. *The Post-political and Its Discontents: Spaces of Depoliticisation, Spectres of Radical Politics*. Edinburgh: Edinburgh University Press.

Tamir, Eran, and Roei Davidson. 2011. "Staying above the Fray: Framing and Conflict in the Coverage of Education Policy Debates." *American Journal of Education* 117:233–265.

Thaler, Richard H., and Cass R. Sunstein. 2008. *Nudge: Improving Decisions about Health, Wealth, and Happiness*. New Haven, CT: Yale University Press.

Thevenot, Brian. 2004a. "New Probe of N.O. Schools Is Launched." *Times-Picayune*, April 20.

———. 2004b. "School Board is Panned in New Poll." *Times-Picayune*, August 14.

———. 2004c. "Sanders Has Raised More than Willard—Political Newcomer Leads in Contributions." *Times-Picayune*, October 30.

———. 2004d. "Superintendent's Powers Reaffirmed—Attorney General Sides with Amato on Law." *Times-Picayune*, December 16.

———. 2009. "Pastorek: State-Run Schools to Persist—Poll." *Times-Picayune*, August 28, 1.

Thevenot, Brian, and Aesha Rasheed. 2004a. "Nagin Offers to Help Schools—City Could Assume Administrative Role." *Times-Picayune*, February 5.

———. 2004b. "Stakes High for School Board's Big Test—Public Confidence Is at an All-Time Low." *Times-Picayune*, July 31.

Tilly, Charles. 1999. *Durable Inequality*. Berkeley: University of California Press.

"Time to Make a Move." 2005. Editorial, *Times-Picayune*, October 10.

Torregano, Michelle Early, and Patrick Shannon. 2009. "Educational Greenfield: A Critical Policy Analysis of Plans to Transform New Orleans Public Schools." *Journal for Critical Education Policy Studies* 7:320–340.

Trounstine, Jessica. 2018. *Segregation by Design: Local Politics and Inequality in American Cities*. Cambridge: Cambridge University Press.

Truman, David B. 1951. *The Governmental Process: Political Interests and Public Opinion*. New York: Alfred A. Knopf.

Tuchman, Gaye, and Barbara W. Tuchman. 1978. *Making News: A Study in the Construction of Reality*. New York: Free Press.

Tuzzolo, Ellen, and Damon T. Hewitt. 2006. "Rebuilding Inequity: The Re-emergence of the School-to-Prison Pipeline in New Orleans." *High School Journal* 90:59–68.

Tyack, David. 1974. *The One Best System: A History of American Urban Education*. Cambridge, MA: Harvard University Press.

Tyler, Tom R. 1998. "Trust and Democratic Governance." In *Trust and Governance*, edited by Valerie Braithwaite, Margaret Levi, Karen S. Cook, and Russell Hardin, 269–294. New York: Russell Sage.

Ullo, J. Chris. 2006. "Prepared Statement of State Senator Ullo." Hearing before the Subcommittee on Education and Early Childhood Development of the Committee on Health, Education, Labor, and Pensions, U.S. Senate. 109th Cong., 2d sess., July 14.

"Unfulfilled Promise for Parents." 2011. Editorial, *Times-Picayune*, May 12, B-6.

U.S. Department of Education. 2005a. "Louisiana Awarded $20.9 Million *No Child Left Behind* Grant to Assist Damaged Charter Schools, Create New Charter Schools." Press release, September 30. Accessed April 19, 2018. https://www2.ed.gov/news/pressreleases/2005/09/09302005.html.

———. 2005b. "Non-public Education: A Vital Part of US K-12 Education." Fact sheet, November.

Useem, Elizabeth, Jolley Bruce Christman, and William Lowe. 2006. *The Role of District Leadership in Radical Reform: Philadelphia's Experience under the State Takeover, 2001–2006*. Occasional paper, Research for Action. Accessed November 17, 2017. https://eric.ed.gov/?id=ED493704.

Vanacore, Andrew. 2011a. "School Changes Survive Assault." *Times-Picayune*, June 3, B01.

———. 2011b. "New Vision for N[ew] O[rleans] Schools Transforms Local Board—Task Force's Governance Plan Phases Out State Control." *Times-Picayune*, June 15, A01.

———. 2011c. "School Application Process to Get Simpler—Parents Can Rank Top 8 Choices; Special Needs Concerns Tackled." *Times-Picayune*, December 9.

———. 2012a. "RSD Finally Makes Enrolling Simpler—Single Application Serves All Its Schools." *Times-Picayune*, February 7.

———. 2012b. "RSD Spells Out Expulsion Rules." *Times-Picayune*, July 17.

———. 2014. "N[ew] O[rleans] School Officials Reach Settlement in Special Education Lawsuit; Monitor to Oversee Reforms." *The Advocate*, December 23.

Vander Weele, Maribeth. 1994. *Reclaiming Our Schools*. Chicago: Loyola University Press.

Van Doorn, Bas W. 2015. "Pre- and Post-welfare Reform Media Portrayals of Poverty in the United States: The Continuing Importance of Race and Ethnicity." *Politics and Policy* 43:142–162.

Vargas, Ramon Antonio. 2010. "Langston Hughes Academy's Former Business Manager Admits to Stealing $660,000." *Times-Picayune*, February 25.

Vasquez Heilig, Julian, Jennifer Jellison Holme, Anthony V. LeClair, Lindsay Redd, and Derrick Ward. 2016. "Separate and Unequal? The Problematic Segregation of Special Populations in Charter Schools Relative to Traditional Public Schools." *Stanford Law and Policy Review* 27:251–293.

Vaughan, Kelly, and Rhoda Rae Gutierrez. 2017. "Desire for Democracy: Perspectives of Parents Impacted by 2013 Chicago School Closings." *Education Policy Analysis Archives* 25:1–26.

Verba, Sidney, Kay Lehman Schlozman, and Henry E. Brady. 1995. *Voice and Equality: Civic Volunteerism in American Politics*. Cambridge, MA: Harvard University Press.

Vergari, Sandra. 2007. "The Politics of Charter Schools." *Educational Policy* 21:15–39.

Waldman, Amy. 2007. "Reading, Writing, Resurrection." *Atlantic Monthly*, January– February. https://www.theatlantic.com/magazine/archive/2007/01/reading-writing-resurrection/305560.

Walker, Hannah. 2019. "Targeted: The Mobilizing Effect of Perceptions of Unfair Policing Practices." *Journal of Politics* 82:119–134.

Walzer, Michael. 1983. *Spheres of Justice: A Defense of Pluralism and Equality*. New York: Basic.

"Was Hurricane Katrina the Best Thing to Happen to New Orleans Schools?" 2010. *Washington Week with Roland Martin*, January. Accessed August 12, 2020. https://www.youtube.com/watch?v=wtLB8MNRimQ.

Weaver, Vesla M., Jacob S. Hacker, and Christopher Wildeman. 2014. "Detaining Democracy? Criminal Justice and American Civic Life." *The Annals* 651:6–21.

Weaver, Vesla M., and Amy E. Lerman. 2010. "Political Consequences of the Carceral State." *American Political Science Review* 104:817–833.

Weir, Margaret, Harold Wolman, and Todd Swanstrom. 2005. "The Calculus of Coalitions: Cities, Suburbs and the Metropolitan Agenda." *Urban Affairs Review* 40:730–760.

Weixler, Lindsay Bell, Douglas N. Harris, and Alica Gerry. 2020. *Voices of New Orleans Youth: What Do the City's Young People Think about Their Schools and Communities?* Survey report, Education Research Alliance, June 8 (updated July 29, 2020).

Welch, Kelly, and Allison Ann Payne. 2010. "Racial Threat and Punitive School Discipline." *Social Problems* 57:25–48.

Wells, Amy Stuart, Julie Slayton, and Janelle Scott. 2002. "Defining Democracy in the Neoliberal Age: Charter School Reform and Educational Consumption." *American Educational Research Journal* 39:337–361.

White, Ariel. 2019a. "Family Matters? Voting Behavior in Households with Criminal Justice Contact." *American Political Science Review* 113:607–613.

———. 2019b. "Misdemeanor Disenfranchisement? The Demobilizing Effects of Brief Jail Spells on Potential Voters." *American Political Science Review* 113:311–324.

White, John. 2016. "A Fresh Turn in the New Orleans Charter Schools Miracle." *Wall Street Journal*, May 27.

Wiebe, Robert H. 1967. *The Search for Order, 1877–1920*. New York: Hill and Wang.

Williams, Jessica. 2010. "It's None of Your Business: Most Charters Don't Comply with Open-Meetings Law." *The Lens*, October 7. Accessed January 28, 2019. https://thelensnola.org/2010/10/07/charter-school-transparency.

———. 2011. "Many Charter Schools Say They Weren't Aware of Open-Budgeting Law, Promise to Comply in the Future." *The Lens*, November 3. Accessed January 28, 2019. https://thelensnola.org/2011/11/03/charter-open-budgeting.

———. 2012. "Audit: Lusher Employee Embezzled $25,000 from School." *The Lens*, December 19.

————. 2013. "Disagreement Raises Question over Who's in Charge at Charter Schools." *The Lens*, March 18.

————. 2014. "You Want Local, Elected School Boards? Charter-based Voting Would Do It." *The Lens*, January 7.

————. 2018. "A Third of New Orleans Students Don't Get into One of Their Top Three Schools of Choice." *The Advocate*, April 16.

Williams, Jessica, and Della Hasselle. 2014. "Children Wait for School Buses along Some of New Orleans' Busiest Thoroughfares." *The Lens*, February 12.

Wirt, Frederick M., and Michael W. Kirst. 1997. *The Political Dynamics of American Education*. Berkeley, CA: McCutchan.

Wohlstetter, Priscilla, Roxana Smyer, and Susan Albers Mohrman. 1994. "New Boundaries for School-based Management: The High Involvement Model." *Educational Evaluation and Policy Analysis* 16:268–286.

Wolbrecht, Christina, and Matthew T. Hartney. 2014. "'Ideas about Interests': Explaining the Changing Partisan Politics of Education." *Perspectives on Politics* 12:603–630.

Wolf, Nikki. 2011. "A Case Study Comparison of Charter and Traditional Schools in New Orleans Recovery School District." *Remedial and Special Education* 32:382–392.

Wong, Kenneth K., and Emily Farris. 2011. "Governance in Urban School Systems: Redrawing Institutional Boundaries." In *Shaping Education Policy: Power and Process*, edited by Douglas E. Mitchell, Robert L. Crowson, and Dorothy Shipps, 216–237. New York: Routledge.

Wong, Kenneth K., and Pushpam Jain. 1999. "Newspapers as Policy Actors in Urban School System: The Chicago Story." *Urban Affairs Review* 35:210–246.

Zanders, Willie M. 2020. *Teachers of the Storm: The Real Story of the 7500 New Orleans Public School Employees Fired after Hurricane Katrina*. N.p.: Self-published.

Zepeda-Millan, Chris. 2017. *Latino Mass Mobilization: Immigration, Racialization and Activism*. Cambridge: Cambridge University Press.

Zimmerman, Jill M., and Debra Y. Vaughan. 2013. "School Choice Outcomes in Post-Katrina New Orleans." *Journal of School Choice* 7:163–181.

Index

Alcée Fortier High School, 19, 175n25
Algiers, 20, 63, 176n27, 183n47
Algiers Charter School Association, 84, 87
all-charter system: decentralization and, 45,
  49, 51, 56, 62, 70, 72, 104, 155–157; discipline and, 44–45, 52, 58–59, 114; enrollment and, 7, 34, 42, 44–45, 46–47, 55,
  93, 96, 98–99, 102–108, 110–111, 114–
  115, 119–120, 143, 152, 154; funding and,
  18–20, 33, 122, 144, 154; jurisdiction
  debate and, 38–39, 45, 53, 182n27; loss of
  neighborhood schools and, 7, 16, 24, 46,
  62–64, 114, 123, 130–135, 149–150, 154;
  opposition to, 5, 21, 35, 39, 45, 87; origins
  of, 31, 33–34, 37–39, 44–47, 50–51; political engagement and, 128–139; portfolio
  management model (PMM), 44, 51–52,
  182n23; protection from opposition, 25,
  45, 53–59, 86, 88–89; recommendations
  for, 152–162; school openings, 47–48;
  selective admissions and, 19–20, 48–50,
  60–65, 86, 112, 147, 196n29; students
  with special needs and, 9, 22, 44–45,
  48–49, 52, 57–60, 63, 79, 115, 157; transportation and, 9, 49–50, 62–64, 155–156.
  See also education policy; governance;
  reform movement
Alvarez and Marsal, 41, 175n18

Amato, Anthony, 39–41
American College Test (ACT), 145–148

Barber, Benjamin, 122, 131
Barr, Steve, 5–6
Benjamin Franklin High School, 19, 188n42
Blackboard Wars, 6
Blanco, Kathleen, 20
Bouie, Joseph, Jr., 54, 162
Bricolage Academy, 6–7, 132–133
Brown v. Board of Education, 29
Bush, George W., administration of, 30–31

Carter, Karen. *See* Peterson, Karen Carter
Center for Reinventing Public Education,
  18, 186n111
Chicago, 101, 125, 160, 163, 192n59, 194n40
class: charter school boards and, 69, 73,
  76, 80–81, 91, 125; effects of education policies and, 10, 17, 48, 51, 94, 96,
  104, 110, 132–133, 141, 154; political
  engagement and, 128–129; role in education reform, 10, 16, 25, 30, 46, 62, 91,
  108–109, 142, 175n21. *See also* systemic
  racism
Clinton, Bill, administration of, 30
community activists, 1, 5, 29, 66, 141; history of, 28–30, 125, 163

J. Celeste Lay is Associate Professor of Political Science at Tulane University and the author of *A Midwestern Mosaic: Immigration and Political Socialization in Rural America* (Temple).

www.ingramcontent.com/pod-product-compliance
Lightning Source LLC
Chambersburg PA
CBHW020346270326
41926CB00007B/335